Six Days or Forever?

Ray Ginger was born in Memphis, Tennessee, and studied at the University of Michigan and Western Reserve University. He is the author of *The Bending Cross: A Biography of Eugene Victor Debs; Altgeld's America: The Lincoln Ideal versus Changing Realities;* and *Age of Excess: The U. S. from 1877 to 1914.* He is at present Professor of History at the University of Calgary.

Six Days or Forever?

Tennessee v. *John Thomas Scopes*

Ray Ginger

OXFORD UNIVERSITY PRESS

London   Oxford   New York

OXFORD UNIVERSITY PRESS
Oxford   London   Glasgow
New York   Toronto   Melbourne   Wellington
Nairobi   Dar es Salaam   Cape Town
Kuala Lumpur   Singapore   Jakarta   Hong Kong   Tokyo
Delhi   Bombay   Calcutta   Madras   Karachi

SIX DAYS OR FOREVER? © 1958 by Ray Ginger. This book
was originally published in 1958 by the Beacon Press,
Boston, and is here reprinted by arrangement with the author.
First issued as a paperback by Quadrangle Books, Inc., 1969
First issued as an Oxford University Press paperback, 1974
Library of Congress Catalogue Card Number: 74-78755

printing, last digit: 20 19 18 17

Printed in the United States of America

For Alice
and Elmer

Contents

1. Law as Symbolic Action   1

2. Hot-Rod Halidom   22

3. An Uncurried Mind   47

4. Darwin and the Adullamites   68

5. "Backward to the Glorious Age"   92

6. God and Caesar   111

7. The Sin   130

8. The Indulgence   149

9. The Stillborn Miracle   167

10. To the Loser Belong the Spoils   190

11. Some Perspectives   218

      Sources and Acknowledgments   242

      Index   251

The difficulty comes from this, that Christianity (Christian orthodoxy) is exclusive and that belief in its truth excludes belief in any other truth. It does not absorb; it repulses. . . .

Culture must understand that by trying to absorb Christianity it is absorbing something that is mortal for it. It is trying to admit something that cannot admit it; something that denies it.

—Entry of June 14, 1926, in *The Journals of André Gide,* ed. Justin O'Brien (New York: Alfred A. Knopf, Inc., 1948), Vol. II, p. 380

Six Days or Forever?

Chapter 1

Law as Symbolic Action

> And the seed of Israel separated
> themselves from all strangers, and
> stood and confessed their sins, and
> the iniquities of their fathers.
>
> NEHEMIAH ix:2

I

The human eye and mind do not readily grasp the unfamiliar. Were two icebergs to collide so that one of them emerged from the water for half or more of its bulk, hung thus momentarily, and sank back to its customary immersion, the event would leave us uncertain. What was it we saw? That part of the iceberg that emerged from the water—was it just more of the same? Or was it wondrously different?

Similarly when massive social forces collide, as they did in the trial of John Thomas Scopes for teaching Darwinism, we can hardly credit the facts. We focus on the easy, because the familiar: the evidences of vanity and foolishness, the brilliant quip and the preposterous statement, a three-time candidate for President hoist on his own canard. Three decades have passed since the trial took place, and perhaps now we can understand the deeper realities that it thrust momentarily into view: the tortured issues of social policy, how the trial expressed the age-old craving of this man and that one, of you and me, to escape by spiritual rebirth from a past soiled with compromise. "And I will sprinkle clean water upon you, and ye shall be clean: from all your filthiness, and from all your idols, will I cleanse you. A new heart also will I give you, and a new spirit put within you: and I will take away the stony heart

1

out of your flesh, and I will give you an heart of flesh" (Ezekiel xxxvi:25-6).

Like so much evil, the Scopes trial began with a sincere effort to do good. John Washington Butler, the Tennessee legislator who sponsored the law that Scopes violated, won the affection, even the respect, of all who met him. He was a broad-shouldered six-footer, with kindly Indian-brown face, ready smile. A straightforward man who, in 1925, had lived all his 49 years on the family farm in Macon County that had been worked successively by his great-grandfather, grandfather, father. Located in north central Tennessee, Macon County did not have a single mile of railroad track. The same year in which he first saw a train, his twenty-first year, John Washington Butler took over the family farm. He also taught school for five years, teaching in the fall, planting his crop in the spring. After that he settled down to raising a variety of plants and animals on his 120 acres. Once a week or so he would go the three miles to LaFayette, the county seat of 800 residents. Every Sunday he went to church.

About 1921 an itinerant preacher who came once each month to Butler's church mentioned a young woman from the community who had gone away to a university. She had returned believing in the theory of evolution and not believing in the existence of God. This set Butler to thinking of his own children: two daughters, three sons. What might happen to them? No need even to go to the universities to be corrupted; Darwin's theory of evolution was taught in the public high schools of Macon County.

The next year Butler was urged to run for the state legislature. He agreed, and his campaign circulars stated the need for a law to prohibit teaching the theory of evolution in the public schools. The Bible said that God had created man in his own image, so man could not have evolved from lower animals as the scientists said. Those were the alternatives, and Butler found the choice easy. "Put not your trust in princes, nor in the son of man, in whom there is no help" (Psalms cxlvi:3). Butler was sure that in the three counties of his district—Trousdale and Sumner were farming country like Macon—99 people out of 100 agreed with him about this. Maybe so. At least, they elected him. As a freshman legislator he was not aggressive enough to introduce his anti-evolution bill, but during the 1924 campaign he resolved that if re-elected he would do his utmost to get the bill passed. It came to that.

On the morning of his 49th birthday Butler was thinking, "What'll I do on my birthday?" And he said to himself, "Well, the first thing I'll get that law off my mind." He sat down in the homely comfortable living room of his farm home before a fireplace with stone jambs (it had been built before the days of fire brick), and composed a bill.

An Act prohibiting the teaching of the Evolution Theory in all the Universities, Normals, and all other public schools of Tennessee, which are supported in whole or in part by the public school funds of the State, and to provide penalties for the violations thereof.

Section 1. Be it enacted by the General Assembly of the State of Tennessee, That it shall be unlawful for any teacher in any of the Universities, Normals and all other public schools of the State which are supported in whole or in part by the public school funds of the State, to teach any theory that denies the story of the Divine Creation of man as taught in the Bible, and to teach instead that man has descended from a lower order of animals.

Section 2. Be it further enacted, That any teacher found guilty of the violation of this Act shall be guilty of a misdemeanor and upon conviction, shall be fined not less than One Hundred ($100.00) Dollars nor more than Five Hundred ($500.00) Dollars for each offense.

Section 3. Be it further enacted, That this Act take effect from and after its passage, the public welfare requiring it.

Butler wrote three or four other versions. In the end he returned to his first effort.

Why had he done it? He explained later: "In the first place,

the Bible is the foundation upon which our American Government
is built. . . . The evolutionist who denies the Biblical story of creation, as well as other Biblical accounts, cannot be a Christian. . . .
It goes hand in hand with Modernism, makes Jesus Christ a fakir,
robs the Christian of his hope and undermines the foundation of
our Government . . ."

Butler was no vindictive, pleasure-hating, puritanical fanatic.
In maturity he looked back with pride to his youthful skill at baseball. He loved music, and his three sons had a band. His religion
looked toward love rather than toward retribution. Clerk of his
own congregation and clerk of the district session of the Primitive
Baptists, he had chosen this sect over the more popular Missionary
Baptists because of a doctrinal issue: "Now *I* don't believe, and *no*
Primitive Baptist believes, that God would condemn a man just because he never heard of the gospel."

Butler carried his bill to Nashville, got a stenographer in the
Capitol to type a clean draft, and threw it in the legislative mill.
Mainly the other members were indifferent. Some thought the bill
would make the state of Andrew Jackson seem ridiculous. An effort was made to pigeonhole it in committee. But Butler called it
out, as he could do under the House rules. And the pressures for
it in Nashville began to build up. A representative from one of the
leading evangelical schools gave a series of five lectures on the
Virgin Birth. Dr. W. F. Powell, pastor of the First Baptist Church,
declared strongly for the bill. His weight counted: the Baptists
were the largest denomination in the state, and Powell lectured
every Sunday morning at the Knickerbocker Theatre to the largest
Bible class in Tennessee.

Baptists could easily view the situation as a variant on the
main chance. Nashville was the national capital of the Methodist
Church, and Methodists, following Wesley's lead in setting less
stock in words than in deeds, in grace than in works, had been
generally inactive in the fundamentalist campaigns against evolution and higher criticism of the Bible. Some Baptist ministers now
saw in the Butler Bill a weapon that could be used to embarrass

their chief rivals in the competition for members. Churches, like other institutions, can be influenced by imperialist ambitions.

Meanwhile there was almost no vocal opposition to the bill. The officials and faculty of the University of Tennessee turned their backs; the legislature was considering a handsome new appropriation for the university, whose president privately disapproved the bill but would say nothing publicly. Officials of the state Department of Education likewise kept silent; the legislature had under consideration a bill to establish a compulsory school term of eight months in the public schools instead of the five or six months' schooling then common in rural counties of the state. Leaders of the Tennessee Academy of Science were not heard from. The main newspapers of the state either approved the measure or ignored it.

And so on January 28, 1925, the lower house passed Butler's bill by a vote of 71 to 5. The next evening William Jennings Bryan, three times the Democratic nominee for President, Secretary of State under Woodrow Wilson, the lifelong apostle of rural America and the acknowledged leader of the crusade against Darwinism, swept through Nashville with his masty physique and his silver voice. His subject: "Is the Bible True?" His reply: It is. Every word of it. Every comma. Jesus Christ was born of the Holy Spirit and the Virgin Mother. He died to redeem man's sins. He was born again. Every miracle recorded in the Bible actually happened. The Bible is the word of God, who dictated it verbatim to the Apostles: "holy men of God spake as they were moved by the Holy Ghost" (II Peter i:21).

As the Butler Bill went to the senate, a Nashville attorney named W. B. Marr, who had heard Bryan's lecture, went into action. He and some friends printed and distributed widely several thousand copies of "Is the Bible True?" About 500 of the pamphlets went to members of the legislature. The anti-evolution lobby, if small, was making itself heard. On the other side, silence. Most voters in the state didn't care a hang either way. Neither did most legislators. But they were politicians who had to stand for re-election. Few of them were willing to give their opponents a chance to say: "Well, there's Bill. He's a good fellow, but he's an atheist. He believes that you are descended from a monkey. I don't. I believe in the Bible." When the measure came to a vote in the senate, only two members spoke against it. Then the speaker of the upper house, Lew Hill, Democrat and ardent Campbellite, took the floor. "Save our children for God!" The vote was 24 to 6.

Even William Jennings Bryan could not affect the steamroller. On February 9 he wrote to a senator, John A. Shelton, suggesting that the bill should not contain any penalty for violations. He pointed out that the joint resolution against the teaching of evolution that he had written and that had been passed the previous year by the Florida legislature did not carry any penalty. This course, Bryan said, was wise for two reasons: A penalty could be used as a diversion by enemies of the bill, as had been done in defeating an anti-evolution bill in Kentucky. Also the law was to apply to an educated class who presumably would obey the law. If they did not, a later legislature could add a penalty for violations. Bryan's letter went for naught. The legislature of Tennessee passed the measure exactly as Butler had written it.

Most legislators did not take the matter very seriously. "The gentleman from Macon wanted a bill passed; he had not had much during the session and this did not amount to a row of pins; let him have it." One senator later claimed that the bill would not have passed at all if students from the local Vanderbilt University had not crowded the galleries during debate and heckled proponents of the bill, but this argument sounds like justification after the fact. Others claimed that most senators felt the governor would veto the bill. That makes more sense.

Austin Peay was a popular governor. And not a bad one. Elected governor in 1922 and re-elected in 1924, he had a progressive program for Tennessee. In his first term he had cleared away the state's financial deficit and given it a balance of $2 million. Then he started spending money. Highways. Schools. Hospitals and prisons. He wanted the compulsory eight-months school term and the largest appropriation in history for the University. To achieve these reforms, he needed the votes of a strategic bloc of rural legislators, men like John Washington Butler. The governor was in a true dilemma. He hesitated. When one of the senators who had spoken against the bill visited him, Governor Peay protested that the measure was absurd and that the legislature should have saved him from this predicament by failing to pass the bill. As the senator left Peay's office, a large delegation of Dr. Powell's Baptists entered. Governor Peay was a Baptist too. On March 21, eight days after the Butler Bill cleared the legislature, Peay signed it. It took effect at once.

The governor explained his action in a special message to the legislature. He noted first that the state constitution mentioned the people's belief in God and immortality. Obviously if man was to be judged after death, he must be judged by some laws, and the only source of those laws was the Bible. The Butler Act did not require the public schools to teach any one interpretation of the Biblical account of Creation. Peay added:

> After a careful examination I can find nothing of consequence in the books now being taught in our schools with which this bill will interfere in the slightest manner. Therefore it will not put our teachers in any jeopardy. Probably the law will never be applied. It may not be sufficiently definite to admit of any specific application or enforcement. Nobody believes that it is going to be an active statute.

If the Butler Act was not intended to be enforced, it can hardly have been a law. And it was not. It was a gesture, a symbolic act. Governor Peay said so: "But this bill is a distinct protest against an irreligious tendency to exalt so-called science, and deny the Bible in some schools and quarters—a tendency fundamentally wrong and fatally mischievous in its effects on our children, our institutions and our country."

The Butler Act was a stump speech; it was each legislator telling his constituents that he very much wanted to be re-elected. It was an expression of the belief of many Americans that law is magic, the sort of belief that led the lower house of the Indiana legislature in 1899 to pass a law fixing the value of pi as 4, that led the Tennessee legislature in 1908, at the behest of the Methodists, to outlaw cigarettes, that led John Washington Butler, that man of sound instincts and kindly heart, to announce that he would introduce a bill to ban gossip in the state. And the Butler Act was prayer, prayer emerging from an overwhelming but vague anxiety.

II

Governor's Peay's message on the Butler Act noted the "deep and widespread belief that something is shaking the fundamentals of the country." The anxiety was nationwide, because some of its major causes were nationwide. In the nineteenth century most Americans had lived on farms or in small towns. While dependent on the impersonalities of the market, they were not directly under the power of any other man who could be pointed out and called by name. A man could, in satisfying ways, still call his soul his own. The emphasis was on character rather than on personality, and the traditional Protestant code of morality was almost universal in a nation that still derived overwhelmingly from British and West European ancestry.

After 1890 this changed with incredible speed. The breath-taking growth of industry resulted in a vast expansion of cities, and the industrial cities overflowed with immigrant laborers from Eastern and Southern Europe. Most of the new arrivals were Catholics and peasants with a moral code that, if neither less strict nor more humane, was yet noticeably different. Overcrowding and poverty meant slums; slums meant political bosses and organized crime. The new immigrant groups came to be voting blocs of more significance than were native-born Americans in one city after another, and acquired influence even in Washington. The erstwhile independent men joined up in the new industrial armies, the new bureaucracies in which each man was subject to the personal dictation of his superior. The farm boy came to the city, and he was often revolted and outraged by what he saw there. And above all, he was frightened and tormented by his loneliness. How can you make them happy up in Detroit, after they've lived on the farm?

All this was summarized in 1926 by the Imperial Wizard and Emperor of the Ku Klux Klan:

> . . . Nordic Americans for the last generation have found themselves increasingly uncomfortable and finally deeply distressed. There appeared first confusion in thought and opinion, a groping hesitancy about national affairs and private life alike, in sharp contrast to the clear, straightforward purposes of our earlier years. There was futility in religion, too, which was in many ways even more distressing. . . . Finally there came the moral breakdown that has been going on for two decades. . . . The sacredness of our Sabbath, of our homes, of chastity, and finally even of our right to teach our children in our own schools fundamental facts and truths were torn away from us.

The sense of losing one's birthright, of alienation, of betrayal, was heightened by World War I. Before the war Christianity had turned increasingly toward the Social Gospel, which sought to face the social problems of industrialism and urbanism and to deal with them in a spirit of practical idealism. The prevailing mood was hope. The representative men were happy men: Theodore Roosevelt, in spite of his splenetic forebodings; Eugene Debs, sure of socialism in the United States in his own lifetime; even Clarence Darrow, certainly one of the most disillusioned men of that generation.

Then came the war. Many persons never stopped thinking that we should stay out of it; not improbably a plebescite in 1917 on the question of American entry would have resulted in negative majorities in the whole region from the Appalachians to the Rockies. Many of those who supported American entry did so, not with sober realism, but with impossible objectives. This would be the last war, and then the world would be safe for democracy. But war itself meant bloodshed and terror, publication of the secret Allied treaties, rejection by the Senate of the Covenant of the League of Nations. The reins of power passed to the flaccid hands of Warren Gamaliel Harding. Everybody—those who had supported American participation as well as those who had opposed it—felt betrayed. Gone now was more than the illusions of the war. Gone was the previous hopefulness, the cheery conviction that progress is inevitable. In its place was a massive distrust, the sort of distrust you would feel if a man stole your silverplate and your wife after you had invited him into your house and fed him at your table. And the distrust was directed toward Europe, things European, anything that could be called European.

Present too, with many, was a vague sense of guilt. For persons steeped from birth in Christian doctrine, the idea of original sin may lead to pervasive anxiety. How much worse for such persons, taught to regard every temporal defeat as divine retribution, to confront the staggering defeat of American purposes in the war. The feeling of having sinned, of being at the verge of eternal damnation, was intolerable, and men had to assure themselves of their basic goodness. This effort required a simple definition of morality: A good man is a man who does not drink, or smoke, or gamble, or commit adultery, or contravene the Word of the Bible, and who punishes the sins of others. A desperate flight backward to old certainties replaced the pre-war belief in gradual adaptation to new conditions. In a convulsion of filiopiety, men tried to deny the present by asserting a fugitive and monastic virtue. Not progress, but stability and certainty. "How blessed that some things, after all, are static—the love of God, the way of life, and the revealing Book, that have not changed through all the centuries." Thus a fundamentalist.

From such roots sprang a multifoliate plant. The Red Hunt, with its insistence that radicalism was a foreign doctrine and that no native-born American could adhere to it, culminated logically in the wave of brutal deportations. The Knights of Columbus, the American Legion, and the Daughters of the American Revolution made a furor about the "pro-British" bias of textbooks on American history; official clamors on the subject occurred in New York City, in Chicago, in other cities from Portland, Oregon, to Boston. New York, Wisconsin, and Oregon were among the states that, as Walter Lippmann wrote, "passed laws designed to do for patriotic fundamentalism what the Tennessee statute had been designed to do for religious fundamentalism." The xenophobia also erupted in the massive, and almost unopposed, demand for restriction of immigration, which resulted in the 1921 and 1924 laws setting quotas based on national origins.

Even before the war, many Protestant advocates of the Social Gospel had believed in prohibition; after passage of the Volstead Act, its strict enforcement became for them a means of solving all social problems. Alcoholic beverages were, simultaneously, European, Catholic, and sinful. A moralizing, if immoral, impulse was likewise basic in the Ku Klux Klan, which in many areas punished adultery as well as Jewish birth, drunkenness as well as Catholic faith, failure to attend church as well as failure to look white: inflicted punishments even on white Protestant Americans. The Klan, in one of its several aspects, was the Ten Commandments swinging a whip. Or rather, some of the Ten Commandments; the moralizing was selective.

Leaders of the anti-evolution crusade, including Bryan, George M. Price, and William Bell Riley, tried too to exploit the current fear of Bolshevism by linking Darwinism to it. Thus T. T. Martin, author of *Hell in the High Schools* and other tracts against evolution, flung down a challenge to the Mississippi legislature when it was considering an anti-evolution bill: "Go back to the fathers and mothers of Mississippi and tell them because you could not face the scorn and abuse of Bolsheviks and Anarchists and Atheists and agnostics and their co-workers, you turned over their children to a teaching that God's Word is a tissue of lies."

All of these movements—the fundamentalist crusade against

evolution, anti-radicalism, immigration restriction, prohibition, the
Ku Klux Klan—originated in the same state of mind, and each
helped to create an atmosphere congenial to the others. But in the
actual struggle for members they were largely competitive with
each other. While a few prominent Klansmen were prompted by
their greed for money to switch to fundamentalist organizations,
such fundamentalist stalwarts as the Moody Bible Institute and
John Roach Straton attacked the Klan. And a statistical study of
Klan membership showed it to be strongest in states where fundamentalism was unimportant, but weak in Tennessee and Mississippi which adopted anti-evolution statutes.

It was charged at the time, by the Harvard theologian Kirsopp
Lake and others, that "large financial interests" might take up fundamentalism as part of their general opposition to revolutionary
ideas. Such instances did occur, but direct support by big business
of the anti-evolution movement accounts at most for a minor part
of its strength. Doubtless other businessmen had the perception to
see what a machinery manufacturer of Fort Wayne, Indiana, expressed: "American business must raise its voice against thought
that is against the best interests of business and denies the theory
of evolution. For evolution is no longer a theory. Science could
not be studied without it. Business is dependent on science."

The social creed expounded in the 1920's by the two influential
business groups, the National Association of Manufacturers and the
United States Chamber of Commerce, clashed head-on at crucial
points with the views of William Jennings Bryan. Bryan stood
squarely for the direct rule of the majority in all matters; the business groups stood equally squarely for rule by an elite because they
believed the great mass of the people were ignorant and could not
recognize their own best interests. The business groups acclaimed
the American system of checks and balances and placed particular
faith in the judiciary, especially the Supreme Court; Bryan believed
in an unrestrained legislature because that branch of government
was most responsive to the popular will. The business groups

thought it was the nature of man to concentrate on material rewards; Bryan spoke for the primacy of spiritual values.

But in other respects these big business groups helped to create good growing weather for the anti-evolution movement. They too preached the overwhelming need for social order, for stony-faced resistance to change. When the Butler Act was violated by John Thomas Scopes, the president of the N.A.M. pointed to "America's greatest menace today—the popular contempt in which many of the laws and much of its constitutional authority are held." The *Manufacturers' Record* was explicitly religious, denouncing theories of evolution as "silly twaddle" and asserting that "one must believe in the Bible in its entirety or not believe in it at all."

The big business groups and the fundamentalists likewise agreed that education should consist in the inculcation of received truths, not in the development among students of certain modes of analysis, not in the discovery of new truths. Truth is known. Teach it. Who knows it? We do. How did you learn it? The fundamentalists replied: God revealed it to us. The business groups replied: We are the elite. We know everything.

And yet, ironically, fundamentalism was in part an effort by Protestant clergymen to regain some of the power and prestige that they were losing to the burgeoning business classes. This condition for fundamentalism, like many others, existed with peculiar intensity in the South.

III

The South is perhaps unique in world history in that the growth of industry, cities, and education stimulated church membership, which rose nearly 50 per cent between 1906 and 1926. This phenomenon was especially marked in the cities; in Memphis, for example, population grew 23 per cent in this period, church membership 62 per cent. Slightly more than a third of the adults in the Southeast were not affiliated with any church; most of these were Negroes or isolated, uneducated whites. Newly arrived in the growing cities, men found themselves faced with an aching solitude and alienation, and they sought an emotional haven in religion.

They also sought emotional excitement that was not given them elsewhere in life, and religion in the South, as earlier on the Western frontier, was often corybantic. The two creeds that claimed three fourths of all church members in the region, the Baptists and the Methodists, were strongly revivalistic. The more ritualistic Protestants were losing ground, and in Tennessee there was only one Roman Catholic in every hundred persons. The arcanum was the Word—or words, which had a special fascination for many Southerners. Mere announcement of a speech would draw an enormous crowd; it would, that is, if the speech met a few simple requirements. It had to be delivered with florid gestures and rotund eloquence. It had to deal in the received words and phrases, so that efforts to follow it would not exacerbate the mind.

But it might torment the spirit. Most Southerners were reared on endless iterations of the same sermon about hellfire and brimstone, about fiery pits and demons with pitchforks. They were conditioned to believe that we are all sinners. Since, like the prisoner in Kafka's *The Trial,* they were not told what specific crime they were charged with, they were not clear just how they could modify their practical actions in order to get right with God; they were left with what the psychologists term "free-floating" anxiety and guilt. Because their humanity was their sin, their sin seemed irremediable. This state of mind, especially if the feeling was not too intense, made them vulnerable to such ritualized acts of expiation as the Butler Bill. "And Aaron shall lay both his hands upon the head of the live goat, and confess over him all the iniquities of the children of Israel, and all their transgressions in all their sins, putting them upon the head of the goat, and shall send him away by the hand of a fit man into the wilderness: And the goat shall bear upon him all their iniquities unto a land not inhabited: and he shall let go the goat in the wilderness" (Leviticus xvi:21-2).

Other Southern institutions did little to offset the theological dominance. Higher education was largely controlled by the churches; each of the major denominations felt constrained to provide at least one college for men and one for women in every Southern state. Although clergymen were being steadily displaced as trustees of these colleges by more opulent businessmen who, if themselves usually conservative in their religious views, were yet more liberal than the clergy, the typical college curriculum consisted of religion and the classics. This limitation was partly due to policy, partly to lack of money; in 1903 the total funds available for higher education in nine Southern states combined were less than the income that year of Harvard. Twenty years later, the entire South held not a single university of the first rank, and its training facilities in engineering and science were particularly poor. The South had no public forums on scientific or social topics. Libraries were rare, poorly stocked, and infrequently visited. Walter Hines Page claimed that the chief element distinguishing Southerners from, say, citizens of Massachusetts was their utter lack of intellectual curiosity. And many Southerners took a perverse pride in their plight. Huey Long knew it was good politics when he declaimed in the Senate: "It is true. I am an ignorant man. . . . I know the hearts of my people because I have not colored my own. I know when I am right in my own conscience."

Although a few fundamentalists sought to show that Darwin's findings were unscholarly, the movement typically catered to the smugly ignorant. A writer in *Christian Fundamentals* declared that almost the only believers in evolution were "the university crowd and the social Reds." A Georgia legislator, Hal Kimberly, who had doubtless never heard of Aquinas' *Summa Theologica,* nonetheless used its distinction between natural and revealed knowledge to reach a conclusion that would have stunned Aquinas: "Read the Bible. It teaches you how to act. Read the hymn book. It contains the finest poetry ever written. Read the almanac. It shows you how to figure out what the weather will be. There isn't another book that is necessary for anyone to read, and therefore I am opposed to all libraries."

The Bible is the medium of revelation. Anybody who wants to

be saved should stake his chips on revealed truth—and the Southern churches never doubted that their mission was individual salvation rather than social reform. The mind and body last but a
day, but the soul is immortal. "Love not the world, neither the
things that are in the world. If any man love the world, the love
of the Father is not in him" (I John ii:15). Not surprising, therefore, that during the entire dispute about evolution no Southern
theological school took a stand against the efforts to ban Darwinism by law. Of the theology professors who grumbled privately
about it, few dared open their mouths. In Tennessee an estimated
fifty ministers held modernist opinions, but only ten would declare
themselves publicly.

It was not that the South had no liberals, or that they were
without influence. Some of the major Southern newspapers had
recently acquired liberal editors; Southern liberals had begun to
achieve the highest political offices. But they were fighting an uphill fight, and many hesitated to dissipate in quasi-religious disputes
the influence they might need on issues of economic policy or of
policy toward Negroes.

Beginning about 1896, the Southern states had launched a rigorous and systematic segregation of Negroes—something that had
not existed even under slavery. So massive a reshaping of society
required more than laws and illegal violence, it required too a reshaping of men's minds. There took place a concentrated effort to
persuade everybody that segregation was natural and inevitable,
that it had always existed, that it was how matters were arranged
by our noble ancestors. The campaign for Jim Crow laws, superbly
analyzed by C. Vann Woodward in The Strange Career of Jim
Crow, was strikingly similar in some ways to the later campaign
for anti-evolution laws: both were greatly facilitated by the lack of
opposition, and both were dependent on a favorable national climate of opinion.

The authentic traditionalism of the South, which grew out of
a relatively simple, homogeneous, and unchanging way of life, was

reinforced by a spurious and manufactured traditionalism enshrined in the myth of the Confederacy. The drive for segregation bred intolerance, and the intolerance spread to other topics. A new idea on any subject would further the habit of discussion, of rational consideration, and these habits would impede the effort to impose segregation. This consideration—in addition to a desire to protect religion for its own sake, or for the sake of social order, or a desire to give harmless diversion to the common folks—may explain why prominent businessmen and lawyers endorsed the anti-evolution movement and why the journal that was virtually the official publication of the Southern textile industry applauded the passage of the Butler Act.

The traditionalism in religion was shored up by the region's ubiquitous ancestor worship. Men voted the way their fathers had, thought the way their fathers had. Cordell Hull testified that in his native Pickett County, Tennessee, a candidate for county office could predict within two or three votes the vote he would get. J. Frank Norris, a fundamentalist leader, told with undoubted effect how a Tennessean had walked up to Clarence Darrow, the chief attorney for John Thomas Scopes, clenched his fist under Darrow's nose and shouted: "Damn you, don't you reflect on my mother's Bible. If you do I will tear you to pieces." John Washington Butler summed the point well; when asked if he knew that many good Baptists believed in evolution, he said yes, and added: "I reckon it's a good deal like politics—the way you've been raised."

But if the South was susceptible to the anti-evolution movement, so were other regions, and the rest of the country was more active in pursuing the moral equivalents of fundamentalism. Two Southerners could write with justice: "In a way it may be said that the Fundamentalist craze was the Southern counterpart of the Northern red-hunt. . . . If Southern reactionaries were more successful in passing 'monkey laws,' Northerners were more active in discharging professors because of their opinions." And Tennessee was by no means the most daddy-ridden of the Southern states; unlike nine of them, it had ratified the Nineteenth Amendment giving women the right to vote.

IV

That the Butler Act was intended as gesture rather than as "active statute," in Governor Peay's words, is confirmed by the failure of the law-enforcing agencies to make any effort to execute it in the classrooms. Teachers taught as they had taught, out of the same books. The Chattanooga *Times* broke its silence to editorialize against the law. And some citizens of the state began to think about seeking a legal test of the Butler Act's constitutionality.

The normal, ordinary way to do this in Tennessee was for a plaintiff to file a bill in chancery court challenging the questionable law. The judge then ruled the law constitutional or not, with his reasons. Appeals could be carried to the court of appeals and to the supreme court of the state. It was rumored that plans were laid to challenge the Butler Act in this way, but that the men who should have been the plaintiffs balked finally for fear of fundamentalist wrath if the law were actually voided by the courts. Such a procedure would have avoided the sensationalism of a criminal trial. But a woman in New York City made the move that started events down a different path.

Lucile Milner was the secretary of the American Civil Liberties Union, which had been organized during World War I to defend pacifists and had continued after the war with the more general purpose of upholding the Bill of Rights. In the course of her regular chore of clipping civil-liberties news from the press, she came upon a three-inch item in a Tennessee paper about the passage of the Butler Act. Seeing the importance of the story, she showed it to Roger Baldwin, director of the organization. As a result, the Board of the ACLU agreed to raise a special fund to finance a test case and to hire distinguished lawyers to handle it. They got off to a slow start. Their first choice as attorney, John W. Davis, who had been the Democratic Presidential nominee in 1924, turned them down. And how could an organization with offices in New York

City find a plaintiff in Tennessee? Finally they sent a story to the Tennessee papers announcing that the ACLU would finance a test case if some teacher were willing to cooperate.

George W. Rappelyea, on May 4, was sitting in his office in a coal yard at Dayton, Tennessee. He was an unimpressive figure: 31 years old, slight, swarthy, untidy, with horn-rimmed glasses and bushy black hair. He had grown up in New York City, and he was a mining engineer. Trained men were scarce in the South. He was in charge of six coal and iron mines for the Cumberland Coal Company, with 400 men under his direction.

Rappelyea saw in a newspaper that Chattanooga had given up its plans to start a case to test the Butler Act. He got an idea, and he telephoned F. E. Robinson, local druggist and head of the county board of education, and Walter White, county superintendent of schools. He argued earnestly with them. The next day he was at them again. They gave in. Then Rappelyea sent for John Thomas Scopes and asked him to come down to Robinson's drugstore. When Scopes arrived, Rappelyea was deep in an argument about evolution with two young local lawyers, Sue K. Hicks (a man whose parents had played him a grim joke) and Wallace C. Haggard. Rappelyea was arguing that the Bible was "mere history"; the two lawyers insisted that it must be taken literally. What, they asked, did Scopes think?

John Scopes was a guileless young man, with blue, contemplative eyes. Only 24 years old, he had graduated from the University of Kentucky the preceding year and had come to the high school at Dayton as science teacher and football coach. His local popularity was very great. Here was the man Rappelyea wanted. Scopes was drawn into the discussion, and found himself observing that nobody could teach biology without using the theory of evolution. Being the person he was, he was trapped. Rappelyea said, "You have been violating the law."

"So has every other teacher," said Scopes. "This is the official textbook," and he went to the shelf in the drugstore, which was also the town's bookstore, and took down a copy of George Hunter's

Civic Biology. This book was officially prescribed for the public schools by the state textbook commission appointed by the governor.

Rappelyea produced the news item about the ACLU offer, and made a proposal to Scopes. "It's a bad law. Let's get rid of it. I will swear out a warrant and have you arrested. . . . That will make a big sensation. Why not bring a lot of doctors and preachers here? Let's get H. G. Wells and a lot of big fellows." Scopes demurred. He did not like the idea of having an arrest on his record. He was a modest man, distressed by the mere thought of being in the limelight. Besides, he believed that "evolution is easily reconciled with the Bible."

But Rappelyea persisted, and finally Scopes agreed. Describing the episode later, Scopes said: "It was just a drugstore discussion that got past control."

Rappelyea wired the ACLU in New York. They replied promptly: "We will cooperate Scopes case with financial help, legal advice and publicity."

On May 7 John Scopes was arrested. Three days later he had a preliminary hearing before three squires. It was charged that on April 24 he had taught the theory of evolution to his class. It was shown that Hunter's *Civic Biology* contained such sentences as: "We have now learned that animal forms may be arranged so as to begin with the simple one-celled forms and culminate with a group which contains man himself." The justices decided there was ample evidence, and Scopes was bound over to the grand jury that would meet the first Monday in August. Bond was fixed at $1,000.

Roger Baldwin announced in New York for the American Civil Liberties Union: "We shall take the Scopes case to the United States supreme court if necessary to establish that a teacher may tell the truth without being thrown in jail."

If Governor Peay and others saw the Scopes trial partly as political speech and partly as pious gesture, such men as George Rappelyea, Sue Hicks, and Dayton merchants viewed it as a civic promotion. This could really put Dayton in the headlines, on the map. It could bring a lot of business to local stores. But it needed celebrities. Who better than William Jennings Bryan, the one man of world reputation in the fundamentalist movement?

So Hicks sent Bryan several telegrams asking him to affiliate with the prosecution in the case. But before Hicks succeeded in reaching him, Bryan announced in Pittsburgh on May 13 that, if the Tennessee officials agreed, he would accept the appointment by the World's Christian Fundamentals Association to represent them in the prosecution of the case. His tone was determined: "We cannot afford to have a system of education that destroys the religious faith of our children. . . . There are about 5,000 scientists, and probably half of them are atheists, in the United States. Are we going to allow them to run our schools? We are not." He was less happy when he actually read the law whose "integrity" he had sworn to protect; he thought it muddled and written in faulty English.

Thus Bryan joined the prosecution, an occurrence that largely determined future events. And a remarkable fact, although few commentators have found it so. State governments sometimes retain prominent specialists and trial lawyers to handle complicated cases before appellate courts, but a simple criminal prosecution in a trial court? Never. And Bryan at that—a man whose brief lackluster career at the bar had ended thirty years earlier.

On the eve of the Scopes trial a Tennessean, an able lawyer and prominent Baptist layman, said to a reporter: "What business do you think William Jennings Bryan, who has not tried a law-suit in twenty-five years, has coming here to assist the bench and bar of Tennessee in the trial of a little misdemeanor case that any judge ought to be able to dispose of in a couple of hours?" The answer was to emerge only gradually. Before the Scopes trial began, few foresaw what kind of ritual it would contain, or what role in it a high priest might play.

Chapter 2

Hot-Rod Halidom

> Faith is the vehicle of knowledge, intellect secondary. Your pure science is a myth.
>
> Leo Naphta, in Thomas Mann's *The Magic Mountain*, trans. H. T. Lowe-Porter (New York: Alfred A. Knopf, Inc., 1944), p. 397

I

Dedicating *In His Image* to his parents, William Jennings Bryan vouched his debt to them "for a Christian environment in youth." The father, Silas Lillard Bryan, was of Virginia farm stock. He migrated to Illinois when 16, and 11 years passed before he graduated from a Methodist college there. He went to Salem, Lincoln's town, read law; when he was 29 he was admitted to the bar and also became county superintendent of schools. The next year he went to the state senate, where he stayed until, in 1860, he became judge of a circuit that covered a half-dozen counties. He held this office 12 years.

Silas Bryan, like any judge, occasionally had one of his decisions upset by a higher court. He was able to take most of these reversals gracefully, but one incensed him. "I know that I was right in that decision because," he said, "I consulted God about it."

William Jennings Bryan was born the same year that his father was elected to the bench. Judge Bryan never missed a chance to impress upon his son that the Bible was divinely inspired. Every day a little before noon he would call Will into the office and read him a chapter of Proverbs with fitting commentary. Later, while a student at Illinois College, Will passed through a period of skepticism. Passed through it. On his 21st birthday he wrote to his future wife Mary Baird that he felt "some trembling" in contemplating the unknown future. "I would dread to be compelled to set forth upon this sea with nothing but the light of reason to aid me. What a blessing it is that we have that guide, the Bible."

Bryan had by this time attained the main features of his rhetoric: the style and the themes. At Illinois College, an offshoot of Yale with a typical classical curriculum, he won a prize for Latin prose, and he debated. He had begun speaking on religion at age 14, on politics when only 20. His college graduation speech was on "Character." Already the habit of oratory was secure. For the rest of his life, the sight of an audience caused Bryan to give off eloquence as spontaneously and abundantly as hot stone gives off steam during a summer shower.

Bryan was admitted to the bar in 1883, and the next year he married Mary Baird. Four years of modest unsuccess in Illinois prompted them to move to Lincoln, Nebraska. In 1890 Bryan ran for Congress, of course as a Democrat—his father's party. The district was normally Republican, but agricultural depression was stirring up all kinds of radicalism, and the tyro won by nearly 7,000 votes. His father's political connections in Illinois got Bryan a post on the important Ways and Means Committee, where he identified himself with the advocates of free coinage of silver. He made a vehement speech attacking President Cleveland for asking the unconditional repeal of the Silver Purchase Act of 1890. Re-elected in 1892, Bryan continued to demand free silver. In 1894 he tried to get the Nebraska legislature to elect him to the United States Senate, but he could not manage it. Out of office temporarily, he withdrew from the practice of law also and turned to journalism, becoming editor of the Omaha *World-Herald*.

Bryan the lawyer was now Bryan the editor and orator, for good. In 1894 and 1895 he was the most active of all the free-silver speakers who toured the country. But his national reputation was still slight when the Democratic national convention met in Chicago in 1896. The strong man of the convention was John Peter Altgeld, governor of Illinois, the man who stirred a tempest by pardoning the Haymarket survivors, then stirred another one by denouncing President Cleveland for sending United States troops into Illinois during the Pullman boycott, the masterly politician whose strategy had stolen control of the Democratic party from the President and the other Eastern conservatives. Strong-willed, forceful, shrewd, more honest than any but the saints, more honest than was good for him, but foreign-born and so ineligible for the Presidency. He tried to get the nomination for the colorless Senator Richard Bland. The convention deadlocked. Four ballots.

Bryan had gotten the floor, almost unknown, only 36 years old, to give what is probably the most famous convention speech in American history. Magnificently he swept into his peroration: "We will answer their demand for a gold standard by saying to them: You shall not press down upon the brow of labor this crown of thorns, you shall not crucify mankind upon a cross of gold." The crowd went crazy, including the delegates. On the fifth ballot, Bryan was nominated for President. He campaigned with unprecedented vigor, traveling 18,000 miles, speaking in hamlets and cities. Meanwhile the rival William McKinley sat quietly on a front porch and smiled, and prosperity returned, and Mark Hanna opened his bags of gold, and the Cross of Gold proved too frail to serve as a ladder to the Presidency.

The day after Bryan erected his verbal cross at the Chicago convention, Governor Altgeld had said to his friend Clarence Darrow: "I have been thinking over Bryan's speech. What did he say anyhow?" The question persisted. Although the Boy Orator was now the leader of the liberal Democrats, many reformers remained skeptical of him. When it seemed, in 1899, that Bryan would again be the Democratic candidate the next year, basic doubts about him were expressed in a letter to Altgeld by Henry Demarest Lloyd, the Christian socialist. Altgeld's reply was the best possible defense of Bryan:

In order to carry an election, you must have a man upon whom enough voters who differ somewhat in individual views will unite in order to give him the majority. . . . Let me further suggest that if Mr. Bryan was to come out and play the role of an educator or an adjutator, he would simply be in a field that is already tolerably well filled . . . The moment Mr. Bryan would enter this field, he would cease to be an available candidate for the presidency . . . Therefore instead of coming out squarely on a radical platform, I think that it is his duty to leave these things to some of the rest of us. Should we get control of the government, there will be no trouble in carrying out any reform for which the people are ripe, and any attempt to carry out a great reform before the people are ripe for it, must prove a failure. I would remind you that Mr. Lincoln never was an abolitionist, and that even after he was elected president, he was opposed to interfering with slavery in the Southern states, yet he became the "great liberator." What we want is to get into the White House a man who is not necessarily radical to begin with, but whose sympathies are with the great toiling masses, who will not be controlled by concentrated wealth, and who will be ready to carry out any great reform just as soon as the country is ready for it.

Even this amount of faith was shaken by Bryan's actions that same year. Although the treaty ending the Spanish-American war recognized American hegemony over the Philippines, Bryan urged ratification upon the Democratic Senators. Liberals thought that bad enough, but Bryan's argument seemed especially disingenuous: Since many European nations are opposed to an independent Philippine Republic, he said, the best course is for the United States to reach out her motherly arms and embrace the Philippines, and then make them independent. The next year, in accepting the Presidential nomination again, Bryan agreed that imperialism should be

made the "paramount issue." It was. Bryan lost even more decisively than in 1896.

In 1904 the nomination went to a conservative Easterner, but
it was Bryan a third time in 1908, and the third defeat was worse
than the second. He was no longer, in Altgeld's word, "available."
But he could still give speeches. A delegate to the Democratic
national convention of 1912, he introduced a sensational resolution
regretting the presence in the convention of two notorious million-
aires, August Belmont and Thomas Fortune Ryan. He then defended his aggressive action by saying that every delegate knew
that "an effort was being made to sell the Democratic party to the
predatory interests of the country." This action and Bryan's violation of his instructions in voting for Woodrow Wilson were widely
credited with getting Wilson the nomination.

The credit was exaggerated, but Bryan's influence was great
enough to make him Secretary of State in the Wilson administration. He was very helpful in lobbying Wilson's domestic program
through Congress. He endorsed the President's coercive policies
toward Mexico. He put into effect a project that had been a favorite of his since 1906 by negotiating arbitration treaties with 30 foreign nations.

Germany signed such a treaty with the United States right
after the war began in 1914. The almost ridiculous was followed—
it happens so often—by the almost sublime. In August, 1914, although American industry was working far below capacity and
Allied orders for munitions would have been politically useful,
Bryan wrote to J. P. Morgan & Co. that "loans by American bankers
to any foreign nation which is at war are inconsistent with the true
spirit of neutrality." By the time this policy was rescinded, Bryan
had resigned his office. The occasion was the *Lusitania* sinking by
a German submarine in May, 1915. President Wilson drafted a
rather stiff note demanding that Germany abjure use of submarines
against passenger vessels. Bryan objected. American citizens
should not travel on ships that were carrying munitions, as the
Lusitania had been. And if this note were sent to Germany, a com-

panion note to Britain should protest against her illegal trade restrictions. Finally, even though Congress had not ratified the arbitration treaty with Germany, Bryan thought its principles should be applied here. The President was not that neutral. Bryan quit office rather than sign the note, saying privately that it would "surely lead to war with Germany." The note was sent. When the policy on war loans was reversed in September, the two crucial steps had been taken that would lead to American entry into the war.

But Bryan would not attack the President. When Wilson campaigned for re-election in 1916 under the slogan: "He kept us out of war," Bryan stumped the West for him. As he went into the Democratic state headquarters in one state after another, he noted especially the large posters that listed the achievements of the Wilson administration, "and not a word," he later recalled bitterly, "about my 30 peace treaties!" Even that did not deter him.

Why had he resigned, anyway? American entry brought a typical response from Bryan. During the Spanish-American war he had raised a regiment of Nebraska volunteers and served a fruitless five months in the United States. Now, 57 years old and running to weight, he volunteered as a private. The offer was rejected.

Bryan turned to another cause: prohibition of alcoholic beverages. His enemies said that as long as he was running for President he never balked at campaign contributions from liquor companies. As late as 1908 he argued for local option in Nebraska. That was the year of his third defeat for the Presidency, and in 1909 he came out as a flatfooted prohibitionist. He was a leading advocate of national legislation. After passage of the Volstead Act, his zeal became international: "Our Nation will be saloonless for evermore and will lead the world in the great crusade which will drive intoxicating liquor from the globe."

II

Bryan came late to the prohibition movement; he came even later to the anti-evolution crusade.

From the publication of *The Origin of Species* in 1859, many religious men had opposed Darwin's theories for fear of their impact on morality. If man had developed from lower species of animals rather than having been created by God in His image, what assurance was there that man had a moral sense and could discern and follow God's law? If the Bible lost its authority as explanation of man's origins, how could it retain authority as a standard for his conduct? These fears found ludicrous forms. Just before the Civil War Josiah Nott, a Southern biologist, and Louis Agassiz of Harvard advanced the thesis that God had created each human race separately, that Negroes and whites had been created as separate species by God. This theory was indignantly rejected by fundamentalists of that day because it conflicted with the account in Genesis; the Bible was the bulwark of social order; the thesis of multiple creation, by subverting the Bible, threatened the entire social system. A writer in 1867 complained that the theory of man's evolution would create a chaos of "defalcations and robberies, and murders, and infanticides, and adulteries, and drunkenness, and every form and degree of social dishonor." In the following decades such fears occasionally were expressed in the firing of a professor by this college or that, in the expulsion of scholars by various Protestant churches.

During those years also, the years when Bryan was earning his reputation in progressive causes, many reformers were vigilantly fighting the applications of alleged Darwinian theory to social problems. Such social Darwinists as William Graham Sumner, a much respected Yale professor, not only justified the status quo as manifesting "the survival of the fittest" but also claimed that society changed gradually and naturally over eternities of time, and that man's efforts to influence the course of social change were futile or harmful. The lengths to which this attitude could carry are illustrated by an episode involving Henry George and E. L. Youmans, founder in 1872 of the *Popular Science Monthly* and the leading American propagandist for Herbert Spencer. Youmans denounced the political corruption in New York and declared that the rich were indifferent or sympathetic to it because it paid them to be so.

George asked: "What do you propose to do about it?" Youmans replied: "Nothing! You and I can do nothing at all. . . . Perhaps in four or five thousand years evolution may have carried men beyond this state of things."

After the turn of the century, explicit social Darwinism died down, and so did the evolution controversy. Then, in 1910, appeared the first of a series of ten small pamphlets, *The Fundamentals,* which expounded as a touchstone for Christians the Five Points: the infallibility of the Bible, the Virgin Birth of Christ, Christ's substitutionary atonement for man's sins, the Resurrection of Christ, the authenticity of all Biblical miracles. On the basis of this creed, *The Fundamentals* declared that Darwinism "can have no possible points of contact with Christianity."

Although fundamentalist activity declined during World War I, the war—by emphasizing the mystical and evil elements in man, by exuding vague anxieties and irrational fears, by equating evolution with "survival of the fittest" and then equating survival of the fittest with "German barbarism," with Nietzsche and the rule of force—eventuated in a postwar climate that proved ideal for fundamentalism. The war also witnessed the creation of a new organization. In 1918 Dr. William Bell Riley, pastor of the First Baptist Church of Minneapolis, led in the formation of the World's Christian Fundamentals Association.

All this happened without Bryan. He had joined the Presbyterian Church in boyhood, and in 1900 he became elder of his congregation at Lincoln. As the most popular Chautauqua speaker in the country for thirty years, he of course needed some religious talks, so he prepared one about Christ called "The Prince of Peace" and one about Christianity called "The Value of an Ideal." But he was blind to the menace of Darwinism. In 1909 he said blithely: "I do not carry the doctrine of evolution as far as some do; I am not yet convinced that man is a lineal descendant of the lower animals. I do not mean to find fault with you if you want to accept the theory . . ."

Then Bryan was reborn. "When I fall, I shall arise: when I sit in darkness, the Lord shall be a light unto me" (Micah vii:8). One factor in alerting Bryan was a book by Vernon Kellogg, a biologist who had gotten to know some German military leaders in Belgium; in *Headquarters Nights* (1917), Kellogg declared that the philosophy of the Germans was Darwinism applied to international relations. Bryan was alarmed also, as he toured the country giving religious talks after the war, by the many expressions of disbelief, especially by college students. He became convinced that the theory of human evolution was the evil instrument that had undermined the students' faith. It devastated him, at the conclusion of a speech in Atlanta, to be told by a college sophomore that Darwinism and Christianity could be reconciled easily; all one had to do was to discard Genesis. "Only Genesis!" Bryan exploded. "And yet there are three verses in the first chapter of Genesis that mean more to man than all the books of human origin: the first verse, which gives the most reasonable account of creation ever advanced; the twenty-fourth verse, which gives the only law governing the continuity of life on earth; and the twenty-sixth, which gives the only explanation of man's presence here."

Alert to any trace of scurf on the student soul, he publicized the report of a religious paper, based on a survey, that at one large university only 10 per cent of the male students were interested in religion, but 50 per cent gambled and 62 per cent drank. Bryan was especially aroused by James H. Leuba's *Belief in God and Immortality* (1916 and 1920). Leuba, a professor of psychology at Bryn Mawr, reported the results of some confidential polls he had taken. Of the 5,500 names in *American Men of Science,* he chose 1,000 as representative. Over half doubted or denied a personal God and personal immortality. Of the biologists replying, two out of three stated their disbelief. Leuba also got from nine ranking colleges 1,000 answers from students, 97 per cent of whom were 18-20 years of age. Only 15 per cent of the freshmen expressed a lack of belief, but 40-45 per cent of the men graduating did so.

Here, thought Bryan, was absolute proof. He hurled himself into the battle. Not only was the theory of evolution destroying our moral standards, he roared, but it was also poor science; there was no evidence of its validity. When he took this line in his address, "Brute or Brother?," at the University of Wisconsin in 1921, President Birge of the University remarked that Bryan would destroy the students' faith by identifying religion with untenable scientific doctrines. The comment was passed on to Bryan, who immediately started a dispute with Birge that lasted a full year. "The real question is," wrote Bryan in the New York *Times* in 1922, "Did God use evolution as His plan? If it could be shown that man, instead of being made in the image of God, is a development of beasts we would have to accept it, regardless of its effect, for truth is truth and will prevail. But when there is no proof we have a right to consider the effect of the acceptance of an unsupported hypothesis." Henry Fairfield Osborn, director of the American Museum of Natural History, wrote in reply that evolution had been Purposeful, not accidental, and that the evidence of evolution actually proved the existence of God.

Bryan got much encouragement, from both Midwest and South. Louis F. Post, a longtime Chicago liberal, the man who had done more than anybody else to stop the postwar deportation delirium, wrote him a warm endorsement. Post declared that man was separated from the animals by "an impassable gulf." The essential feature of man was that God had breathed life into him so that he became a living soul. Post would accept even Genesis as literally true if "indefinite periods" were substituted for the six days of the Creation. Bryan, much pleased by this support, replied: "I am very much in earnest in my opposition to Darwinism because I have abundant evidence of the evil influence it is exerting. I am trying to protect the students from atheistic professors by showing them that it is not necessary to reject the Bible—that there is no proof of animal origin."

Contrary evidence—what Bryan regarded as contrary evidence —continued to pile up. In February, 1923, he was jubilant about the discoveries in the newly opened tomb of Tutankhamen. "King Tutankhamen," he chortled, "appears to have been a man . . . If

ever man came from the ape we must have quit coming before the
Egyptian king took the throne. Man seems to have arrived on our
earth a good while ago, judging from the fact his civilization of
3,000 years before Christ was in quite a high state of progress." No
doubt of it, Darwin was wrong. A newspaper clipping reporting
these comments by Bryan was sent to Clarence Darrow, who in no
way shared Louis Post's enthusiasm about the religious views of
Bryan. Bryan, he thought, was worse than a boor, he was a dangerous boor. And Darrow soon found a way to express his attitude.

When the Chicago *Tribune* editorialized against Bryan's efforts
to proscribe the theory of evolution, Bryan replied in a letter to the
editor. Here was Darrow's chance. His terse but lengthy letter
rated the front page of the *Tribune* on the Fourth of July, 1923,
and was reprinted in full by many other newspapers.

Commenting on a questionnaire that Bryan had publicly addressed to those professors who claimed to believe simultaneously
in Christianity and in the theory of evolution, Darrow agreed that
answers to Bryan's queries might help to clarify the issue; "likewise," he continued, "a few questions to Mr. Bryan and the fundamentalists, if fairly answered, might serve the interests of reaching
the truth—all of this assumes that truth is desirable." Then came
55 questions to Bryan about the Bible. Did he believe in the literal
truth of every word of it? Was the story of the Creation factual or
allegorical? "Did God curse the serpent for tempting Eve and decree that thereafter he should go on his belly? How did he travel
before that time?" Darrow asked questions about the Flood, the
age of the earth, the origins of man.

Bryan was an artful politician; he would state his case in his
own way. This was not it. He didn't answer Darrow's questions,
which lay fallow to crop up again, two years later, in an unforeseen
context.

Bryan's campaign was meeting opposition. Even in his own
Presbyterian Church he had been humbled. A delegate to the General Assembly of the church in 1923, Bryan was nominated to be
moderator, the denomination's highest office. In the voting he led

on the first ballot, and again on the second. He turned to another candidate, Charles F. Wishart, and said confidently, "I'll win on the next ballot." But he didn't. Wishart did, a man only nine years in the church, the president of Wooster College that harbored a biologist, Horace Mateer, whose religious liberalism had already stirred Bryan's indignation. And Wishart further humiliated Bryan by refusing to name him as vice-moderator. Bryan did not offer the congratulations that the vanquished customarily advances to the victor.

Four days later, Bryan introduced a resolution in the General Assembly that would have denied any part of the church's educational fund to any school that taught, "as proved a fact," any evolutionary theory that connected man with any other species. During the debate, Bryan declared: "I am now engaged in the biggest reform of my life. I am trying to save the Christian Church from those who are trying to destroy her faith!" But his resolution was sidetracked in favor of a milder one. In spite of this personal defeat, Bryan could find considerable solace in the affirmation by the General Assembly of the fundamentalist Five Points.

And reactions elsewhere were encouraging. The governor of North Dakota wrote him in 1922 to praise his activities and to denounce professors who subverted their students' Christian beliefs. Bryan personally argued the iniquities of Darwinism before the legislatures of Kentucky, West Virginia, his own adopted state of Florida, and Georgia. After he addressed the Kentucky legislature in 1922, an anti-evolution law failed of passage in the House by a single vote. In Florida he was completely successful; the legislature in 1923 passed a resolve written by Bryan himself. It was essential, said the resolve, that the public schools should not be sullied by "sectarian views" or by "teachings designed to attack the religious beliefs of the public." Therefore it was "improper and subversive to the best interest of the people" for any teacher in those schools to teach "atheism or agnosticism or to teach *as true* Darwinism or any other hypothesis that links man in blood relationship to any other form of life." The resolve provided no penalty for violations, thus avoiding the tactical error that Bryan thought had been made in Kentucky.

III

Bryan, the Great Commoner, was, in some respects, a most uncommon man. He held one of the highest offices in the country, and ran three times for the very highest. A magnificently handsome man, possessed of a voice like an organ, he was adept at caressing a crowd with the sin they loathe so much. His popularity on the lecture platform spawned a fortune estimated at "some hundreds of thousands of dollars"; Bryan invested it in real estate in Nebraska, Oklahoma, Texas, and Florida. For several years he had a winter home in Florida, and in 1922 he transferred his permanent residence and citizenship there. He lived at Coconut Grove in a substantial mansion. It was called Marymount. He had a favorite saddle horse. In the winter of 1924-25 he spoke daily at noon, under the palms, to the tourists at Coral Gables. Not about Florida real estate, reported Mrs. Bryan, but "of Florida generally, of its advantages and pleasures." On Sundays from December to May he drew an average of 4,000 persons to his Bible classes at Royal Palm Park.

Yet, although he was clearly a man already made, Bryan continued throughout his career as spokesman for the man on the make. On his speaking tours he learned what the common people wanted, and he then told them in his sonorous similes they were right. From beginning to end, Bryan thought the people should have whatever they desired. The role of the politician was not merely to vote as his constituents wanted, it was to reassure them constantly that what they wanted was the Good, the True, and the Beautiful.

Many of the reforms he championed were worthy ones: woman suffrage, the Federal income tax, free silver in 1896, which was hardly the ridiculous nostrum that it was termed by his Republican contemporaries and later historians. But there are also the anti-evolution laws. There is a law Bryan drafted that would have made it a crime, punishable by loss of citizenship, for any American to drink an alcoholic beverage while abroad or on the high seas. And there is the fact that Bryan never took up any reform until it could poll a big vote.

This is not necessarily to Bryan's discredit. As Altgeld pointed out in his controversy with Henry Demarest Lloyd, democratic reform needs agitators; it also needs politicians who can get in front of the big parade and let it push them into public office. Bryan's widow used another argument in explaining why he was so tardy in taking up the cause of prohibition. Until 1912, she said, he had opposed making prohibition a national issue because it would have diverted attention from the economic reforms that were already national issues. So far, so good. But there was a deeper reason. To Bryan, truth and virtue were determined by the popular will. He resented the experts in government as much as he resented the plutocrats in business. He insisted that ordinary people are fully competent "to sit in judgment on every question which has arisen or which will arise, no matter how long our government will endure." The important political questions are moral questions, and the heart of the common man is good.

Majority rule, to practical minds, is likely to seem the most practical way of running a government. It is a political expedient, a way of settling disputes that require settlement, and preferable to the alternatives only because it is less disruptive. Like the alternatives, it rests ultimately on force, not on wisdom; it is less disruptive exactly because it requires less exercise of force.

This was not what majority rule meant to Bryan. His doctrine had originated in the mystical intuition that all men are equal in the eyes of God. But Bryan secularized it, so that all men became equally wise, equally just, equally creative. What had been a denial of worldly standards was transformed into a mechanism for managing a government. As Walter Lippmann wrote of Bryan: "The spiritual doctrine that all men will stand at last equal before the throne of God meant to him that all men are equally good biologists before the ballot box of Tennessee."

And so Bryan advocated all measures that would extend direct

democracy in government: the initiative, the referendum, direct
primaries. He demanded the same sort of majority rule in the
church. His practical program against the theory of evolution was
a straightforward demand that the issue be debated in every congregation and decided by a majority vote. The minority, if it
would not acquiesce in the result, should be forced to withdraw.
Such a program did not infringe on freedom of conscience in any
way. Each person had a right to think and speak as he pleased, but
these were individual rights. "The moment one takes on a representative character," wrote Bryan, "he becomes obligated to represent faithfully and loyally those who have commissioned him to
represent them."

Similar procedures applied in the schools. The teacher was the
representative of the parents. He should do what they wanted done.
If you hired a man to paint your house, Bryan said, you would expect him to use the colors you selected. Likewise if you hire a man
to teach your children, he should use the facts you select, the ideas
you select. Most of the people were Christian; Darwinism was anti-
Christian; Darwinism should not be taught. "By what logic,"
asked Bryan, "can the minority demand privileges that are denied
to the majority?"

The logic is clear enough to anybody who believes in objective
reality; from this belief it follows inevitably that the content of science courses should be determined by specialists who have studied
the facts of nature. But Bryan's ear was ill-tuned to the cacophony
of ordinary facts; reality of this coarse sort played always on the
soft pedal. The voices of God and the people thundering over the
prairies were continuously drowning out the sounds of the grass-
hoppers and the crickets.

Once at least, so Mrs. Bryan reported, Bryan was unable to
cope with a religious task. He was to speak at a waterfront mission
in New York City. As he looked at the battered, underfed, miser-
able men around him, he felt inadequate. Later he told Mrs.
Bryan: "It takes a man who has been saved from the depths to
reach men like these. I cannot do it. I lack the necessary past."

This humility was rare. His customary stance was wild-eyed exuberance. "I feel sure of my ground when I make a political speech, but I feel even more certain of my ground when I make a religious speech." Such certainty does not often lead to self-restraint. It did not in Bryan. His oratory contained the maddest fancies of vocabulary and figure. "What did he say, anyhow?" Altgeld had asked. The question never occurred to Bryan. Words are words, a way to move people; words need not connect either with thoughts or with things.

Anybody who has read a few of Bryan's political speeches will not be surprised to learn that he liked huge meals of greasy food. For all his intimate association with men and women who demanded the compulsory prohibition of alcoholic beverages, his attacks on food showed no moderation and little decency. One hot day in St. Louis, a bystander was amazed to see him eat an enormous platter of sauerkraut and frankfurters, served originally for four men, and then call for another helping. Equally memorable is an eye-witness account of a breakfast eaten by Bryan in Virginia during the 1900 Presidential campaign: "An enormous melon, 2 quails, a formidable slice of ham with 6 eggs, batter cakes immersed in butter accompanied here and there with potatoes and small delicacies for sidedishes, all of which he washed down with innumerable cups of coffee with milk."

IV

In theology also, Bryan lived high on the hogma. "You believe in the age of rocks: I believe in the Rock of Ages," he told his opponents. At the Presbyterian General Assembly of 1923 he shouted: "More of those who take evolution die spiritually than die physically from smallpox." His real clincher was: "I have just as much right as the atheist to begin with an assumption, and I would rather begin with God and reason down than begin with a piece of dirt and reason up."

In labelling his opponents who questioned the plenary inspiration of the Bible, Bryan projected some of his own qualities; he

called them "complacent" and self-indulgent, he accused them of
"egotism—an insufferable egotism." Behind these traits in Bryan
was a desperate intolerance of the ambiguous, the uncertain. Repeatedly he voiced a demand to know, for sure: "Why should the
Bible, which the centuries have been unable to shake, be discarded
for scientific works that have to be revised and corrected every few
years?" The agnosticism of Robert Ingersoll moved him to ask:
"how could anyone find pleasure in taking from a human heart a
living faith and substituting therefor the cold and cheerless doctrine,
'I do not know.'" Bryan the grown man, even as Bryan the college
senior, had to have a guide and protector. Religion rested upon
"man's consciousness of his finiteness in an infinite universe"; recognition of this compelled man to lean "upon the arm that is
stronger than his."

Bryan could not accept both the flawed nature of man and the
responsibility of each individual for his own deeds. Mature men
realize that life is uncertainty, and also realize that liability to error
does not mitigate the demand for action. Since life cannot be
solved, it continues to give pleasure, and the pleasure arises from
our efforts to cope with a varied and endless sequence of problems and contingencies. In a sense the consciousness of a wise person is always divided, one part of it acting with conviction, while
another part stands aloof, appraising, never forgetting that all
human action is based on limited insight and that it may get results far different from those it seeks. But with Bryan, it was
whole hog or none. He could qualify nothing. He ate with both
hands and talked in stentorian tones. His perception changed every
shade of gray into a dismal black or a dazzling white. He saw no
object as it really was. The people were an Absolute Good, the
gold power was an Absolute Evil, as was Darwinism.

In the 15th century, says Johan Huizinga, life was a series of
extremes: silence and sound, darkness and light, summer and winter. If a man was sick, he was sick unto death; if he was happy, his
heart brimmed over; if he was rich, he was very rich. So with
Bryan: if he believed, his commitment was total.

But his mind, medieval or not, was not always incoherent. His attacks on the theory of evolution were based on a cohesive argument: Civilization cannot exist without morality. Morals rest on religion. Religion rests on belief in God. Belief in God rest on the authority of the Bible. Darwinism undermines belief in the Bible.

It would not do to say that morality could rest upon reason. A person's character is formed in his youth, before his reason matures. "What shall guide the child in youth?" Bryan asked. Nor is that all; even the mature reason can be distorted by ignorance and self-interest. No judge is permitted to decide a case to which he is a party. If one looked closely at any so-called rational system of ethics, he would see that its conception of virtue was borrowed from a moral system based on religion.

This view allowed no room for compromise with the theory of evolution, "the source of the poison which is bringing disorder into the church." Bryan was not carked about the believers in Darwinism who were also atheists or agnostics; very few Christians would listen to them anyway. The worst enemies were the men who professed both Christianity and evolution. Their contradictory doctrine was "an anaesthetic that deadens the Christian's pain while his religion is being removed." Bryan had the insight to see that nobody can be open-minded about the divine inspiration of the Bible; the man who says he is open-minded is in fact denying what Bryan asserted.

Nor could one go through the Bible picking and choosing, as some modernists did, between the reasonable and the unreasonable miracles ("If God is infinite in power, he can perform any number of miracles as well as one"). If one part of the Bible is divinely inspired, all parts are. Once subject any part of the Bible to the censorship of science, and the insane procedure cannot be halted short of the bitter end. Authority is authority, and faith is faith. Bryan did not mean that we should accept some Biblical passages as myths that emphasize spiritual truths. "Give the modernist three words, 'allegorical,' 'poetical,' and 'symbolical,' and he can suck the meaning out of every vital doctrine of the Christian Church and every passage in the Bible to which he objects.*

Bryan had as little respect for scientists as for humanistic scholars. He scorned "those who measure men by diplomas and college degrees." He was wroth at the "scientific soviet" that was trying to control the schools. And yet, Bryan insisted that he was in favor of science. Truth revealed in the Bible could not conflict with truth discovered by science. All truth was from God. But what if they seemed to conflict? The answer was easy: The truth that science claimed to discover had not been discovered at all. It was not truth, but wild guesses.

To reach this outcome, Bryan used the vocabulary of science, such words as *evidence, proof, truth, reason*. Listen to him. The "proof that God actually speaks to man" was "the influence the words have exerted on hearts and lives." The validity of the blood atonement as the road to salvation could "be proved by experience. Hundreds of millions bear joyful witness to it." The "strongest evidence possible" for "the truths that the Bible contains" was the fact that millions of people had died in defense of their validity. On the subject of the Virgin Birth: "The modernists have no evidence to offer to contradict the Bible record. In not a single one of the sixty-six books of the Bible can they find a sentence, word or syllable to justify a rejection of the explicit language of Matthew and Luke." This was no small matter: "If the Virgin Birth be rejected, how shall the deity of Christ be proved?" The first verse of Genesis "gives the most reasonable account of creation ever advanced." After all this evidence, proof, reason, and truth, where does he arrive? "There is only one argument that can be made to one who rejects the authority of the Bible, namely, that the Bible is true."

* Confer Reinhold Niebuhr: "The vice of all mythical religion is that its interpreters try to reduce its supra-history to actual history. Thus the myth of the creation is constructed into an actual history of origins when it is really a description of the quality of existence. The myth of the Fall is made into an account of the origin of evil, when it is really a description of its nature." *An Interpretation of Christian Ethics* (Copyright 1935 by Harper & Brothers; New York: Living Age Books, 1956), p. 93.

Using this method of analysis, aided ofttimes by vacuous analogies, Bryan refuted to his satisfaction the evidence for evolution. Having asserted that no scientist had ever been able to show how any specific species evolved, he reasoned that God had created each species "separate and distinct." Thus Bryan—a man who never in his entire life dissected animal flesh until it was cooked—could reach conclusions about physiology contrary to the conclusions of all physiologists: "Anatomy presents convincing evidence that man's body was designed by an Infinite Intelligence and carefully adapted to work required of him. . . . all his parts show that man is not a haphazard development of chance, but a creation, designed for a purpose."

That disposed of Darwin. Bryan did not hesitate to draw practical implications. "A teacher receiving pay in dollars on which are stamped 'In God We Trust,' should not be permitted to teach the children there is no God." Everything depends on the will of the parents: "teachers in public schools must teach what the taxpayers desire taught." Here was the marriage of Bryan's two chief principles; the rule of the majority, the infallibility of the Word. Marriage, yes, but a feckless affair, sterile of normal offspring, producing its deformed children in unnatural ways. By ignorance, out of anxiety.

Bryan was determined to defend as literally true every word of the Bible. In the deepest sense, he had to defend it; he needed reassurance and certainty, and since childhood he had learned to rely on the Bible as the source of reassurance and certainty. But if he defended all Christian theology, he did not defend all parts of it with equal intensity.

Unlike many fundamentalists, Bryan was not impressed by the notion of original sin. He lacked a sense of the irrational and the corrupt in man; it is hard to imagine that he ever writhed in anguish at the thought of his own wickedness. He held rather to the more common American opinion that men are basically good—not rational, but good; he believed that sound religious instruction can lead the worst sinner into the ways of the Lord. "But if we walk in the light, as he is in the light, we have fellowship with one another, and the blood of Jesus Christ his Son cleanseth us from sin" (I John v:6). A man can know whether he is a true Christian, said Bryan, by a simple test: "If the sinlessness of Christ inspires within him an earnest desire to conform his life more nearly to the perfect example, he is indeed a follower; if, on the other hand, he resents the reproof which the purity of Christ offers, and refuses to mend his ways, he has yet to be born again."

Rebirth. Rebirth and salvation and immortality. Here, for Bryan, is the core of Christian doctrine. "I am the resurrection and the life: he that believeth in me, though he were dead, yet shall he live" (John xi:25). In denying that a man who "refuses to mend his ways" is a true Christian, Bryan seems to endorse the doctrine of salvation by works. "But the mercy of the Lord is from everlasting to everlasting upon them that fear him, and his righteousness unto children's children; To such as keep his covenant, and to those that keep his commandments to do them" (Psalms ciii:17-18). But this doctrine wars and struggles in Scripture with another road to redemption. "For thou, Lord, art good, and ready to forgive; and plenteous in mercy unto all them that call upon thee" (Psalms lxxxvi:5). "Not by works of righteousness which we have done, but according to his mercy He saved us" (Titus iii:5). In the Bible these two doctrines live together, not amicably, but in the most rigorous tension. It is Christ's injunction that man should love God *and* his neighbor. No man can be certain of salvation, because no man can know that he has passed the test.

Convulsively, compulsively, in a frenzy of creative forgetting, Bryan collapsed this tension. And inevitably he embraced the softer, easier terms of it. Bryan did not reject the general pattern of Christian rebirth, from Darkness through Suffering to Light; what he did was to emphasize the Blood Atonement. Magically, struggle and suffering are no longer the portion of each individual man. Christ struggled and suffered for us all. "If one believes in a God who is all-loving, as well as all-powerful," wrote Bryan, "the scheme of substitutionary suffering is not only believable but entirely natural." And Christ was saved for us all. "Christ, by His resurrection, has made immortality sure," wrote Bryan; "He has transformed death into a narrow, star-lit strip between the companionship of yesterday and the reunion of tomorrow." Here, at last, at long last, was certainty. A cenoby everlasting.

In order to hold up this keystone, Bryan had to defend the arch. If the Bible was not inspired, there is no proof of miracles. If the Virgin Birth did not occur, there is no proof of Christ's divinity. If Christ was not divine, He did not suffer for us all, but only for Himself. If Christ was not bodily resurrected, He was not saved for us all. "For if the dead rise not, then is not Christ raised: And if Christ be not raised, your faith is vain; ye are yet in your sins" (I Corinthians xv:16-17).

But the dependence of morality on religion that Bryan stressed so much—what of that now? It still exists in his thinking: in fact, we can see more clearly just how he conceived the nature of the dependence. Virtue, to Bryan, was not a quality that a man achieved; it was a quality that a man accepted, as shown by Bryan's belief that it was both possible and just to force others to accept it. Virtue came not as a result of the accumulation of good habits within a man because of his struggles with himself and his world; a man received virtue, by transfusion from God, much as he might receive blood plasma. All he needed to do was to relax, not to harden his veins against the needle. So Bryan's theology is remarkably lacking in moral tension. He could be so easy-going about it that he was not in the least disturbed to call Christianity "the Gospel of the Second Chance." He gave his listeners an even larger placebo by telling them: "it is more than that; it is the gospel that offers forgiveness to any who come in true repentance, no matter how often or how deep they may have fallen."

Not only was salvation easy, it was instantaneous: "He saves, not by the slow process of education, but by a change of heart—the New Birth."

V

For William Jennings Bryan, the immaculate conclusion of the Scopes trial would have been the confession and repentance, the Resurrection, of John Thomas Scopes. There is no evidence that Bryan ever conceived of this specific man as the object of his efforts; probably he never did. But surely Bryan was going to Dayton, Tennessee, not as a lawyer goes to court, but as a preacher goes to a revival meeting. He would preach the Word, and thousands, perhaps millions, of sinners would hit the sawdust trail. And his services were accepted in the same spirit. If the purpose of the trial was to convict Scopes, Bryan was a blunt accessory. But if the purpose of the trial was to stage a religious celebration—one that would arouse the populace, win promotions to higher office for politicians, and make Dayton a place to reckon with—Bryan was ideal as high priest.

Not that Bryan's motives were solely directed toward the welfare of his fellow man. He was prurient for popularity, so much so that he had seriously compromised himself the preceding June at the Democratic national convention in New York. When the minority of the platform committee tried to add to the plank on religious liberty a specific denunciation of the Ku Klux Klan, Bryan spoke against the amendment. He said that it would give undue prominence to the Klan and that it would create intolerance and strife. This position kept him in line with those sections, the South and Midwest, where his influence had always been greatest.

And now, at the Scopes trial, he could take his place at the head of the American people. "For the first time in my life," he told a fundamentalist conference on May 14, "I'm on the side of the majority."

The same day, John Randolph Neal became chief counsel for Scopes. Neal was already a controversial figure in Tennessee. In 1923, when he was dean of the law school at the state university, a professor had selected James Harvey Robinson's *Mind in the Making* as a textbook. This volume had been a chief fundamentalist target, and a campaign began against the professor. The president of the university discharged him. That caused a bigger uproar. Before it died down, Neal and four other professors were also fired. Neal, a man of independent means, promptly opened a private law school in Nashville. He ran for governor in the Democratic primary against Austin Peay. The issue was evolution. Neal was swamped. Now he had a chance to get even.

If Bryan and Neal were happy, the defendant was writhing. Not from fear. From embarrassment. In agreeing to the case, Scopes had thought it would be a local affair, a quiet law case among friends. He never expected it to interfere with his plan to spend the summer selling Fords for 5 per cent commission. When the case hit the front pages, he was abashed. But he talked the situation over with his father, who told him he had an unusual chance to serve his country.

The great cause at stake was stated for the press by Scopes' lawyer, who denied that the defense had any intention of waging a fight for the theory of evolution. "The question," said John Randolph Neal, "is not whether evolution is true or untrue, but involves the freedom of teaching, or what is more important, the freedom of learning." Having thus posed the issue, Neal was promptly displaced as senior defense counsel by a man who did not agree with him.

Clarence Darrow first thought of himself in relation to the Scopes trial while visiting the novelist James Branch Cabell in Richmond, Virginia. The two men discussed the case with Joseph Hergesheimer, another novelist, and H. L. Mencken, whose caustic ebullience was making the *American Mercury* into the house organ of irreverent youth. Darrow was asked if he would not like to defend Scopes. He said that he would. But instead of publicly announcing his willingness, he went quietly to New York City to discuss some legal matters with Bainbridge Colby and Dudley Field Malone.

The three lawyers had achieved different kinds of prominence. Darrow, a huge, unkempt, shambling man of 68 years, was as well known as any trial lawyer in the country. Colby was a prosperous New York lawyer who, like Bryan, had been prominent in reform politics. Also like Bryan, he had been Secretary of State under Woodrow Wilson. Even some of his friends thought him a stuffed shirt. Malone was Irish by birth, Catholic in upbringing, and a divorce lawyer for the international set. He was the youngster of the trio, 43 years old, virile and fair-complexioned and vibrant.

As the three lawyers conferred in New York, they noticed in the newspapers that Bryan had volunteered to aid the prosecution. The response almost suggested itself: "Well, we will offer our services to the defense," was the way Malone phrased it later. They did. John Randolph Neal was pleased to accept the offer, especially since they promised to serve without fee and to pay their own expenses.

The elements of the trial were becoming apparent: Scopes, certain to be unobtrusive. The erratic Neal, whose ways would cause the defense some excruciating moments. Bryan, committed to defending the literal truth of every word in the Bible—a commitment that would turn to ashes in his mouth. The 55 questions that Clarence Darrow had put to Bryan in the pages of the Chicago *Tribune*. And, of course, Darrow.

Chapter 3

An Uncurried Mind

> I applied mine heart to know, and
> to search, and to seek out wisdom,
> and the reason of things, and to
> know the wickedness of folly,
> even of foolishness and madness.
>
> ECCLESIASTES viii:25

I

Picture a boy, sitting, his mother combing his hair. He is squirming and resentful. He does not want his hair to be trained and orderly.

But the same boy will hardly be conscious of how the tines of usage and custom bite through his scalp to form those neural connections compatible with the received truths. The grooves in the brain, shaped in this fashion during a man's lifetime, grow imperceptibly into a three-dimensional network. But not a tangle—no, the mind has been parted, and each connection fits snugly into its proper niche. Since the channels never cross, no new connections can be formed. The man is predictable, tamed. In church he bends his head and bows his knee. The sight of a flag prompts him to salute. But at a ball park he will shout in vulgate and curse the umpire. The same man does all these things.

But now imagine a boy whose scalp was trained by his parents to be tougher than most, so that subsequently the tines of society are often turned aside from their intended mark. The expected order, the predictability, is lost. The grooves in his mind intersect at odd junctures; they form a complex and unique pattern. Impulses are forever leaping from one groove to another. The mind is uncurried, untamed. Such a man may end up scoffing at our heroes and mocking our pieties. Clarence Darrow was like that. No man can claim to be his own parish, but Darrow reached hard and far toward that goal.

Any society, almost any relation between two people, draws its cohesion from certain conventional dicta that the members conspire to mumble to one another. A roster of such propositions for the United States of 1925 would have included these:

God's ways rule the world, and they are generally beneficient.

Therefore progress is inevitable.

Man has free will.

Most men typically behave in rational ways.

Formal education is likely to make a person more decent.

People who are deeply religious are more likely to be virtuous than atheists or agnostics.

Morality and virtue can be defined by a few clear and simple rules.

The United States as a nation, and the people within it as individuals, are better than foreigners who have not enjoyed the countless benefits of the American way of life.

In the United States, anybody who is willing to work hard can be a success in life.

The American judicial system produces results that, however rough-hewn at times, can still (without irony) be called justice.

If criminals are punished promptly and efficiently, there will be fewer crimes.

> Negroes are, whether for reasons of heredity or upbring-
> ing, inferior to white people.

> My group—whether businessmen or trade unionists or
> Congressmen—is more virtuous than other groups.

The coherence of American society, the unity of the American
people, were widely presumed to rest on a shared faith in this apo-
dictic code. But Clarence Darrow dissented from every plank in it.
Not by mild, sly, veiled questions, but by raucous and ruthless No-
saying, day after day and year after year. Since few believers can
credit the existence of even one man who never believed, his dis-
sent was inevitably viewed as apostasy.

But it was not. In plain fact, he never did believe. His mind,
like the minds of us all, had been textured by habituation to the
world around him. But that world, in Darrow's youth, was not the
common, ordinary American world. His father was peculiar. If
Silas Lillard Bryan trained his son to acceptance of the normal beliefs, Amirus Darrow grew subversion in his children as some men
grow rose bushes. He had fostered a green thumb for it since the
time when, a year after he graduated from the Meadville Theological Seminary, he had departed from the ministry, the church, and
all traffic with worldly and other-worldly creeds.

Amirus was the town eccentric of the little village of Kinsman
in northeastern Ohio. He earned a modest living by making furni-
ture and being the local undertaker. His wagon served as a hearse;
between funerals, he used it as a chicken coop. A bookish
freethinker, he was less involved in practicalities than in pondering
the big questions of human existence that the Bible asks and that
Meadville Theological had not answered. So he was engrossed in
what the theory of evolution had to say about the origins of man,
and he eagerly read the books of Ernst Haeckel.

Into this atmosphere of 19th-century rationalism Clarence Darrow was born on April 18, 1857, the fifth child and second son in
the family. Clarence liked to play baseball and to dream. His one

contact with physical labor lasted less than a day and caused him to seek a trade at which he could live without working. He found it: law. He went to school at Kinsman, a year at Allegheny College, a year of law school at the University of Michigan, then reading law in Ohio until he was admitted to the bar in 1878. He got married, had a son, practiced law for nine years in various towns around northeastern Ohio. At Ashtabula the liberal social views he had learned from Amirus were reinforced when a banker lent him Henry George's *Progress and Poverty* and a judge lent him John Peter Altgeld's *Our Penal Machinery and Its Victims.*

Altgeld was a county judge in Chicago, where Darrow's older brother was living. In 1887 Darrow, without clear purpose or firm ambition, drifted along there, seemingly a typical half-trained lawyer from a little farming town. But Chicago was booming, and Darrow boomed with it. His rise in Chicago legal circles was incredibly rapid. Soon after his arrival he entered into various reform movements; he also became an effective stump-speaker for the thieving Democratic machine of Hinky Dink Kenna and Bathhouse John Coughlin in the First Ward. This political hackwork, and the close ties he had established with Altgeld, launched Darrow's law career. A Democratic mayor gave him a city job in 1889; the next year Darrow was put in charge of all civil litigation for the city government. He left that post to become general attorney to the Chicago & Northwestern Railroad. So his early success, up to the time he went into private practice in 1893, was at civil rather than criminal law, at paper work rather than trial tactics.

The Prendergast case of 1894 was an omen. Robert Prendergast, a deluded adolescent, shot and killed the mayor of Chicago. At his trial he was found mentally competent and convicted of murder. Darrow was hired to handle the appeal. The only legal grounds open to him—that Prendergast had become insane since his trial and conviction—were impossibly narrow. Prendergast was hanged. This was the only client Darrow ever lost to an executioner, although he later defended more than 50 persons charged with first-degree murder. The case was important to Darrow in other ways. It gave him his first intimate view of the sort of psychological evidence that he later used so effectively. It gave him a chance to argue that every man's character is rigorously determined by his birth and upbringing so that none of us is responsible for his own actions. Therefore no man can justly be punished, and no group of men has a right to condemn another man to die.

The Prendergast case was followed immediately by the Pullman boycott, and Darrow was retained to defend Eugene Debs and other strike leaders against charges of violating an injunction and of conspiring to obstruct interstate commerce. Although Debs went to jail for contempt of court, the case gave Darrow a national reputation in labor law. In every big labor case, the trade unions wanted Darrow. For two decades his major practice was in this field and he was counsel in major cases all over the country: in 1898 the Kidd conspiracy trial in Wisconsin; in 1902-3 the hearings before the Anthracite Coal Strike Commission; in 1906-7 the trial of Moyer and Haywood for conspiring to murder a former governor of Idaho. These cases were front-page news from Maine to California. The name of Darrow was known in every little town in the country. He was having fun, taking only cases he liked, handling the cases as he pleased, living as he pleased, making perhaps $20,000 a year and more whenever he wanted it.

No case was more sensational than the McNamara trial of 1911. In the midst of a bitter strike at Los Angeles, dynamite wrecked the building of the anti-labor *Times,* causing the death of twenty men. The men arrested for the crime were John J. McNamara, secretary-treasurer of a national AFL union, and his brother Jim, a wispy, frail, sad-eyed man with guts of steel and a bantering humor. The American Federation of Labor and the influential Socialist Party shouted that the McNamaras were innocent. Darrow was hired to defend them.

But the McNamaras were not innocent. Although Darrow soon saw that he had no chance to win, he kept working to win, and trying to make a deal for clemency. The deal was made. On December 1, with no previous hint to the public, Jim McNamara stood up in court and pleaded guilty. His brother John pleaded guilty to a lesser crime. With self-righteous anguish the leaders of organized labor implied that Darrow had deceived them into thinking his clients innocent. And the prosecution, aglow with victory, indicted Darrow himself on two charges of conspiracy to bribe jurors.

When Darrow came to trial on the first count, he was represented by one of the ranking criminal lawyers on the West Coast. An acquittal came easily. But Darrow ran out of money before he was tried on the second charge. He could not collect evidence. He could not hire a lawyer. He defended himself, always a difficult task, and he did it in the hardest way possible. Instead of deserting Jim McNamara to save himself, Darrow changed the plea in his own defense into a plea for clients already in prison. Jim McNamara, said Darrow, was no murderer, but a man who had fought for the workingmen, and had fought with the only weapons he could find in a pitiless war. McNamara had planted the dynamite, but he had not meant to kill anybody; the deaths of those twenty men were due to a tragic accident. Here is the measure of Darrow's recusancy. With his reputation, his right to practice law, his right to walk the streets and live as he pleased, with all these at stake, he still would not say that society was right and Jim McNamara was wrong. "God forbid that I should justify you; till I die I will not remove mine integrity from me. My righteousness I hold fast, and will not let it go: my heart shall not reproach me as long as I live" (Job xxviii:5-6).

Considering Darrow's argument, he was lucky not to be convicted. But the jury couldn't agree, and the indictment was later dropped. Darrow went back to Chicago, 56 years old, ill, broke. His integrity was suspect. He had no clients. His former friends in the trade-union leadership could not bear to hear his name. His law firm was dissolved, and Edgar Lee Masters, his partner since 1903, had become a vindictive enemy. Thus, twenty years after he had largely abandoned general practice, Darrow suffered the death of a second career, in labor law. Now he was to be reborn into a third, in criminal law.

But the pregnancy was accidental, the gestation period lengthy and cluttered with irrelevancies. For some time Darrow just muddled along. His law practice was slow and various. Some of the criminal cases that came to him were interesting, but not enough so to win notice outside his own city; even an alert resident of New York City might have wondered what had happened to Clarence Darrow, so infrequent and so modest were the newspaper notices about him. Only with World War I and its aftermath did Darrow become a national figure again. A zealous advocate of American entry into the war, he traveled all over the country stating his views at giant mass meetings. He was surprised at finding himself on the same platform, physically and programmatically, with such men as Samuel Insull; writing to his son, Darrow marveled that he was "right in it now" with the men who had always been against him. Soon Darrow was right out of it again. As the Red Hunt continued and mounted after the war, he was defense counsel in several big sedition trials: Ben Gitlow in New York; Arthur Person in Rockford, Illinois; a group of anarchists in Milwaukee; twenty leaders of the Communist Labor party in Chicago.

Gradually Darrow got back on his feet financially. He began to slow down, and actively made preparations to retire from practice. Increasingly he gave his reduced energy to writing, lecturing, debating. And then he took on the most difficult case of his career.

Nathan Leopold, Jr., and Richard Loeb, two teen-agers on the south side of Chicago, were driving around in their car one afternoon in May, 1924. They picked up Bobby Franks, a 13-year-old boy they knew. They killed him with a hammer, mutilated his body with acid and stuffed it into a culvert. After that they tried to collect $10,000 ransom from his father. They were caught, and confessed. Additional evidence was obtained. The state had an airtight case. Instantly the newspapers set to work building up hysteria. They could scarcely have asked for better marks. Both defendants were intellectuals, Jews, homosexuals, and rich. The crime was brutal. Loeb and Leopold said they had done it from a desire to commit a perfect crime. And they persisted in boasting about their action.

Darrow took the case, although he wrote a friend that it would be "a hard struggle to save the lives of the boys." This was his sole aim. The defendants, he agreed, were unfit to be set at liberty. He delayed the trial as long as possible to let the climate cool off. Then he entered a plea of guilty and fell back on a little-used clause in the Illinois statutes providing that, in murder trials where the defendant pleaded guilty, the judge should hear evidence in mitigation of the crime before passing sentence.

Darrow saw these hearings in terms of a single question: How can I create a community atmosphere that will enable the judge to exercise mercy? If he could do that, the judge would be all right; after all, Darrow and the judge had both campaigned in behalf of Hinky Dink Kenna more than 30 years earlier. So Darrow brought four neurologists and psychiatrists to court to testify about the psychic condition of Loeb and Leopold. Darrow scraped together every biographical fact he could find. And, in a summation that lasted three full days, he put these facts together into a coherent story. Neglect by their parents. Improper attention by a governess. Nietzsche and crime stories. Strength and weakness. Emotional dependence. Delusion and dream. The quest for recognition. Boys who want to be gods.

Every day he talked, and every night he read the newspapers. Especially the headlines, and day by day they shifted. He worked back and forth over the same evidence. He mentioned a fact, dropped it, picked it up again four hours later and saw it in a new light. After three days he stopped talking. The judge sent Loeb and Leopold to prison for ninety-nine years. The strain on the judge of doing what he knew he should do was so great that he had a nervous breakdown.

Darrow's argument had saved the lives of Loeb and Leopold.

A year later, it was used against John Thomas Scopes. Scopes was guilty, so his prosecutors argued, by association with Darrow.

II

In his attitude toward government, Darrow was directly opposed to his conservative contemporaries. Continuously from his first days in Chicago, even when he was general attorney to a railroad, he agitated and chicaned for labor legislation; workmen's compensation, eight-hour laws, abolition of labor injunctions, public works. He wanted the welfare state. In every campaign he supported the most radical of the anti-monopoly movements, even to the point of public ownership of basic industry. In general a liberal Democrat, he hobnobbed with the Populists in 1896, with an independent reform party in Chicago a few years later, with the Socialists off and on for four decades. He believed in Jefferson, Henry George, Altgeld, and Debs.

But he despised the police state. Almost an anarchist, he wrote a book in praise of Tolstoi's doctrines of non-resistance. He was a defense lawyer by understanding as well as by vocation. Only in the Loeb-Leopold case did he fail to use every effort to get his client entirely acquitted. And he would never help to prosecute anybody for anything. The intensity of his feelings on this score expressed itself repeatedly. For instance, after he returned from Los Angeles in 1913, Darrow was hired by the Amalgamated Clothing Workers in connection with a violent strike. Fights on the picket lines were frequent. One day a union picket was stabbed. He died. The union said a scab had done it. They knew the man. Would Darrow make certain the police did something about it? No, he would not; even though at the time he had few clients, even fewer union clients, he would not.

This was Darrow's attitude toward government. He thought the job of the state was to bolster and expand every man's capacity for self-expression, not to restrict it. No enthusiastic drinker, he missed few chances to violate the Volstead Act and to talk about his derelictions after they had occurred. He also talked about them, one suspects, when they had not occurred. Even worse than prohibition were the infringements on free speech. Darrow never said whether he believed a man had a right to get up in a crowded theater and shout "Fire"; perhaps he found the issue too difficult to resolve.

But when a law restricted the exposition of science, there was no issue. Such laws were an abomination. Darrow's interest in science had begun with childhood and his father. He continued to have an enraptured, if rather lazy, interest in scientific affairs. He read the newspaper accounts and an occasional book. But his interest quickened and deepened after he returned to Chicago from the McNamara trial. With idle time and an idle mind, Darrow organized several of his friends into a Biology Club. Usually they met in the evening at Darrow's apartment near the University of Chicago, and most of their speakers were faculty members there. When Fay-Cooper Cole, an ethnologist, went to Darrow's home to speak in 1914, he found about 25 members present. Darrow explained to them: "It is our practice to bring a man here from the university and let him talk to us, teach us all he can, ask him questions, learn all he knows and then we get rid of him and get another one."

This group was still meeting in 1925. Numbering by that time nearly 75 members, it had held pretty steadily, in a relaxed way, to the goal that Darrow had stated in organizing it: "Here we have been guessing all our lives. It would be a darn good thing to find out the facts." Speakers were drawn from increasingly diverse fields of study: George Burman Foster of the English Department, Anton J. Carlson the physiologist, Frederick Starr the anthropologist, Charles Judson Herrick the biologist, T. V. Smith the philosopher, Shirley Jackson Case the theologian. If the Scopes trial became a discussion of science—or of religion—Darrow would have it over Bryan hands down.

But Darrow was no scientist. At best he was an interested layman, who looked to science chiefly to provide analogies and insights into the human condition. The questions that interested Darrow were the questions the Bible asked, the questions that small-town philosophers like Amirus had argued so avidly in small towns like Kinsman. Is there a God? Did He create the earth? Was man created in His image? Does man have free will? Is he immortal? Is life worth living? Darrow debated these questions incessantly on public platforms, and he always replied with a flat negative or a noncommittal shake of the head. What he wanted from science was evidence on these questions. Sometimes all he wanted was examples. For instance, when Jacques Loeb was releasing from his University of Chicago laboratory the results of his work on tropisms, Darrow used these facts about plants and animals to support his own argument that man is a machine.

Two years before the Scopes trial Darrow wrote his longtime friend Fremont Older, the San Francisco editor, who had just been seriously ill. Darrow was glad for himself, but sorry for Older, that the latter had recovered. Life, wrote Darrow, was a "damned humbug, and not worth while." Yet he knew that he, like everybody else, would resist dying. "It is instinctive in the organism and we cannot help it. . . . I am quite sure that you cannot do anything with your mental equipment, whatever that is, to prevent your physical reaction which makes you fight death." Darrow was certain that "one's thoughts and philosophy have nothing whatever to do with his conduct. His reactions are purely mechanistic and cannot be changed."

Human existence he saw as irretrievably chaotic. Not only pain, but pointless pain. Truth, Justice, Love—these are not realities. At worst, deceitful words; at best, mirrors that send back to man the projections of his own mind. Man believes because he must believe, because he is too weak to face life without believing. All of our perceptions, everything about us, our very motives, are ambiguous and uncertain. The affairs of men, Darrow said repeatedly, are a continuous irony. This theme he returned to constantly, as in his memorial address for Altgeld in 1903, when he broke off a torrential attack on big business and its political servants with the statement: "In the commercial revolution of this generation, many wise, humane and righteous men have found themselves with the reactionary forces that are strangling liberty and destroying popular government throughout the world."

He was so convinced that each man's life is a tormented jumble of good and evil that he could see his own life in this same way. At the time, when his reputation as a reformer and labor sympathizer was enormous because of his part in the Pullman boycott, he did not hesitate to become attorney for an electric company. His seeming opportunism was criticized by many friends, and Darrow wrote to one of them that he did not doubt that the company had used bribery to get its franchise from the city council. Yes, he had been hired to get the franchise amended in ways that favored the company as much as possible. Judged by "the ordinary commercial and legal standard of ethics," he was right in doing so. But "judged by the higher law, in which we both believe," wrote Darrow, "I am practically a thief. I am taking money that I did not earn, which comes to me from men who did not earn it, but who get it because they have a chance to get it. I take it without performing any useful service to the world, and I take a thousand times as much as my services are worth even assuming they are useful and honest."

Years earlier, Darrow explained, he had discussed these matters with a friend named Swift, whose father owned a drugstore. When the father died, Swift took all the patent medicines out in the yard and broke the bottles. He renounced his estate, left town without money, refused to compromise with the world. Eventually, during the 1893 depression, he raised a Coxey's army and marched to Washington. Swift, said Darrow, is a man who "has perhaps done some good in his way by refusing to compromise with evil." But is there no other way to do good at a time when "society is organized injustice" consisting of "two classes, the despoiler and the despoiled," a time when society is ruled by business and "business is legal fraud"?

Darrow chose another way, and chose it deliberately. "I came to Chicago. I determined to take my chance with the rest, to get what I could out of the system and use it to destroy the system. I came without friends or money. Society provides no fund out of which such people can live while preaching heresy. It compels us to get our living out of society as it is or die. I do not choose yet to die although perhaps it would be best." If he were to abandon this course, he would be prompted, not by principle, but by fear of public reproach. He admitted that he cared very much what his friends thought of him, but he would not let it influence his actions. Yet he carefully made clear where he drew the line. "If I let my professional business change my views of life, or allow it to influence me as a citizen to the support of measures in which I do not believe, I am wrong. Otherwise as I see the light, I am doing my duty."

Darrow would not say that his friend Swift was wrong. But neither would he admit that he was wrong. This in 1895: "the only way any person or deed can be judged is by the purpose and the full results."

But who knows the purpose? Who so wise that he can comprehend the full results? Here is the basis of Darrow's opposition to all punishment. Perhaps some men, like Loeb and Leopold, are so violently irrational that society in self-defense must restrict their freedom. But punishment is barbaric, barbaric because self-righteous, self-righteous because it refuses to recognize that no man transcends the limitations of human beings by donning a judicial gown or taking his seat in a jury box.

This conclusion was reinforced by Darrow's knowledge of the way that judicial processes actually worked. Courts were no instrument of justice; courts were "a cockpit for lawyers to fight in." Victory was to the best lawyer, not to the righteous cause. And nearly always the state had better lawyers than the defendant. Most judges, moreover, had first served as prosecutors; they thought like prosecutors; they were wealthy men; their business and social associates were wealthy men. All in all, poor people and outsiders and deviates were likely to be treated roughly in the courts.

Darrow was much criticized for the way he handled his cases. It was charged, condescendingly, that he really was not a good lawyer, meaning that he did not "know the cases." But his early success, be it remembered, was won by doing paper work in civil cases for a railroad and for the city government. He could have been a good book-lawyer, but he scorned this approach to the law. To rely on precedent was to accept the fetters of a savage past. And it was not, he insisted, the way to win cases. A trial is not won or lost in court; a trial is won or lost in the community. Judges and juries are moved by winds of opinion that seep into courtrooms from the newspapers and the streets and the market place. Look, for example, at Loeb and Leopold. They had been sentenced to die in the headlines; they had to win their commutation in the same arena.

Not only courts, but all the institutions of society, are "to a great degree reflections of the spirit of the age." This is true of the schools. Education means nothing but increasing the power of the individual. But power to do what? Society determines that. In one age, the schools train for war; in another, for religion; "now it is typically education for producing and getting wealth." But in every age the school system "has no independent initiative of its own, but is a reflection of the dominant forces, which shape it to their own image." The only way, then, to influence the schools— the issue in the Scopes trial—is to alter the "dominant forces" in the community.

Religion too was slave to the ruling passion of the modern age. Enumerating in a 1921 debate the main Christian doctrines—non-resistance, love, reliance on prayer, forgiveness, renunciation of earthly riches—Darrow declared that they had no relation to daily life. Men wanted to make money, that was all. Christianity had been harnessed to the cause of business. Christianity was the group of wealthy Chicago businessmen who built a tabernacle for

Billy Sunday "because they thought it was cheaper to pay working-men in religious dope than to give them money."

Knowing that Henry Lloyd and many others he respected were deeply religious, Darrow still dissented from their views. In 1932 he wrote to Jane Addams about her published collection of memorial addresses, *The Excellent Becomes the Permanent*. "Of course," he told her, "I like the human side, the charity, the kindness, but I don't like the mysticism. If I know anything, I know that I am not alive after I am dead, and that the same applies to every other form of life." Anybody who truly believed in immortality would not "travel over the world in agony, and be cut up until he has no semblance of himself, just to stay here a week longer; he does it because he dreads and fears death." Darrow didn't even like the title of the book. "The permanent (if there is any such thing) becomes excellent, because it survives, and in no other way." He was sorry to make such objections. *"I appreciate all you have been and done,"* he wrote, "but I have so long been striving for realities—and seeking to look life in the face, that I cannot do otherwise, even with one I respect and admire as much as I do you."

Darrow had his views, and he had to stick by them until they changed, but he was certain of nothing. His uncertainty led to skepticism and curiosity. "The real student may believe a great deal, but does not feel absolutely sure of very much, if anything. He knows that what is true from one standpoint or in one age is not necessarily true in another, and that truth is a relative and not an absolute quality."

This humility, this belief that nobody knew anything for sure, brought Darrow—how different his road from the one Bryan followed—to a belief in democracy and majority rule. But Darrow was no worshipper of the majority. The individual had rights against any majority. The majority, in fact, usually could not see or feel far beyond the dinner bucket. The majority was usually inert, likely to be wrong when it stirred itself, prone to foolishness and cruelty. The real sources of reform and social progress were the agitators, the occasional men of spiritual vision who had the courage to stand alone. Men like John Brown, Voltaire, the martyrs for Irish freedom, Eugene Debs, Jim McNamara, John Peter Altgeld.

In his memorial address for Altgeld in 1903, Darrow answered the charge that Altgeld had been a demagogue in quest of votes. Altgeld, he said, was a wise man, and every wise man knows that it is the powerful and the rich who can bestow power and riches, not the poor and the weak. Altgeld had chosen to serve the poor and the weak knowing full well from the beginning that they would turn against him in the end. They had done so; when election day came in 1896, the workingmen even forgot where the ballot boxes were. This, said Darrow, was what happened to agitators; look how the slaves had failed to rally to John Brown, failed precisely because they were slaves.

Society puts up monuments to military heroes who went out on the battle field "with 10,000 comrades, moved and inspired by drum and fife, dreaming of victory, of glory, of honor . . ." But, said Darrow, "moral courage has ever been greater than physical bravery." The real hero was not the man in military uniform. The real hero was the man like Altgeld, in civilian clothes, "and these spots upon the garment, these are not epaulets or brass buttons, or even the heart's blood of the hero; these are spots of mud which have been thrown by the filthy hands of the filthy mob, the mob in broadcloth and the mob in rags, for whom he risked his reputation and his life."

It was inevitable that a man with these views about government, about science and religion, about the significance of the individual, about human fallibility, would despise what William Jennings Bryan was trying to do.

III

Clarence Darrow was a close observer of the American scene, and one of its shrillest features was the anti-evolution movement. After Bryan joined up in 1920, it swept through all parts of the

country. Rural communities—because they were isolated from
modern science and industry, because they were dependent on farming and thus likely to be dubious of the powers of human reason to
solve ultimate problems—were especially subject to fundamentalism, but recent migrants from country to city were hardly less so.
And the campaign to drive Darwinism from the public schools was
doubtless aided by a recent precedent for banning unpopular subjects; during World War I, many public school systems, and the entire states of Delaware, Iowa, and Montana, had proscribed the German language.

At the van of the fundamentalist movement marched preachers. Church membership declined after the war; a way had to be
found to bring people back into the pews. And the fundamentalist
minister, sparsely stocked as he was in food for the intellect, tried to
compensate by a well-larded dread-bin. Some of the leaders themselves were frightened because they realized, as Bryan did, that the
doctrine of substitutionary salvation rested on the entire theological structure. "No Adam, no fall," wrote one; "no fall, no atonement; no atonement, no Savior. Accepting Evolution, how can we
believe in a fall?"

Such cries of alarm helped to build fanatical, if small, movements in state after state. These movements sought to coerce legislatures while the majority of the voters (instead of ruling)
watched, indifferent, or were themselves vaguely anxious to stay
right with God and their fellow men. In 1921 an anti-evolution
rider was attached to the appropriations bill in the South Carolina
legislature; it was removed only by the joint committee of the
houses. The following January a teacher in Kentucky was fired for
teaching, in contradiction to the Bible, that the earth was round.
The annual convention of the Southern Baptists, the largest denomination, decreed that evolution and the Bible were in irreconcilable
conflict. The next annual convention, 1923, endorsed the opinion
that scientists must begin investigations by conceding the plenary
authority of the Bible, including the Virgin Birth, Atonement,
physical Resurrection, and the Second Coming of Christ.

That year the anti-evolutionists scored their first legislative victories. Oklahoma, as part of a free-textbook law, banned from its public schools any book giving "a materialistic conception of history, that is, the Darwin theory of creation versus the Bible theory of creation." Then the Florida legislature passed Bryan's resolution. In Texas, J. Frank Norris, whose church in Fort Worth would soon become the largest Baptist congregation in the world with 8,000 members, succeeded in driving out three professors at Baylor and even one at Southern Methodist. An anti-evolution bill passed the lower house of the legislature and was favorably reported by a committee of the senate, but died on the calendar. And the authorities of Kentucky Wesleyan College (Methodists again) suspended five members of the faculty who denied that evolution contradicted the Bible.

Alarmed by these inroads, 35 prominent citizens, including 15 scientists, issued a "Joint Statement upon the Relation of Science and Religion." Drafted by Henry Fairfield Osborn, director of the American Museum of Natural History, and his friend Robert A. Millikan, it suggested a position that Osborn developed more fully in his books: science proves the existence of God. The statement said that science sought to learn "the processes of nature"; religion was "even more important" because it tried to develop "the aspirations of mankind." Science portrayed God as "revealing Himself through inbreathing of life into its constituent matter, culminating in man with his spiritual nature and all his Godlike powers."

No state legislature formally banned the theory of evolution between 1923, when Oklahoma and Florida acted, and 1925, when Tennessee passed the Butler Act. During those two years the movement achieved its goal in other ways. In 1924 Governor Cameron Morrison of North Carolina rejected a biology text recommended by the state board of education. His grounds? "I don't want my daughter or anybody's daughter," he said, "to have to study a book that prints pictures of a monkey and a man on the same page." The state board of education saw his point and co-operated with him. In California the state board of education went on record as favoring the teaching of Darwinism only "as a theory but not as an established fact"—in essence, the Bryan position, which he had written into the joint resolution adopted in Florida. As far north as Minnesota an anti-evolution society was strong enough to worry the liberals, who perhaps worried easily.

The Anti-evolution League of America started a national "Bible-Christ-and-Constitution Campaign against Evolution in Tax-supported Schools." At the General Assembly of the Presbyterian Church South in 1924, the fundamentalists were strong enough to secure a reaffirmation of an 1886 declaration that Adam was not born of animal parents. In Arkansas the Baptist State Convention decreed that no Baptist institution could employ anybody, not even a janitor, who believed in Darwinism.*

Still, even in Dixie the fundamentalists could be beaten. In North Carolina an anti-evolution bill was introduced in the legislature early in 1925. Due largely to stiff opposition by President Harry W. Chase of the University at Chapel Hill, President William L. Poteat of Wake Forest, the Raleigh *News and Observer,* and the state Academy of Science, it was defeated in the lower house by 67 to 46.

The movement against evolution was strongest, clearly, in the South and the border states, and it was far from negligible in the Midwest and in California. The absence of public victories elsewhere does not force us to conclude, as has one recent writer, that the rest of the country was free from "serious embroilment" in the controversy. It is impossible to know how many communities quietly dropped objectionable textbooks or quietly discharged objectionable teachers. Even more important, it is impossible to know how many writers modified their textbooks, or how many teachers changed their classroom presentation, to avoid conflict with the anti-evolutionists. The most prevalent, and the most serious, type of censorship is always self-censorship. "The threat of legislation

---

* Lest this seem incredible, we should recall that in 1947 the most prominent Baptist layman in the country issued an Executive Order setting standards of belief for all Federal employees, including janitors.

like that in Tennessee," wrote Walter Lippmann at the time, "is almost as effective as the actual legislation itself, and that such a threat exists as a determining influence on education in many parts of this country, no one, I think, will deny."

To illustrate. In 1923 Kirtley Mather (who was to go to Tennessee two years later as an expert witness in the Scopes trial) was professor of geology at a Baptist college in Ohio. There was considerable rumbling among the college trustees and elsewhere in the denomination about Darwinism. One day the president of the college stopped by Mather's office for a two-hour talk about these questions: How did evolution relate to Christianity? What did Mather think of a certain zoologist on the faculty? Mather was glad to explain how and why he based his own courses on the concept of evolution; he had the security of being a deacon in the Baptist church. He also warmly defended the scientific competence of his colleague (who was not Baptist but Jewish). Soon the president got rid of the zoologist.

Some Southern newspapers were glad to point out that such episodes were not confined to their own region or to sectarian schools. Said the El Paso *Times*:

> In New York state, supposed to be the natural haven of freethinkers on all subjects, scores of ex-teachers are looking for odd jobs . . . because they dared, in defiance of the Lusk law, to believe in some economic system other than the capitalistic . . .
>
> The outstanding fact about any community is that, constitution or no constitution, public school teachers have less personal liberty than any other class in town.

This repression was especially severe at the time of the Scopes trial. In April, 1925, the American Civil Liberties Union, releasing a survey of restrictions on teaching in schools and colleges, said that more restrictive laws had been passed in the preceding six months than at any time in the country's history. The various statutes banned the teaching of evolution, or required daily Bible reading in the schools, or forbade the employment of radical or pacifist teachers. Roger Baldwin, director of the ACLU, attributed this repression to the growth of class conflict that had followed the Russian Revolution. It seems likely that big business had little direct responsibility for the anti-evolution campaign, but it had contributed heavily to the distrust of intellectuals, the scorn for idle curiosity, and the belief that teachers should teach whatever the community authorities desired to have taught. While William Jennings Bryan wanted to determine truth by counting votes, many businessmen thought the proper test was to count bank balances. The groups could unite on Bryan's dictum: "the hand that writes the pay check rules the school."

This doctrine seems callous, even brutal, but it has always been the dominant one in American education.

Chapter 4

Darwin and the Adullamites

> Certain doctrines and opinions
> . . . have descended like heir-
> looms . . . and thus do certain
> dogmas, political and religious,
> . . . continue to be handed down,
> unsubjected to the test of philo-
> sophical examination.
>
> Thomas Hamilton, *Men and Man-
> ners in America* (Edinburgh: Black-
> wood, 1833), Vol. I, p. 131

I

In mid-May, 1925, feeling ran high in Dayton, Tennessee, against the city of Chattanooga. John Scopes could not be indicted at Dayton until the next regular meeting of the grand jury in August. The editor of a Chattanooga newspaper tried to take advantage of this delay by proposing that his town should stage an immediate test case under the Butler Act. Dayton was angry at this threatened loss of its hour in the sun. Many a businessman reacted as if it were immoral for another city to capture his prospective customers; a retaliatory boycott of Chattanooga wholesalers was proposed. Dayton warned other cities not to intrude on its jubilee.

A mass meeting was called to register a duly strenuous protest. George Rappelyea, the man who had put Scopes up to it all, should have been a hero at the meeting. But he chose to use the occasion to speak against the Butler Act. When he said that "there are as many evolutionists in Dayton as there are monkeys in Chattanooga," the owner of the town's main barber shop became enraged and shouted, "You can't call my family monkeys." He bit Rappelyea. They scuffled a little before they were separated.

Rappelyea was widely disliked in Dayton: because he was a New Yorker, college trained, and boss over 600 men, or because he had seduced Scopes into sin, or because he proclaimed his own right to speak about religion and patriotism by declaring that he was the direct descendant of a man who had come to America in 1623. Some of Scopes' many friends had another reason. Not understanding that Rappelyea had signed the original complaint against Scopes as a legal maneuver, they thought it a betrayal of friendship. They planned to waylay the villain and punish him properly. Scopes stopped them. Then some of Rappelyea's friends thought of abducting him as a publicity stunt, but word leaked out in advance. The hoax was abandoned when half the town, in a different spirit, showed its eagerness to help.

The competition from Chattanooga was burked by John T. Raulston, judge of the circuit of seven counties that included Dayton and Rhea County. If Dayton businessmen saw the impending trial in terms of more customers, Judge Raulston saw it as prestige and votes. Born in the mountain town of Gizzards Cove, Tennessee, he had lived in the area all his life. The biggest cases that ever came before him involved bootlegging and murder, neither of which attracted much notice within his circuit and even less outside. Here was a chance at something big, a chance for a new life for Dayton and for John Raulston. The judge was more than just a Republican politician, he was also a lay preacher in the Methodist Episcopal Church. He did not hesitate. Happily, no hesitation was called for, since duty to God, duty to country, and duty to himself all called for the same course.

Judge Raulston summoned a special session of the grand jury, which met on May 25. Press photographers took lots of pictures of the judge and other persons prominent in the case. Walter White, the county superintendent of schools, became plaintiff instead of Rappelyea. After the grand jury of thirteen men, nine of them farmers, was sworn, the judge read them the Butler Act and the first chapter of Genesis. Seven boys, students in Scopes' science classes, appeared as witnesses. The grand jury took an hour to return the indictment, and Judge Raulston ordered a special term of court for July 10 to try Scopes. It seemed that the challenge from Chattanooga had been staved off; Dayton, at last, was to have another chance at fame and fortune.

The town of Dayton was originally called Smith's Cross Roads. The name was changed in 1876 as eastern Tennessee began to burgeon. The population of Chattanooga, 38 miles southwest of Dayton, grew from 6,000 in 1870 to 49,000 by 1900; Knoxville, somewhat farther away and to the northeast, became a lusty wholesaling center. Dayton shared in this growth after the Cumberland Coal & Iron Company started a blast furnace there and brought several hundred men from Glasgow, Scotland. By 1895 Dayton had 3,500 people. It even had a slum, so it could fancy itself a city. But in the depression after 1893 the blast furnace, its market shrinking, cut back its operations, and half of Dayton's residents moved away.

Then came Peter Donaldson, who defied the stereotypes by being a wild-eyed Scotchman. He got control of the blast furnace, and he set out to corner the iron ore of the world. Dayton boomed until, in 1913, Donaldson's project collapsed. Nearly a thousand men lost their jobs; the iron company's payroll of $50,000 a month fell to nothing. Even during World War I the blast furnace did not reopen. Dayton's next benefactor was the local banker, A. P. Haggard, who scouted out a sound industry for the town, a hosiery mill, and got the money to open it.

But the economy of Rhea County depended chiefly on its farms. This was fruit country, peaches, tomatoes, and the world's greatest strawberry beds. In 1925 the strawberry crop promised to be the biggest ever, and Rhea County, in contrast to much of American agriculture at the time, was enjoying a marked prosperity. Not, of course, that the expected income would be distributed at all evenly. Of the 1,200 farms in the county, two of every three were smaller than 100 acres. But of the five farms in Tennessee with more than 5,000 acres, two were in Rhea County. A similar concentration had taken place in Dayton, where A. P. Haggard was head of every important enterprise including the city commission.

Although Dayton was county seat of this thriving farming county, its business section was limited to two blocks on Market Street running north, and one on Main running west to the Cincinnati, New Orleans, and Texas Pacific Railroad. The one express train a day came in the early morning. There was also bus service to Chattanooga, automobiles were not uncommon, and the important streets were neatly paved. Dayton was proud that its tax rate was about the lowest in the state, and that its electric and water plants were owned by the town.

But Dayton was not so daring in its social arrangements. Whiskey had been banned by local option since 1903. Dayton had no gamblers and no abandoned women—unless one chooses to think that all of its women had been abandoned. They did not smoke cigarettes or wear cosmetics or bob their hair. They never attended trials. No woman had ever served on a jury in the county. The women's clubs stayed out of civic affairs. That was men's business. White men. The town's 200 Negroes observed the law and stayed in their prescribed place.

Dayton was not a particularly religious town; only half of its 1,800 residents were church members. But the church members imposed their rules on everybody else. In Dayton, unlike the state as a whole, Methodists were more common than Baptists, and Methodists generally were more concerned with personal actions than with doctrinal orthodoxy. But not in Dayton, where the ministers resolved at a meeting that "the holy Bible contains and is itself the fountain of true wisdom." Agreeing to raise funds to prosecute Scopes, they explained: "we do not believe that the right of free speech or religious liberty warrants any man or set of men to teach our children any theory which has as its purpose or tend-

ency the discrediting of our religion." This even though John
Wesley had held that some Biblical texts were in error and that life
had reached its current form as a result of gradual change.

The only piety that could contend with religion was patriotism.
This was the volunteer region of the Volunteer State. The local
hero was Alvin York, the one-man army of World War I, the uneducated, devout Tennessee mountaineer who had, almost single-
handed, captured an entire machine-gun battalion of Germans.
But the intense patriotism of the area did not deter men, during
the war, from voting as they had always voted. In 1912 most of
the Republicans in Rhea County showed that they were really populists by jumping to Theodore Roosevelt; in 1916 they returned to
the fold and carried the county for Hughes. Just as reporters at
the Scopes trial would find a religious division between town and
countryside, so in politics: the county was Republican, Dayton was
Democratic. And everybody always voted for his own party.

Only in 1920 did enough voters switch tickets to change the
outcome. Cordell Hull, the Congressman from the district, had
been a Representative since 1906. Occasionally his Democratic majority had fallen as low as 1,500 or 2,000. But in 1920 he played a
leading role in agitating for the Versailles Treaty and the League
of Nations. Even some of his best friends cooled toward him.
They would not exert themselves to get out the vote. He lost by
300 votes—his only electoral defeat. Woodrow Wilson was no idol
of Rhea County: some men were angry because he had betrayed
them; others were uneasy or guilt-ridden that they had betrayed
their fathers and their God. They were willing to let the sinful
world sink into the lake of fire; they sought only to isolate themselves from temptation.

Any cloistered paradise in Rhea County was sure to be ruled,
politically as well as economically and socially, by a minority. In
the state as a whole, 90 per cent of the adult males had voted in the
Presidential election of 1888. Then the right to vote was limited
to those who paid a poll tax. The percentage of adult males voting declined steadily: 70 per cent in 1892, 58 in 1904, 46 in 1920, 34

per cent only in 1928. In Rhea County the total vote in 1920 was 2,413; in 1924, 2,412.

But Rhea County, for all its efforts to stultify human beings, sometimes failed. After John Scopes was indicted, a reporter went to interview the foreman of the grand jury. John Rose, 71 years old, was picking strawberries on his farm. He said that at the Methodist Sunday School, where he had been superintendent for thirty years, he told his class that "this hellfire and brimstone stuff is all bosh." He also thought that man was constantly bettering himself and his environment. In his boyhood, he said, the Irish potato had been the size of a hen's egg; the tomato had been "a little, ridgy, one sided thing" in no way like the modern Ponderosa. "The cow was a crumply-horned animal that gave about a half a gallon of milk a day the three months she wasn't dry—and the milk wasn't as good as that we feed our hogs today. And the razor back hog looked like a hound dog. Stand it beside our current Poland China—then ask me if I believe in evolution."

Such philosophizing was rare. Most men, as always, were thinking of practical matters. They began to repair and paint the courthouse in Dayton, a three-story brick building that stood in a grassy two-acre plot on Market Street. The local businessmen, expecting 2,000 visitors for the trial and knowing that Dayton's three hotels could accommodate only a tenth that number, asked the Pullman Company to sidetrack cars at Dayton during the trial, and asked Cordell Hull to secure tents from the War Department. The United Press reported that the trial would be held in a ball park where 10,000 persons could be seated, that a jazz orchestra would play every afternoon and evening at a resort eight miles from Dayton, that Judge Raulston had agreed to have brief daily sessions of court in order to keep the extra customers in town longer.

Bryan and the Butler Act were under fire from several sides. Jesse W. Sprouls, one of the professors ousted from the University of Tennessee in 1923, said that Bryan's policies would set public education back a generation. Wilbur Glenn Voliva, overseer of

the Christian Apostolic Church at Zion City, Illinois, denounced
Bryan as inconsistent because he did not say the earth was a flat
surface. If Darwinian biology and Copernican astronomy should
both be overthrown, said Voliva, "the millennium will be at hand.
Amen!" The American Medical Association convention unanimously condemned restrictions on the teaching of evolution and
also the prosecution of Scopes.

Governor Peay expressed his "profound contempt" for these
criticisms. Tennessee had a perfect right to protect the religion of
its students from "stuff that no science has established and which
belongs in no reputable textbook." The Scopes trial was a simple
matter; it should not last more than an hour. And the Butler Act
was a wise law: "In my judgment, any state had better dispense
with its schools than with the Bible. We are keeping both."

Other areas began efforts to enforce the statute. The board of
education of Carroll County, in western Tennessee, announced
that it would not employ any teacher who believed in evolution. In
the central part of the state, the school board of DeKalb County
said that it would not sign a contract with any teacher until it had
learned his views on Darwinism. But Rhea County was setting the
pace.

II

The young Dayton lawyers who were on the staff to prosecute
Scopes were gleefully chortling about the defendant's disreputable
counsel: Malone the backslider and Darrow the disbeliever. "All
we will have to do," enthused one of them, "is to get the fact that
Mr. Darrow is an atheist and does not believe in the Bible, if this
be a fact [he hardly dared credit it], across to the jury and his
case is lost."

The same thought was deeply disturbing to some leaders of
the American Civil Liberties Union. As in most voluntary organizations, the national board and national committee of the ACLU
ordinarily accepted the recommendations of a few paid officials
and other insiders, especially in regard to specific legal cases. The

usual leader of this policy-making group was the ACLU's director, Roger N. Baldwin, but in early June, 1925, he was engrossed in a criminal anarchy case that had grown out of a silk strike in New Jersey. So far as the Scopes trial was concerned, ACLU policy depended chiefly on Forrest Bailey, who on June 1 became associate director in charge of the daily executive work, leaving Baldwin free to direct research, writing, and publication; on Felix Frankfurter, professor of law at Harvard; and on Walter Nelles, ACLU general counsel, soon to become professor of law at Yale.

All three wanted to maneuver Darrow and Malone out of the Scopes defense. Malone was too much a member of the international set, too closely identified with woman suffrage, a born Catholic, a divorced man, a divorce lawyer. Darrow was a notorious agnostic. He wasn't really a good lawyer. His presence in the Dayton courtroom would evoke mention of Loeb and Leopold who were identified in the public mind with "over-education."

Bailey, Frankfurter, and Nelles thought the case required a lawyer of unchallenged religious orthodoxy (preferably a Protestant), a respectable and conservative attorney who would conduct the trial on the sole issue of the constitutionality of the Butler Act. Mentioned as qualified were John W. Davis, Democratic nominee for President the previous November; Charles Evans Hughes, Republican candidate for President in 1916; ex-Representative Martin W. Littleton of New York; Senator Thomas J. Walsh of Montana who had conducted the Teapot Dome investigation; and Frank P. Walsh of Kansas City and New York, cochairman of the War Labor Board during World War I.

As the conflict about Scopes' counsel manifested itself in rumors and dope stories, John Randolph Neal added to the confusion. Another 21 years were to elapse before, in 1946, he would run simultaneously for Governor and United States Senator in both the Democratic primary and the general election. But the seeds of such behavior could already be seen in 1925. Although the newspapers persisted in calling Neal "a brilliant attorney" and "Tennessee's foremost authority on constitutional law," he was also recognized as an eccentric who was usually unshaven, who hated to squander any of his ample income on haircuts, and who was careless in dress (and also, as events were to show, careless about more vital matters).

On May 28, Neal announced in Dayton that the defense would seek to hire John W. Davis. The same day, he announced that Scopes was entitled to engage any lawyer he wanted, and that the services of Malone and Darrow were "greatly desired by both Mr. Scopes and myself." Two days later, the office of John W. Davis announced that he would not go to Dayton even if he were invited. John Scopes tried to dispel the uncertainty by saying: "I know of no two lawyers in the country who are more capable of defending a great cause than Mr. Darrow and Mr. Malone." Scopes said he would be "an imbecile" if he refused their offer to help.

But who was Scopes? Merely the defendant. The campaign against Darrow and Malone had hardly begun. On June 6, Scopes, Rappelyea, and Neal went to New York for a defense conference. Darrow showed up at the ACLU offices late, hulking, breathless, carrying a heavy suitcase. The others present were four lawyers active in the ACLU: Nelles, Frankfurter, Samuel Rosensohn, and Arthur Garfield Hays, the only insider in the organization who would say vociferously and continuously that Darrow was the right man to handle the case. At the conference it was politely but insistently urged upon Scopes that an orthodox lawyer should have charge of his defense. Scopes, this callow, modest young man from the backwoods, listened politely. His drawl was seldom heard. The conference recessed on Sunday, June 7, so Scopes went sightseeing and got a crick in his neck from looking at tall buildings. Country boy. He and Neal went to the American Museum of Natural History, where Henry Fairfield Osborn warned him not to let his defense become tainted with radicalism. Osborn also announced that he would shortly publish a book dedicated to Scopes.

On Monday the country boy went back to the ACLU offices to

confer some more. He listened quietly to everything they had to say. Then he said he wanted Darrow. His self-effacing steadfastness won out—for the moment. The executive committee of the ACLU voted to support Scopes both morally and financially. Forrest Bailey announced to the press that the chief counsel for Scopes would be Darrow, aided by Bainbridge Colby, Neal, Malone, and Rosensohn. Scopes told the newspapers there had been "no friction" at the conference, which had gone off "very smoothly."

The news came from Dayton that the school board intended to leave Scopes' job vacant until the trial was over. They bore him no animosity at all. One member said, "We'll take care of Scopes all right if he wants to come back."

But Scopes said in New York that he would probably be found guilty since "it's pretty hard in Tennessee to find twelve men who wouldn't want to convict me." Scopes was busy. He and his lawyers conferred with two famous psychologists, James McKeen Cattell and Charles B. Davenport. He missed the automobile that was to take him to a Civic Club dinner in honor of him and Darrow, was forced to walk there, lost his way. He was glad to leave New York for Washington, where he inspected the original copy of the Constitution at the Library of Congress. Accompanied by Neal, he reverently looked into the chamber of the Supreme Court. Then he went back to Tennessee. It was reported that a motion-picture company had offered him $50,000 to appear in a production. Other offers from syndicates would have added another $100,000. Scopes denied that any offers had been made.

Darrow returned to Chicago. His role was momentarily secure. But Malone was vulnerable, and the attack turned to him. Allegedly on Frankfurter's insistence, Malone was told that he was not needed in Dayton, but that he could help by doing legal research in New York. Malone heatedly declared that he would not "be the goat." His clerks, he said, customarily looked up his references for him. And there it stood.

Some leaders of the ACLU continued to worry. The press

said that the Scopes prosecution intended to discuss in the trial the
ACLU's attitude toward pacifism and radicalism during World War
I. The New York *World* declared that Scopes' supporters included
"atheists, free thinkers, free lovers, Socialists, Communists" and
"just talkers." Sue Hicks, member of the prosecution staff, ecstati-
cally noted that the ACLU had represented "pro-communists." He
was also delighted that Scopes had the support of President Nicholas Murray Butler of Columbia, who was tarnished by his criticism of prohibition.

But worried or not, the ACLU did not limit itself to the constitutional issue in announcing its objectives in the trial. They
were:

To educate the public on evolution.

To show that science and religion are not incompatible.

To demonstrate the necessity of having education un-
hampered by restrictive legislation.

At least temporarily, Darrow's approach had won out. The defense strategy was necessarily formulated in more legalistic terms;
it was to show that the law was unconstitutional because (1) it
violated freedom of religion by making the Bible the test of
truth, (2) it was unreasonable in the light of modern knowledge
of evolution, (3) it was indefinite because no two persons construed the Bible exactly alike. The defense also wanted to show
that laws such as the Butler Act were, as Arthur Garfield Hays
wrote later, "born in ignorance—ignorance of the Bible, of religion, of history, and of science."

Critics of Bryan and the Butler Act were numerous: the president of the American Turnerbund; George Gilbert Murray, re-
gius professor of Greek at Oxford, who called the impending trial
"the most serious setback to civilization in all history"; the pastor
of the First Congregational Church in Washington who was President Coolidge's religious adviser; George Bernard Shaw; the Unitarian Laymen's League; the Georgia Federation of Labor. But

the most telling opposition came from Tennessee. In the very city where the legislature met, Vanderbilt, a private school and therefore not subject to the law, announced that it would continue to teach evolution; Chancellor Kirkland predicted that the men responsible for the Butler Act would "reap a harvest they did not expect" because the law would stimulate "far more inquiry" into Darwinism by students. When the University of Tennessee had a parade before its annual circus at Knoxville, the floats of four fraternities satirized the law. One float exhibited a moonshine still inscribed "Bootleg Evolution." Another shouted "Long Live Darwin." Governor Peay announced that the state textbook commission had adopted a new biology text written by two high school teachers in New York City. One of them, when interviewed, said that of course they both were evolutionists.

On June 13 at Dayton, Judge J. L. Godsey as a lawyer for Scopes filed a motion to quash the indictment because the Butler Act was unconstitutional. Before the motion was acted on, Scopes made formal application to the school board for reinstatement in his job. Walter White, the superintendent, was at first startled, then announced that the application would have to wait until the trial was over, and that he would not recommend anybody as a teacher who was not a fundamentalist.

In mid-June, the anti-evolutionists were actively pressing their campaign in a half-dozen Southern states and in Iowa, Minnesota, Oregon, and North Dakota. Delaware passed a new law requiring the reading of the Bible in the public schools. In Tennessee the state board of education added the Bible to the curriculum of elective studies for which schools could give credit.

Not surprisingly, Bryan was confident about the outcome of the Scopes trial even though, as he told the reporters, he had not served as a lawyer in any case in 28 years. Writing on June 11 to W. B. Marr, the Nashville attorney who had actively sought the passage of the Butler Act, Bryan thought it good that "an outspoken believer in evolution" like Darrow was to conduct the defense since "he will furnish us with abundant material." In the correspondence between Bryan and Marr, which dealt mainly with citations of cases, Bryan pointed out the major strategy of the prosecution: to exclude the testimony of natural scientists and of Bible experts, by which the defense would try to prove that the Butler Act was unreasonable and indefinite. "If," wrote Bryan, "we can shut out the expert testimony, which is intended to prevent the enforcement of the law by proving that it ought not to have been passed—a perfectly absurd proposition—we will be through in a short time."

On June 19 Bryan went to Atlanta, Georgia, where he conferred with the Tennessee members of the prosecution. Three days later, as Albert Einstein was declaring in Berlin that "any restriction of academic liberty heaps coals of shame upon the community which tolerates such suppression," Clarence Darrow arrived in Dayton to get the lay of the land. He also gave the commencement address at John R. Neal's law school, where he said that we should elect to the legislatures men who would repeal laws instead of passing more. "Some time," he said optimistically, "we may have a movement to let people alone." Back in Chicago on June 25, Darrow made public a letter from Luther Burbank saying that perhaps the Scopes trial was being taken too seriously. "It appears to me as a great joke," Burbank wrote, "but one which will educate the public and thus reduce the number of bigots."

III

Clarence Darrow was invited to address the convention of the Tennessee Bar Association at Memphis on June 26. Although on June 24 the invitation was withdrawn, the convention heard other critics of the pending trial. A state senator from Fayetteville, a former president of the Association, offered a resolution objecting to the "using of a criminal or other trial before any court of our state as an advertising medium," and he specified which trial he meant. The Butler Act was denounced by Robert S. Keebler, a Memphis attorney who had been born in the East Tennessee mountains and reared a strict Methodist. Keebler argued that the law was invalid because it violated the constitutional injunctions to cherish science and to uphold religious and intellectual freedom. His speech raised an acrimonious discussion that led to a ruling by the chairman that the whole subject was out of order. The convention voted, 86 to 53, to strike the entire speech from the record.

This suppression served chiefly to draw attention to Keebler's remarks. The ACLU printed 2,000 copies of the speech and distributed them around the country, in conjunction with its campaign to raise money for Scopes' defense. Although an independent committee had been formed to control the fund, in fact the responsibility rested with the ACLU. Estimating that the case might require $10,000 if it went to the federal Supreme Court, the acting chairman of the ACLU said that public interest was greater than in any case "since the Dred Scott decision."

The ACLU had at last accepted the participation in the trial of Dudley Field Malone, and he went south to look around. Malone also announced the fruits of an offer of scientific advisers for the trial that had been made a month earlier to the ACLU by Michael I. Pupin, president of the American Association for the Advancement of Science. Included among the eleven scientists who had agreed to testify were Pupin and Henry Fairfield Osborn.

While Malone was trying to spread enlightenment in Tennessee, a Baptist minister in Brooklyn was calling evolution "a lie of hell" and Scopes "an ambassador of the devil." The publicity was too much for John Scopes, who went into seclusion, but not before he had been asked in an interview whether he was a Christian. "I don't know," he said. "Who does?" A lot of people did. The school board of Paducah, Kentucky, was so sure of its own rectitude that it dismissed one of Scopes' sisters from her job teaching mathematics because she would not disavow Darwinism.

George Rappelyea resigned as superintendent of the Sunday School at his Methodist church. The resulting void in his life he filled by fixing up quarters for the defense lawyers and expert witnesses at the Mansion. This eighteen-room house, the largest in

Rhea County, had been vacant for a decade. It stood on a little hill a mile from Dayton. An old faded brown with yellow trim, it had no lights, no window-screens, and the plumbing didn't work. Some local folks thought it was haunted. Rappelyea fixed it up in a style suitable for famous lawyers and scientists, with Japanese mats and iron cots.

Darrow and the other defense lawyers met in New York on July 1 and discussed presenting witnesses who would reconcile the Bible with Darwinism. In Dayton, Rappelyea's minister, agreeing to testify for the defense, said he did not think the Bible had been "written in heaven, printed on India paper, sewed with silk, bound with calfskin, and tossed out the window." The convention of the National Education Association decided to by-pass the whole issue of evolution. The American Federation of Teachers denounced the Butler Act as "unenlightened dictatorship." A biologist at the University of Minnesota made known his views on Darwinism by pointing to the "strange resemblance" between a pink chimpanzee and a woman emerging from a hot bath. Hendrik Van Loon said that Europe thought of the coming trial as a "free-for-all vaudeville show," and Julian Huxley agreed with Wilbur Glenn Voliva that Bryan, if he were consistent, would insist that the earth was flat. A Dayton merchant named Darwin hung out a red sign proclaiming in huge letters that "Darwin is right"; beneath, in tiny print, "inside." This particular Darwin could see no conflict between the Bible and the theory of evolution.

These criticisms rankled. A Tennessee state senator justified his vote for the Butler Act by replying to Nicholas Murray Butler: "I suppose he thinks it was a bunch of ignoramuses who helped break the Hindenburg line." William Jennings Bryan explained that the law did not interfere with the right of John Scopes to think and to say whatever he pleased. "The law," said Bryan, "is simply an effort to control the public schools." John Washington Butler, saying that his law was meant to "protect our children from infidelity," added that evolutionists had written to him proposing that all Bibles be burned. Butler talked like Bryan: "There is no controversy between true science and the Bible." The theory of evolution was "only a guess."

The people of Dayton were worried that they still might lose the trial altogether. Darrow announced in Chicago on July 3 that John R. Neal would apply to the federal district court at Nashville for an injunction to halt the Scopes trial. The purpose, said Darrow, was to get a quick decision on the constitutionality of the Butler Act. He also pointed out that a federal decision on the point would have more effect in other states than a decision of the Tennessee supreme court.

This dismayed Dayton. On the Fourth of July the streets were filled with knots of people talking about the new developments. The representative from Rhea County in the legislature said that any move to take the case elsewhere was "an injustice to Dayton." Nor did he conceal his reason for this belief: "The people here have given a lot of time and gone to a great deal of expense and trouble to prepare for the visitors."

The press reported a split among the defense: Neal wanted to go to trial at Dayton, and Darrow threatened to withdraw from the case unless the move in federal court was pressed. Darrow did not care how many customers remained image rather than reality to Dayton. More prescient than his critics, he underlined a danger to the defense. "Unless we land in the Federal courts," he said, "the whole matter of evolution, pro and con, may be ruled out in Dayton. In other words, the case might resolve itself into the simple question of whether or not Scopes taught evolution in his classes."

July 5 was a day of great anxiety in Dayton. Crowds wandered uneasily up and down Main Street and gathered in front of Robinson's drugstore, while John Neal went off to Cooksville, where Federal Judge John Gore was fishing, to argue the application for the injunction. About 8 P.M. the news was telephoned from Chattanooga to Dayton and chalked up on one of the drugstore windows. Judge Gore had turned down the application.

Now the town could finish its preparations in confidence. The front of the Aqua Hotel was painted a harsh yellow and cots were placed in the corridors. The Dayton Progressive Club announced that visitors would get a medal showing a monkey wearing a straw hat. The police commissioner declared: "We will make it hard for crooks to work here and there will be little business, if any, for the bootleggers." Citizens trimmed their lawns and merchants painted their stores. John Scopes strolled about town in his shirt sleeves, being stopped often by somebody who wanted to shake his hand; local residents treated him as if he had gone out and landed a big convention for Dayton. A reporter sidled up to a slouch-hat mountaineer and asked what he thought of the evolution case. "Case of evolution?" was the mildly excited reply. "Land's sake! Who's got it?" Another reporter was fined $2 for using profanity in a public place.

As the trial date of July 10 approached, the cast began its migration to Dayton. First came Bryan, whose train made a special stop to deposit him in Dayton in the late morning of July 7. Greeted by a huge crowd at the station, he paused only a moment before friends whisked him away to a local home where he would stay. Bryan's abundant and aging figure was emphasized by his striped trousers, dark coat, and white tropical helmet.

That evening the Dayton Progressive Club had a welcome dinner for the fundamentalist leader. Before Bryan's address, he had a private chat with Scopes and John Neal. Scopes was amused by Bryan, who had stopped eating white bread because he was on a diet but who ate potatoes and corn and heaped sugar into his tea. "Why," laughed Scopes, "he didn't know that there is three times as much starch in potatoes as in bread."

The next day Scopes, without coat, collar, or hat, rode through Dayton sitting on the gas tank of a low yellow racing car, his arm linked in that of a girl with bobbed hair. Bryan stalked grimly around, wearing a starched gray shirt cut into a V at the throat, with the sleeves cut and hemstitched above the elbows. He was carrying a palm-leaf fan and wearing the white pith helmet he had bought in Panama. Occasionally he stopped at a grocery store to buy a bunch of radishes, which he ate while walking along the street. If he was defeated in court, he said, he would campaign for a constitutional amendment to ban Darwinism in the schools. Two defense lawyers, Hays and Malone, were en route from New York with the Reverend Charles Francis Potter of the West Side Unitarian Church, who was to be guest of George Rappelyea.

Clarence Darrow boarded a train in Chicago, announcing at the time that Bainbridge Colby had withdrawn because of involvement in another case in New York. Doubtless Darrow was just as happy, since early in the preparation for the trial Colby had gotten in a fierce controversy with Arthur Hays which involved both personality and policy.

Judge Raulston and his wife drove in from their home in Winchester. H. L. Mencken rolled gustily in from Baltimore and went through the town in search of targets for his witty and vigorous prose. The town was already flooded with reporters, two days before the trial. All of the wire services had their big men there. Two movie cameramen had joined the large group of press photographers. A crew of workmen began installing radio equipment, quite a novelty, in the courthouse for the Chicago *Tribune*. Telegraph wires were run into the courtroom itself; phone booths were installed just outside in the corridor.

The issues of the trial were dividing Catholic from Catholic, uniting fundamentalist to fundamentalist. On July 9 two prominent lay Catholics arrived in Dayton and offered their aid to Bryan, and a former president of Marquette University at Milwaukee said that evolution "is subversive of morality and undermines the foundation of the state." But Father John A. Ryan called the Butler Act unconstitutional and said that Catholics knew that the Bible and science could not conflict. The editor of the Catholic *Commonweal* denounced Bryan's plan for an anti-evolution amendment to the Constitution as an effort to impose a state religion. No awareness of this split in the Church was shown by the president of the Methodist League for Faith and Life when he declared that he had "vastly more fellowship with the Church of Rome than with any Modernist in any church."

Big, quiet-voiced John Washington Butler, having arranged for somebody else to do the threshing on his farm, arrived in Dayton as correspondent for a press association. He did not interview as many people as interviewed him. Euphorically remarking that he had read Darwin's two chief books and that he did not object to his children doing so, he said, "They will find out the truth."

Near the courthouse the streets were jammed with hot-dog stands and fanatics: T. T. Martin, white-haired and frenzied secretary of the Anti-Evolution League; a blind mountaineer who trotted around tirelessly wearing a sign that announced he was the greatest authority on the Bible; a large number of nitwits who greeted everybody with, "Brother, thy tail hangs down behind." But some reporters said that Dayton had "not one indigenous freak." More typical of the local people, they said, was the man who had met a Bostonian, promptly agreed to give him shelter, handed him the house key and said, "The house is yours."

Many of the visiting eccentrics had come from the surrounding hill country to flirt briefly with sin. To them, Dayton was "this wicked town." One tall raw-boned woman in calico and sunbonnet, a Holy Roller, spirited her children away to her mountain retreat in the conviction that "the mark of the beast" was on the inhabitants of Dayton. "They'll go down to the lake of fire. I ain't got no business at this here trial. I'm going to stay away for something might happen to the courthouse." But some of the townspeople too were doggedly pious. A stenographer, educated in Chattanooga, who worked for George Rappelyea, was asked to type some letters for the Reverend Charles Francis Potter. "No," she said, "I will not take any dictation from a Unitarian." One native asked belligerently: "If God wanted to write a perfect book he could, couldn't he?" Another insisted: "Well, brother, my way's the safest; just believe what the Bible says and quit trying to figure out something different."

But Joseph Wood Krutch liked the candor in Dayton, where

everybody was willing to give an opinion. It was different in Knoxville, where the president of the University would talk to Krutch only in confidence, where a leading trustee of the University had taken him aside to whisper in his ear, where one man had spoken for many: "Of course it's a damn fool law—but I won't be quoted." Krutch declared that Tennessee was playing such a "sorry role" because "bigotry is militant and sincere; intelligence is timid and hypocritical . . ."

Certainly Judge Raulston was militant. In a statement to the press he said: "If man, without inspiration, attempts to delve into the mysteries of God he finds himself overwhelmed in perplexities. Therefore, I am much interested that the unerring hand of Him who is the Author of all truth and justice shall direct every official act of mine." But what was the judge militant for, as he circulated around the streets? Thinking ahead to the expiration of his term on the bench in 1926, he passed rapidly from one group to another shaking hands. In the hotel dining room he gleefully told a reporter: "It's a big case. All the big men on both sides will be there. Never any case like it before. . . . They say it's all in the New York papers. Of course they'll appeal it and it will go to the supreme court."

Here was the man who would hold the scales of justice. Nonetheless, Henry Fairfield Osborn said that the trial would do great good by clarifying the issues. In his book, *The Earth Speaks to Bryan,* he advised the defense that Bryan himself had stated the main issue in his article in the New York *Times* in 1922:

The Real Question Is, Did God Use Evolution as His Plan?

Beside this question all of the others—"such as personal rights, rights of opinion, rights of free speech, constitutional rights, educational liberty"—were insignificant. "If Scopes has been teaching the truth to his students he will win," wrote Osborn; "if he has been teaching untruths he will lose, and will deserve to lose."

Clarence Darrow agreed. Although he thought that references to God were impertinent, he did regard the truth of evolution as the main issue. His whole approach to the trial was to establish this truth by means of scientific testimony. The right witnesses, from many sciences, had been lined up. So Darrow did not bother to arrive in Dayton until the very night before the trial was to open. Every automobile in town was at the railroad station when his train pulled in. Darrow came out of the train into the hot Tennessee evening, John Scopes greeted him warmly, and they took their places before the movie cameras.

IV

When Clarence Darrow arrived in Dayton on the evening of Thursday, July 9, William Jennings Bryan was at the apex of a day that had been busy, exhilarating, almost giddy. That morning, with the opening of the trial just twenty-four hours away, he had appeared at the courthouse, the very scene of the expected triumph, to address the sixteen members of the county board of education. Introduced by Walter White, the superintendent of schools, as "the greatest man in the world and its leading citizen," Bryan asserted that he was an educated man who held seven doctorates of law and numerous other degrees.

Was this the man who had written: "The most learned man in the world cannot *explain* a watermelon, but the most ignorant man can *eat* a watermelon and enjoy it"? Yes, it was. Bryan told the educators that education, while important, was not primary. "To educate a man without giving him religion," said Bryan, "is like sending out a ship without a pilot. If we have to give up either religion or education, we should give up education." Bryan appealed to the sectional pride of his listeners, assuring them that the South's pious fervor distinguished it from less godly parts of the country. Formerly, political reforms had come from the agricultural West; henceforth, he predicted, religious reforms would come from the South.

Bryan and John Washington Butler stood together, their hands on a Bible, while their photograph was taken.

That evening Bryan expanded upon his themes of the morning. He had been asked to have dinner with the other members of the prosecution at Morgan Springs Hotel, a resort inn at the famous iron springs high on the crest of Walden's Ridge. But in the late afternoon a terrific thunderstorm broke. Streak after streak of lightning split the darkening sky. The heavens opened and the rain fell as an omen and a portent. Although it had been rumored that Bryan would make a speech after dinner, the newspapermen looked at the flooded streets and were dubious about getting up Walden's Ridge in their cars.

And then, like another sign from on high, the storm slackened. Bryan and his company started up the mountain. Up the gravel and clay road, around sharp and dangerous turns in the darkness, a climb of six miles into the low clouds. Six miles toward righteousness, while thunder growled in the distance and an occasional lightning flash illumined the way. "And the Lord came down upon mount Sinai, on the top of the mount: and the Lord called Moses up to the top of the mount; and Moses went up" (Exodus xix:20).

At the Morgan Springs Hotel, on the top of the mount, they ate dinner in silence. Even at Bryan's table, where he sat with his hosts, he did most of the talking. The others seemed overwhelmed by their proximity to him. The guests at the surrounding tables seemed embarrassed, even awed. Conversation was held only in whispers. The meal finished, Bryan rose and left the room. Chairs scraped as his guests got up and silently followed after the prophet.

Outdoors it was very dark. The rain had stopped. In the background the dark trees tossed in the wind. Bryan strode to a little slope in front of the inn, and took his position atop some rocks that formed a small eminence. A ray of light from the hotel door fell upon his figure, making him dimly visible against the overcast sky. Before him sat a crippled old man in a wheelchair, gazing upward at him with rapt face. Only one other person was close to Bryan, a tall mountain man who stood like stone, motionless, one hand holding out a glass of water in case Bryan should want it. The crowd gathered around on chairs or the porch railings or stood in the shadows.

Two aspects of the Scopes case, Bryan said, could properly be discussed before the trial. One was the contention of some big-city newspapers that a jury of Dayton residents was not competent to pass on the issues involved. What do they want, asked Bryan: a jury of scientists? Merely to say this was to condemn it. American institutions held that a jury was capable of deciding all issues of fact. In no state was there an educational requirement for jury service. "According to our system of government," Bryan insisted, "the people are interested in everything and can be trusted to decide everything, and so with our juries."

Second, said Bryan, the case raised "an entirely new question, viz., can a minority use the courts to force its ideas upon the schools?" The majority (wise, as majorities are always wise) had placed constitutional restraints upon itself "so as to prevent sudden action in times of excitement." But now an arrogant and irreligious minority was trying to do what the humble and religious majority would never do: impose its ideas upon the schools. If the evolutionists were a majority in Tennessee they could elect the legislature and repeal the Butler Act. This course was closed to them, and would always be closed by the wisdom and piety of the people, so the Darwinians were relying on the courts to coerce parents and voters into acquiescence. To this impious few, evolution was a religion; to most of them, the only religion they had.

Not so the common people, said Bryan; not so the South. He stood there in the dimmed light, his hair streaming, his arms going in the magnificent gestures that had made him famous. He looked ten feet tall, and his great voice rolled and reverberated from the rocks and the trees. The audience was hushed, silent.

Bryan spoke his pleasure at being among the simple people of the world. After praising the people of the South for their political allegiance to him, he eulogized the way they had held to the piety of their forefathers. Ever since he moved to Florida, said

Bryan, he had been conscious of a growing religious interest. Now, partly as a result of the Scopes trial, a great revival would sweep the country, beginning in the South and spreading with whirlwind rapidity. If this crusade moved on to other nations, as Bryan thought it would, the force inspiring it would be the humble faith of Southerners in the Bible as the revealed word of God.

As Bryan summoned the South to enlist in the army of the Lord, two voices spoke to him. One voice he heeded, the one that came from the air above him. "These words the Lord spoke unto all your assembly in the mount out of the midst of the fire, of the cloud, and of the thick darkness, with a great voice: and he added no more" (Deuteronomy v:22).

But Bryan heeded not the other voice, that rose from the mountain beneath him, from some of the oldest rocks containing fossil invertebrates, the Cambrian rocks; from the Ordovician rocks bearing primitive fishes and some of the earliest fossil corals; from rocks formed in the Silurian age when scorpions and some modern fishes had come into existence; from the black slate cropping out at the foot of Walden's Ridge and from the limestones lying above it, both slate and limestone being part of the Devonian and Mississippian series formed in the Great Age of Fishes.

Chapter 5

"Backward to the Glorious Age"

> The world is to be carried forward by truth, which at first offends, which wins its way by degrees, which the many hate and would rejoice to crush.
>
> William Ellery Channing, "The Abolitionists," *Works*, 11th ed. (Boston: George G. Channing, 1849), Vol. II, p. 161

I

On Friday, July 10, 1925, at the partially renovated Mansion outside Dayton, Clarence Darrow ate breakfast surrounded by reporters. Darrow seemed very genial and hearty to Emanuel Haldeman-Julius, a former socialist whose Little Blue Books flowed from Girard, Kansas, to carry sex, psychoanalysis, and freethought to all parts of the land, for only five cents a copy. The pudgy and prosperous publisher said airily that the pending trial showed "how people need to be debunked." Darrow asked: "If you take the bunk away what do you have left?" When somebody mentioned the Little Blue Books, Darrow commented: "You can Fordize literature, but you can't Fordize intelligence."

It was a hot day, terribly hot. The defense contingent moved up the dusty street to the courthouse, passing the soft-drink and sandwich stands along the curb, the vendors of religious books and watermelon, the peddlers auctioning calico and notions, the open-air tabernacle flung up by evangelists. The buildings in Dayton were festooned with banners. People from the neighboring hills had come on foot or riding in wagons fitted out with chairs and settees. Some of the men, sober of face and tight-lipped, were carrying rifles. The atmosphere was 90 per cent carnival, 10 per cent chastisement.

At the courthouse the lawn was crisscrossed by newly installed water pipes. Privies had been hastily built to comfort the expected crowds. The raw planking had been partially covered with printed signs: "Read Your Bible." A similar sign hung above the porch to the courthouse. Inside, a staircase led up to the courtroom on the second floor. The judge's bench was newly stained with a dark cherry color. Here, his back to two windows, sat John T. Raulston, middle-aged, florid, raw-boned, his perpetual smile somewhat like the grimace of a man who had eaten a green persimmon. "Jist a reg'lar mountin'eer Jedge," he called himself.

Darrow arrived, playing his role to the limit, clearly amused, thinning hair drooped across his reticular forehead, coat dangling from the crook of his arm, suspenders flaunted over his tan shirt, soft collar and white string tie. He met the McKenzies of the prosecution. J. Gordon McKenzie, county judge and criminal lawyer, was earnest and neat and looked like a businessman. His father Ben G. McKenzie was the dean of the local bar, a practicing lawyer for 32 years. His pink round face was usually chuckling; ten times a day his sides shook as he said: "No, suh, I wear no man's collar, no, suh!"

Darrow glanced at Ben McKenzie's rotund form and said: "Well, I see you, too, wear suspenders."

McKenzie said: "Yes, Colonel Darrow, we have to keep our pants up down here in Tennessee just like you do up there in Chicago."

After that it was "Colonel Darrow" consistently. Everybody had a title. Ben McKenzie was called "General." Even Dudley Field Malone was denominated "Captain," but that first morning he seemed uncomfortable, with a cigarette in one hand and a handkerchief in the other. John Scopes looked embarrassed and boyish in a blue shirt and a hand-painted bow tie. Besides Malone, the only person who persisted in wearing a jacket was the attorney-general of the circuit of seven counties for which Raulston was judge, a position that made A. T. Stewart the legal head of the prosecution. But the idol of the crowd was William Jennings Bryan, whose arrival prompted the entire courtroom to applaud. Bryan smiled and smiled. It was the 29th anniversary of his Cross of Gold speech.

Mrs. Bryan was there, in her wheelchair, as she would be at every session of the trial. Also Bryan's son, as another visiting member of the prosecution. The son was 38 years old, a Los Angeles lawyer whose taste in clothes ran to high fashion. He smoked cigars, said nothing about politics or religion or evolution but would talk endlessly about fishing. William Jennings Bryan, bent on surviving after death, had named his son "Junior"; Bryan also, his yearnings for peace tempered by his yearning for titled glory, had sent his son to Culver Military Academy in Indiana.

More than a hundred American reporters, and two from London, sat at the press tables. H. L. Mencken shared a table with Watson Davis of Science Service. John Washington Butler squeezed his big frame into a chair and settled back with the nonchalance of a veteran reporter. The courtroom was filled to its capacity of 400 and the walls were lined with added spectators when Judge Raulston called on the Reverend Mr. Cartwright to open court with prayer. With mixed reactions the defense lawyers—Darrow and Malone and John Neal and the burly Arthur Hays—heard the minister intone: "we come to Thee this morning, our Divine Father, that we may seek from Thee that wisdom to so transact the business of this court in such a way and manner as that Thy name may be honored and glorified among men." Bryan stood with head bowed while the prayer emphasized the omnipresence of God and the imminence of the Last Judgment. Darrow's eyes wandered around the room.

A brief delay was necessary. The judge was on the bench, the lawyers ready. But it was doubtful that John Scopes was a proper defendant; his indictment in May had been handled so summarily —after all, Dayton had been in danger of losing the trial to some other town—that nobody was sure it was legal. The neglect was repaired. A new grand jury was empaneled, and Judge Raulston, not the least embarrassed by his earlier unsightly haste, read the Butler Act to the 13 jurors. Then, in his evangelist's voice, often wiping his face with a moist handkerchief, he read the Creation story from Genesis: "And God created man in his own image, in the image of God created He them, male and female, created He them."

Three students of Scopes, boys of 14 and 15, were wanted to tell the grand jury what he had taught them in class. But they were friends of his who did not want to see him in trouble. They took to the woods. John Scopes was sent to find the fugitives and persuade them to testify. He did so. By 11 A.M., the grand jury had returned an indictment. Now at last the case of *Tennessee* v. *John Thomas Scopes,* No. 5232, could go forward.

II

The police chief of Chattanooga, loaned for the occasion to Dayton, announced: "No smokin' when co't takes up." It was time to pick the trial jury. Judge Raulston said: "Step up here a minute, Colonel Darrow." The sound of the title startled Darrow; he looked around as if expecting somebody else to answer. Then he understood, and he grinned eupeptically as he tugged at his galluses and shuffled to the bench.

Darrow wanted to know right away whether the judge would permit scientific testimony, and, if so, about when this point in the trial would be reached. The scientists who would be offered as witnesses were, he pointed out, busy men, and it would be wrong to waste their time by having them come to Dayton in vain or sit around idly once they got there. But Judge Raulston said that he would not rule on the admissibility of the scientific testimony until after both sides had outlined their respective theories of the case, and that could not be done until the jury had been chosen and sworn. Stewart made it clear that the state did not think that any scientific testimony about Darwinism or the Bible would be competent.

Thus, in the first session of the trial, the major issue was defined. Could the defense seek to prove that the theory of evolution was valid and that it did not necessarily conflict with the Bible? Or would the issues be limited to the factual question of whether Scopes had violated the Butler Act? On the resolution of this issue would depend the nature of the trial. If the issue was narrowly limited by the court, the defense had no case to offer.

Judge Raulston wanted everybody to have a good time, especially the photographers. The proceedings were punctuated with nonlegal requests:

"Put your face a little more this way, Judge."

"Come a little more forward, Mr. Darrow."

When Stewart said he thought they could pick the jury in less than a day, Darrow indicated his doubts. No phase of a trial seemed to him so important as selecting the jury; if you could get the right men in the jury-box, the case was half won. In major cases he not infrequently used two months and hundreds of veniremen before finding twelve men who suited him. On one occasion he had left the trial of a case in Idaho, returned to Chicago, spent six weeks there in selecting the jury in another case, and then had gone back to Idaho, feeling that the most important part of the Chicago trial was over. Even in the Scopes trial, where the maximum penalty that could be imposed on the defendant was a modest fine and where the major issues were matters of law that would not be decided by the jury anyway, Darrow said he wanted "a reasonable liberty of examination, to see that we get as impartial a jury as is possible."

It turned out that only 16 veniremen were present in court. When the judge explained that additional ones, if needed, would be simply rounded up by the sheriff from among the bystanders, Darrow said he was surprised that a regular jury list was not used. The local custom, replied Raulston, was to do so only in felony cases in which the defendant insisted on it, but he would be formal in this instance even though Scopes was charged merely with a misdemeanor.

After lunch the judge showed that his call for prayer that morning had been only an instance of his chronic trait of ordering life by scrambled ritual and symbol. The Christian doctrine that "a little child shall lead them" (Isaiah xi:6) was concentrated in the fundamentalist conviction that the wisdom bred of age and education was jejune beside the purity of youth and ignorance. The fundamentalists wept for childhood, worshipped it; almost their ideal was to remain childish for life. A man aware of the innocence of childhood was a man who merited re-election as judge. Judge Raulston, looking ahead to the end of his term in 1926, got a child to come up, perch on the corner of the judicial bench, and draw the names of veniremen from a hat. The altar of childish judiciousness, and the judge beaming happily the while.

As the panel of Tennesseans moved man by man into the witness chair to be questioned by Darrow, many reporters were intrigued by the masterly performance. The gangling Chicago lawyer talked easily and conversationally, but he gazed hypnotically at each man as he flattered by tone of voice or by the phrasing of questions. Darrow was allowed great latitude in his interrogation; when Stewart objected, Judge Raulston said that Darrow could find out whatever he wanted to know in order to decide whether to challenge a man. But Darrow didn't like the method of challenging. In Illinois, a lawyer could temporarily accept a venireman onto the jury, and then get rid of him later by means of a peremptory challenge. But now Darrow found that he had only three peremptory challenges, and that he had to exercise one while questioning the veniremen or he could not do it at all. Once a man had been accepted on the jury, he was there for good. Under this system, Darrow complained, "you never know which one to challenge." He liked to see what the choices were before he took his pick.

Darrow accepted the first man, the second. The third was an ex-miner, now a farmer, named Jim Riley. His white shirt contrasted strongly with his dark blue glasses. Darrow asked if he had ever talked to anybody about evolution, or heard any sermons about it. Riley said No.

Darrow: "Ever hear Mr. Bryan speak about it?"

Riley: "No, sir."

Darrow: "Ever read anything he said about it?"

Riley: "No, sir; I can't read."

Darrow: "Well, you are fortunate."

Riley was accepted on the jury. Then it was suggested to Darrow that perhaps Riley's dark blue glasses meant that his eyesight was bad; perhaps he could not read for that reason. Darrow recalled Riley to ask. Everybody was impressed by the straightforward dignity of the reply: "No, I am uneducated."

Tom Jackson, a square-jawed ex-soldier, was asked if he had formed an opinion about evolution. "I have," he said, "and I got my information from the Bible." Darrow excused him from the jury, but as Jackson passed him, Darrow said in his deliberately audible undertone: "I believe you are a damn square man."

The Reverend J. P. Massingill, who ministered to four congregations in the country north of Dayton, had a different effect on Darrow. When asked if he had ever preached for or against evolution, Massingill tried to evade the question. Finally he blurted out: "Well, I preached against it, of course!" The audience applauded. Darrow asked: "Why 'of course'?"

He knew why. He knew that such aggressiveness often arises from a fear of doubt. As another sign of that lacy cloud of guilt to which fundamentalism made effective appeal, even those veniremen who were not especially religious felt compelled to apologize for their backsliding. A man like J. R. Thompson (a well-groomed portly man with a white goatee and a cold cigar, a United States marshal for five years during the Wilson administration) was enough at ease to say banteringly that he might not listen so closely when the lawyers were talking, but when he said that he belonged to the Methodist church he added that he was "not a good member, not as good as I ought to be." And Bill Day, a retired farmer, said that he had read the Bible but not "like I ought to."

In about two hours and a half, contrary to Darrow's expectations, they had the jury. Only 19 veniremen had been examined in agreeing on 12. The state had not bothered to question 13 of them at all.

Again Darrow ran up against the local customs. When Stewart said that he preferred not to have the jury sworn until Monday, so that if a juror became ill over the week-end a replacement could be chosen on Monday morning, Darrow protested that the jury should be sworn at once; if this were done, no juror could discuss the case outside the courtroom without violating his oath and putting himself in legal jeopardy. But Judge Raulston said the local practice was to read the indictment and hear opening statements by both sides before the jury was sworn. To do all this, he added, would carry them past the regular 4:30 adjournment. So, the judge being in no hurry to see the trial concluded, court adjourned early.

As the jurors filed out the door, John Scopes' father Thomas stood at the door looking them over. "Say, brother," he commented, "that's a hell of a jury!" Nine of the jurors were farmers. Five had lived in Rhea County since birth. Six were Baptists, four Methodists, one a Campbellite, one a non-belonger from a Baptist family. Besides the illiterate Jim Riley, three had testified that they read no books other than the Bible. These were men who had compensated for the narrowness of their own experience by ignoring the experience of others.

But this isolation had bred a noncommitment that might become receptivity. In the examination of the jury panel, one venireman after another testified that he had never heard any discussion of evolution until after Scopes was indicted and that, while there had been a "right smart" of it since that time, he himself had not paid much attention to it. Eleven of the 19 veniremen had stated this general fact. Ten of the 11 were taken onto the jury.

Was it possible that the South was not, after all, a solid phalanx drawn up to repel the infidel invaders from New York and Chicago? Darrow had at least been encouraged to try some discreet filibustering. If he could not seduce any birthright virgins, maybe he could spy out some weak sisters and lure them into the ways of knowledge.

III

As the trial opened, the Chattanooga *News* predicted: "The people of Tennessee, the south, even of the world, will become more familiar with the theory of evolution than they ever were before." But the Dayton authorities meant to do what they could to influence the discussion. Although Bryan was given a permit to speak on the courthouse lawn, a Brooklyn modernist was denied one; A. P. Haggard, the town's head commissioner and wealthiest citizen, said he was fearful that a hostile crowd might harm the modernist. Two days later the city officials cancelled all permits for public preaching in Dayton for the duration of the trial.

The weather was so sweltering that Ben McKenzie suffered heat prostration, but the visiting Yankees stayed active. In court on Friday, Stewart had agreed that the admissibility of scientific testimony should be taken up on Monday as a special motion by the defense; that night and the next day Scopes' lawyers were at the law library preparing their argument. But Stewart changed his mind. On Saturday he drove out to the Mansion to say that the matter should not be argued in advance, but should come up in the ordinary course of events. An advisory opinion in advance by the judge, said Stewart, might constitute a technical error in the trial record. After a discussion, Neal and Malone agreed, and Stewart drove back to town. But when Darrow heard about the change, he insisted that they go through with the original plan. We should not have to ask a dozen scientists to come down here and sit around for a week or two weeks, he argued, only to be told that they cannot testify after all. Now Neal was up and away to Dayton to find Stewart and tell him that the defense had changed its mind.

Thus the pattern of the trial took shape—one false start after another (with John Randolph Neal as errand boy, but so far nobody realized how lackadaisical an errand boy he was). The immediate procession of errors was not ended. The defense lawyers had thought that Stewart's agreement, made in court on Friday, was binding. Now they learned that they had no legal rights in this respect because in Tennessee a stipulation had to be made in writing. So all the confusion was without offspring: the defense decided not to insist on the special procedure but rather to wait until it was time for the scientific witnesses to testify before arguing the propriety of their testimony.

Out at the Mansion the defense forces were having a congenial, often an uproarious, time—all without benefit of alcohol. Rabbi Herman Rosenwasser of San Francisco, in Dayton to testify as a Bible expert, had brought with him a Hebrew copy of Genesis. Every evening he would conduct a class in translation. First he would render the Hebrew into German, with a choice of maybe a half dozen German words for each Hebrew character. Then he could pick and choose again in turning the German into English. The transmutations were startling: the words in Psalms (cxlviii:6), "He hath made a decree which shall not pass," should be translated, "He hath made a law of nature which He doth not transgress."

The prosecution also was preparing for scholarly warfare. Bryan wired to the Reverend John Roach Straton of Calvary Baptist Church in New York, asking if he could come to testify. Straton was hot for Deity and headlines—he had long been roasting Henry Fairfield Osborn and the American Museum of Natural History—and he wired back that he would be delighted to serve. He offered to prove that Scripture and evolution were "thoroughly incompatible." He added even more exciting news:

> Can also give valuable information regarding refusal of scientists in museum here to accept fossil horseshoe sole, antedating alleged time of man's appearance on earth, taken from cretaceous gravel antedating entire

> alleged evolution of horse from little five-toed animal,
> &c. Have pictures, affidavits from research experts whom
> scientists have turned down.

And closed with a blessing: "God guide you!" Doubtless Bryan appreciated the blessing; if he could not understand the rest, probably he should be forgiven.

Alfred W. McCann of New York rejected Bryan's invitation to testify. Although he had written *God or Gorilla?*, one of the most pretentious attacks on Darwinism, McCann did not like the Butler Act. He explained: "the spirit of this generation must feel outraged by the spectacular methods invoked to put a muzzle on the teachings of any cult, however erroneous."

In Dayton the conflict kept alive over the week-end. Charles Francis Potter, the New York Unitarian minister affiliated with the defense, had been invited to speak Sunday morning at the local First Methodist Church, North. But several parishioners protested to the pastor, Howard G. Byrd. Potter decided not to speak. Then Byrd resigned his pulpit. Meanwhile William Jennings Bryan was preaching about the Bible before a large group at the rival Methodist Church, South. He argued that God must have had a reason for making man ignorant rather than learned. And in passing on men's qualifications for Heaven, God does not ask for diplomas. References to Heaven were adroitly coupled with references to Florida—its wonderful climate, its business prospects. The kind of sermon that sells plenty of real estate.

For John T. Raulston, these triumphs of righteousness were marred by reports that he would have serious competition for re-election in 1926. A Democrat whom he had beaten only by 120 votes in 1918 (and 1918 was a bad year for Democrats) was rumored to be considering another try. It was even said that Raulston would have to fight off the challenge of another prominent Republican for his party's nomination.

Thomas Scopes was having a good time. Down from Paducah, Kentucky, for the trial, he told a reporter in his soft drawl that "a father just naturally has to stick by his own blood and flesh, ma'am, no matter what they've done." Not that John had done anything bad; the father said he was an evolutionist himself. The son spoke from inside his yellow racing car: "Don't blow so much, dad."

IV

Blowing began in earnest in the courtroom on Monday. A bad day for it too: hot, stifling. A small electric fan had been found to cool Judge Raulston. The jurors waved fans bearing a toothpaste advertisement: "Do your gums bleed?" Attorneys and audience sat in shirt-sleeves, shifting stickily. The judge delayed opening court so that radio engineers could adjust the hook-up; he was proud that this was the first trial ever broadcast. "My gavel," he exaggerated, "will be heard around the world."

After prayer, Stewart rose to read the indictment, that Scopes had taught in the public schools of Rhea County "a certain theory and theories which deny the story of the divine creation of man as taught in the Bible, and did teach instead thereof that man has descended from a lower order of animals . . ." The wording followed the Butler Act, but its interpretation, involving, as it did, the propriety of the scientific evidence, became a hotly debated issue.

When the indictment had been read, John Randolph Neal offered a motion to quash the indictment on 13 grounds. Some of them split words so spectrally as to make even the defense a little sheepish; those were stated and forgotten. But it was more seriously urged that the Butler Act violated six clauses of the Tennessee constitution: II(17), providing that no bill in the legislature could embrace more than one subject, which had to be clearly stated in the title; XI(12), requiring the state to "cherish science and literature"; I(3), that "no preference shall ever be given, by law, to any religious establishment or mode of worship"; I(9), on freedom of speech; I(8), on due process of law; and II(8), stating that all laws must be of general application. The defense argued further that statute and indictment were both void "for indefiniteness and lack of certainty." Finally, both statute and indictment were held to violate the federal Constitution, 14th Amendment, Section 1, forbidding infringement of life, liberty, or property without due process of law. These were, from the defense viewpoint, the constitutional issues.

Neal asked the judge to defer judgment on this motion until all the evidence in the case had been heard—a pointless request, since nobody hoped that even the scientific testimony would convert John Raulston. But Stewart insisted that the motion should be decided before the jury was sworn, and the judge so ruled.

Oral argument on the motion began at once, with Neal leading off. He did little more than repeat in jumbled fashion the points in the motion. Probably his speech was doing the prosecution more good than harm, but Stewart asked that the jury, still not sworn, be sent from the courtroom. Darrow objected. Stewart would be "more at ease" if the jury were not present.

Darrow: "We'll be less at ease," good-humoredly.

Raulston: "Let the jury retire."

The jurors filed out, even though the state constitution said that in criminal cases the jury should be judge of the law as well as of facts. Not that it mattered: reporters looked out the window and saw the jurors sitting in the courthouse yard listening to the arguments over the loudspeakers.

But nobody listened closely. Soon they hardly listened at all, as Neal meandered along, to be followed by Hays who excited a little interest by reading a statute he had drafted which decreed the death penalty for anybody who taught the Copernican theory in the public schools. If the Butler Act is valid, said Hays, so is this. The comparison was not original with him; both supporters and opponents of the Butler Act had already used it to flog Bryan.

That morning saw occasional flurries, but, all in all, Neal, Hays, Ben McKenzie, and Sue Hicks put on a dull show. Constitutional law is a poor topic for a hot day. Had the trial continued thus, the audience would have flowed out like a tide and silted up along the curbstones, under the shade trees, on the front steps, around the cracker barrels. But after lunch Stewart made a gymnastic, sarcastic reply to the defense motion. In an hour he had rejected every point of it.

This case, said Stewart, involved no religious question at all; the constitutional guarantee of freedom of religion applied only to worship in churches. When Malone asked if the law did not prefer the Bible to the Koran, Stewart said sharply: "We are not living in a heathen country." The Butler Bill was purely and simply an effort by the legislature "to control the expenditure of state funds, which it has a right to do." To prove this, he construed the recent *Meyer* v. *Nebraska* into a ruling by the Supreme Court that a legislature had plenary power over the curriculum in public schools. He also leaned hard on the *Leeper* case, in which Tennessee's uniform-textbook law had been challenged; the state supreme court had ruled that control of the public schools had to lodge somewhere and that the legislature was the proper place.

Just as Ben McKenzie had jested that any 16-year-old boy in Tennessee could tell what the Butler Act meant, so did Stewart say that he saw nothing vague or indefinite about the indictment. (*Plain as the nose on your face. The Word is there. Just read It. It means what It says.* Showing again that in a ritual, words do not have meaning; words are meaning. Whoever violates the Word has desecrated the Thing, since word and thing are one. The first book of Samuel [xxviii] tells how the right words can even call forth the dead; names are so powerful that a god whose name is properly uttered has no choice but to gratify the petition.)

Stewart taunted the defense lawyers by asking if they were unsure what Scopes had been accused of. "You did not prepare a brief here to defend him on a charge of arson, did you? He is not here for transporting liquor, and he knows it."

Darrow opened with light-hearted courtesies (no intense beginnings: an express elevator may carry the body but it abandons the spirit). He grinned and thanked the judge for giving him the title, "Colonel," and Raulston grinned and said that Darrow should take it back to Chicago with him. Darrow was talking easily and genially: abruptly, he was talking about the man "responsible for this foolish, mischievous and wicked act," a man who came "from Florida." Casual again, he conceded that the legislature had the right to prescribe a course of study in the public schools. But its prescriptions had to be reasonable; it could not abolish reading and writing and set up the Bible as the sole subject of study. There was no doubt that the statute was vague and contradictory, because it forbade anything that conflicted with the Creation story of the Bible. But the Bible was not one book; it was 66 books, written over a period of a thousand years. The Bible was not a book of science; it was a book of religion and morals, which served millions as consolation and solace in time of affliction.

"My friend the attorney-general says that John Scopes knows what he is here for." Darrow paused, and lashed out. "Yes, I know what he is here for—because the fundamentalists are after everybody who thinks. I know why he is here. I know he is here because ignorance and bigotry are rampant, and it is a mighty strong combination, Your Honor." The powerful shoulders writhed upward, rippling the wet shirt, rumpling the limp collar. His left hand caught at his blue suspenders; the right arm, formerly wagging in mere wrist movements, now became the boom of a sail, and the sail whipped by an invisible tornado. The crescendo rose, and his right hand slapped the left palm in brisk staccato. Judge Raulston's grin sagged into total disbelief. Darrow shifted again, shifted subject and tone. Back to the indictment, chaffing his opponents. "Let me show you a real indictment, gentlemen, in case you ever need to draw another one. You don't mind a little pleasantry, do you?"

He talked along, his manner seeming relaxed and offhand; his organization, loose and repetitive. This was guise. His arguments were as carefully composed as a mural. He led the audience back and forth across the facts, showing each fact from calculated viewpoints, playing the light across it now from this angle, now from that. His palette astonished by its range of hue and tonal value. And for each fact he found the right color. If he missed it the first time, he wiped out what he had done, and came back later and tried again. Always he watched his audience, judging whether he was getting across to them with the facts, and with the meaning of the facts, the emotional color of the facts. He worked at it until content and style had fused completely and been absorbed into the spectators.

He used words as an artist uses paint. Catch the eye here with a yellow, but don't startle by it. The eye carries easily from the yellow to the earth-browns, carried by line that is camouflaged but yet moves onward. (Relaxation the keynote. Make the jurors like you. The matter as unaccented as a wheat field, the voice trifling as a breeze.) Here the spectator feels uneasy, for here on the canvas the starlings fly overhead by the thousands, and their black shadows fall over the warm golden earth; no bird more terrifying than starlings, for like censors they devour the seeds and nothing will fructify and the warm golden earth will be wasteland; see how the starlings thicken the telegraph wires into a heavy sagging black; even insensate matter is bloated and festered by the censor starlings (and the shrill alarming cry of the birds mutes into a restful drawl). Unexpectedly the eye finds itself back at that patch of yellow pigment where it began: the pigment is the same, but the eye sees it differently, coming now to the yellow from the brown and subdued gold and the terrifying black. (The lawyer crossed and recrossed the canvas of the argument, painting with color and light and memory, highlighting the canvas with shadows like the starlings' shadow and with scarlet like the Crucifixion.)

Anybody knew, said Darrow, that "to think is to differ," and the Butler Act was constitutionally void because it was an effort to coerce agreement about religion. "There are no two human machines alike and no two human beings have the same experiences and their ideas of life and philosophy grow out of their construction of the experiences that we meet on our journey through life. It is impossible, if you leave freedom in the world, to mold the opinions of one man upon the opinions of another—only tyranny can do it." His manner, almost negligent an instant earlier, was emphatic; once more his right arm swept like a scythe slashing through the weeds planted by his opponents.

Time for a joke; time to say again that the Bible is not a scientific treatise. "This law," said Darrow, "makes the Bible a yardstick to measure every man's intelligence, and to measure every man's learning. Are your mathematics good? Turn to I Elijah ii. Is your philosophy good? See I Samuel iii. Is your astronomy good? See Genesis, Chapter ii, Verse 7. Is your chemistry good? See—well, chemistry [the slow shrug]—see Deuteronomy iii:6, or anything that tells about brimstone." (Of course the references were hasty frauds, but serviceable enough.)

Now to interweave the frightful black and the glorious scarlet. "Your Honor knows that fires have been lighted in America to kindle religious bigotry and hate. . . ."

The Court: "Sorry to interrupt your argument, but it is adjourning time."

Darrow impatiently asked for another five minutes.

The Court: "Proceed tomorrow."

Darrow went ahead without permission. "Today it is the public school teachers, tomorrow the private. The next day the preachers and the lecturers, the magazines, the books, the newspapers. After a while, Your Honor, it is the setting of man against man and creed against creed until with flying banners and beating drums we are marching backward to the glorious age of the sixteenth century when bigots lighted faggots to burn the men who dared bring any intelligence and enlightenment and culture to the human mind." He had finished, and court adjourned.

In sweeping to his climax, Darrow had folded his arms and caught his elbows in his hands. One sleeve ripped badly. Now the comely Mrs. Darrow came up to him in the front of the courtroom to say with embarrassment: "Clarence, don't you think you'd better put on another shirt?"

"Well, Ruby,"—he smiled—"don't you think it's too hot today for two shirts?"

Darrow strolled out with his wife, he in his torn and sodden shirt, she in a printed crepe frock and a violet hat ornamented with fluted silk. One woman looked at him and exclaimed, "The damned infidel!"

A native of Dayton came up to say: "Mr. Darrow, if I could have heard you before, I would never have spoken of you as I have in the past."

"That's all right, that's all right," said Darrow warmly.

Here came Ben McKenzie to throw his arm around Darrow and say in a voice choked, truly or falsely, with emotion: "It was the greatest speech I ever heard in my life on any subject."

Darrow patted the upholstered back and said, "It's mighty kind of you to say that."

Buckshot Morgan, another local man, wanted to know if that was all "this evolution business" meant. "I might as well have gone fishing," he commented; "folks ain't going to waste their time listening to wickedness when it ain't more interesting than that. Do you think"—he was wistful—"that a fellow could grasp more of the wickedness of it if he had an education?"

Since the preceding day, when Ruby Darrow arrived in Dayton, the Darrows had occupied an entire house by themselves. (She always took good care of his physical comfort. He enjoyed the coddling.) But Monday night after his speech he went out to the Mansion to see his associates. (Women were not much as intellectual companions.) All of the men sat in one of the large, sparsely furnished rooms. Dayton's electric current failed (the water supply had failed that afternoon). A few candles were lighted. The men heard the thunder swell and rumble, saw the lightning flash.

Darrow chuckled. "Boys, if the lightning strikes this house tonight, it is the hand of providence."

But Darrow was making friends in Dayton. Even before the trial started, the secretary of the Dayton Progressive Club had said of Loeb and Leopold: "I can understand how those boys just had to do that because of the way they were raised," and another member of the Club had said of Darrow's plea for them: "He made us understand the relation of cause and effect." Now personal acquaintance was extending this sympathy. It was not easy to remain hostile to a man as winsome and tolerant as Darrow proved to be. They liked his negligent ways, the spellbinding oratory of his speech. Even Attorney-General Stewart called him courteous and able. The earlier tense rejection by many Tennesseans of Darrow, Scopes, and Darwin was changing into conversations about the issues. Small groups of men, interested but not frenetic, stood on the courthouse lawn or in the streets. There were, it seemed, matters here that needed some looking into.

Of course the businessmen were disappointed. Chief Commissioner Haggard and the president of the Dayton Progressive Club estimated the town would lose money, so heavy were the extra expenses caused by the trial. But Haggard was pleased by the publicity; that Monday night an estimated 200,000 words—enough to fill a book of 500 pages—were telegraphed out of Dayton by the reporters.

Chapter 6

God and Caesar

> If I lose faith in Genesis, I'm
> afraid I'll lose faith in the rest of
> the Bible; and if I want to com-
> mit larceny I'll say I don't believe
> in the part of the Bible that says
> "Thou shalt not steal." Then I'll
> go out and steal. The same thing
> applies to murder.
>
> John T. Raulston, speech in New
> York City, November, 8, 1925

I

Having shocked the judge on Monday afternoon by his as-
sault on the Butler Act, Darrow opened the following day with
another challenge. As soon as court was called to order on Tuesday morning, he rose to ask whether any of the jurors were present. None responded. In their absence, said Darrow, he wanted
to object to opening each session with prayer.

He spoke in a soft voice. Most spectators could not hear him.
But the words struck John Raulston like physical blows. It seemed
that Darrow had dared the Almighty to strike him dead.

The judge recovered enough to say that it had been his custom
to open court with prayer, and that he would overrule the objection.
Darrow spoke again. The prosecution, he said, claimed that the
case involved a conflict between science and religion. Therefore
it was especially important that the jury should not be subjected to
extralegal influences.

111

Ben McKenzie could not bear to be a spectator in such a situation: spectators tense and expectant, rising from their seats, standing on tiptoe, craning their necks. Who would crush this impious
man? McKenzie deflated these hopes of retribution by saying
merely that the state supreme court had already ruled that it was
commendable to seek divine guidance for a jury.

Darrow said that he did not mind if the jurors or anybody
else prayed in secret, but it was not right to turn the courtroom
"into a meeting house."

Stewart would not tolerate this. He harshly denied that the
case involved any conflict between science and religion. It was entirely proper to open court with prayer, and the devout people of
Tennessee would have no sympathy with the objections made by
"the agnostic counsel for the defense." He said the word "agnostic" in a tone razored with insult. Darrow shrugged and shook
his head as he smiled at Stewart, but Arthur Hays shouted an objection to Stewart's language. Dudley Field Malone, his face flam-
ing, replied hotly that he was not an agnostic. The defense counsel, he explained, had discussed the matter among themselves. They
had not objected to prayer on the first day of the trial, but con-
tinuation of the practice would reinforce the hostility to Scopes
which already existed in Dayton because of the "widespread propaganda."

Malone stood facing the judge. Stewart on Malone's right and
Darrow on his left were looking past him at each other.

Stewart: "So far as creating an atmosphere of hostility is
concerned, I would advise Mr. Malone that this is a God-fearing
country."

Malone snapped: "And it is no more God-fearing country
than that from which I came."

Here was occasion for Bryan to take the floor, but he did not.
He remained seated, wearing neither coat nor tie; above his collarless shirt the muscles moved in his throat and jaws as he nibbled
the edges of a palm leaf fan, his false teeth shredding the dried
leaf.

The argument went on, and the judge pleaded for peace, and there was no peace. Darrow insisted that the case involved religious issues; how could it be otherwise when the statute forbade any doctrine of man's origins that conflicted with the Bible?

Raulston cut them off. He did not see how the prayers could influence himself or the jury, so he would continue them: "I believe in prayer myself; I constantly invoke divine guidance myself when I am on the bench and off the bench; I see no reason why I should not continue to do this." Raulston was not one to taunt the Deity or the voters.

Nor was the Reverend Mr. Stribling, a stout, middle-aged man of unclerical attire, who prayed: "we ask that Thou will enlighten our minds and lead us to understand and know truth in all its every phrase, we ask it in the name of our Blessed Redeemer, Jesus Christ, amen."

The judge explained that he would need another two hours or so to finish his consideration of the defense motion to quash the indictment. Now Scopes' lawyers took the chance to also file a demurrer, based on the same grounds as the motion to quash. Raulston said that he would rule on both together.

Eager as the judge was to get back to his law books, he said to the photographers: "If you want to make any pictures, I will give you fifteen minutes."

Darrow, determined to have a proper record for the expected appeal, asked that a defense objection should be entered to each specific occasion of prayer in the future, and Raulston so ordered. Court adjourned for him to do some legal thinking.

As the judge was walking to the Aqua Hotel, he was joined by William K. Hutchinson, a young reporter for International News Service. Hutchinson glanced at the bundle of papers under Raulston's arm and asked if that was the decision on the motion to quash. Raulston, eager to cooperate with the press, said: "No, the decision is being copied right now by my stenographer."

Hutchinson: "Will you read that decision this afternoon?"

Raulston: "That is my intention."

Hutchinson: "Will you adjourn until tomorrow?"

Raulston: "Yes, I think so."

Hutchinson walked away.

At 1 o'clock, a policeman in the courtroom rapped for order, then merely announced that court would convene at 2:30. At 2:15 Judge Raulston appeared in court, tight-faced and stern, to say that if any member of the press released information about his decision before it had been read in court, that person would be punished for contempt. The trial was not actually convened until 3:45.

Hays asked permission to present a petition and to read it. Stewart objected vehemently. Hays insisted.

Stewart: "Will you please keep your mouth shut?"

The judge agreed to hear the petition, which proved to be a statement that the fundamentalist prayers that had been offered in court were "not spiritually uplifting" and were "occasionally offensive." The petition, which asked that clergymen who were not fundamentalist should be also asked to offer prayer in court, was signed by a rabbi, two Unitarian ministers, and a Congregationalist pastor. The two Tennesseans among the signers were both from Knoxville.

The judge said that he would refer the petition "to the pastors' association of this town—" He was drowned out by guffaws from the newspapermen, who thought he was being shrewdly jocose. But the laughter in turn was overwhelmed by cheers and stamping feet; only then did the reporters realize that Judge Raulston thought he was being impartial in sending the petition off to the fundamentalist clergymen of Dayton.

The judge broke the levity abruptly by saying that he had a "very serious matter" to take up. He had spent four hours dictating his ruling on the motion to quash and demurrer to a "reputable court stenographer in secret." But newspapers were already on sale in distant cities purporting to say what his ruling was. Obviously John Raulston smelled wrong-doing; somebody must have sneaked a look at his secret manuscript. Therefore, said the judge, he would not read his ruling until the next morning; and he cleared the courtroom of all except newsmen to discuss the news leak.

Malone and Neal, tiring of the repeated delays, asked Raulston to at least rule on the admissibility of the scientific testimony so that the trial would keep moving forward. The judge was adamant; he would do nothing else until this outrageous breach of ethics was cleared up. A telegram was read: A St. Louis paper contained a story that the law had been held constitutional by the judge. Raulston named a committee of five reporters to investigate and report to him as soon as possible.

As court recessed, Bryan was asked by a bystander if he believed Joshua had commanded the sun to stand still. He replied angrily that while he would always answer honest questions, "somebody told you to ask me that question. It is asked with no other purpose than to insult me." He stalked away. By contrast, when Mrs. Bryan was being assisted from the courtroom, Dudley Field Malone showed his most gracious smile and asked if he could help. The defense lawyers differed from the prosecution in smiling more readily, mixing more easily, and giving bigger tips to the telegraph messengers. The distinction was not lost on the townspeople of Dayton, and certainly helped to soften them for Darrow's subversion.

But Scopes' lawyers no longer felt so cordial toward all of their opponents. Darrow had been called an "agnostic"; Hays had been told to keep his mouth shut. A newspaper report said that the defense lawyers expected the trial to become a knock-down brawl. This outlook further increased the chagrin of the jurors, who had been barred from the courtroom for two days and so had not witnessed the rancorous disputes. Now they were faced with the possibility of even bigger fights in the future, from which they might again be excluded.

The Chattanooga *Times* was also distressed, both by the "crusade against intelligence" in Dayton and by the timorous "skulking up alleys" of Tennessee's educated citizens. "Had they had the courage and boldness to speak out when this thing began," the

Times editorialized, "they might have saved themselves and their state from the humiliation that has come upon them."

More mortification for Tennessee grew out of the investigation of the advance story about Judge Raulston's decision. On that Tuesday evening, on the huge screened porch of the second-floor flat above Dayton's hardware store, the investigating newsmen held a mock court. The culprit called before this court was William K. Hutchinson, who had sent out the offensive story for INS. Where, demanded the investigators, had Hutchinson gotten his story? The reporter said that he had overheard Darrow congratulate Bryan on winning the first round by getting the judge to uphold the constitutionality of the Butler Act. Bryan, said Hutchinson, had admitted that this would be the decision. The mock court decided that Hutchinson had done no wrong in publishing the story, and he went to bed very happy that he had managed to palm off on his colleagues a fiction about the source of his information. But later that night Hutchinson was awakened by a friend. The INS office in New York was on the telephone, said the friend; they wanted to know in strict confidence the real source of Hutchinson's story. Under these circumstances he told the facts. But this time Hutchinson had been taken in by a colleague who had concocted the non-existent phone call.

II

Wednesday began routinely, with Bryan posing for a publicity photograph in front of the "Ask Us about Tampa, Florida" truck. But then the pattern broke. First the chairman of the Dayton Minister's Association asked Charles Potter, the New York Unitarian, to open court with prayer; some fundamentalists would have found it less painful to yield to Darrow's argument and omit the prayer altogether.

Then Stewart apologized for having told Arthur Garfield Hays to shut his mouth. Hays replied graciously: "there are two qualities I much admire in a man. One is that he is human and the other is that he is courteous. The outburst on yesterday proves

that the attorney-general was human, and the apology proves that
he has the courtesy of a southern gentleman." John Randolph
Neal suggested that Stewart should also apologize for having
called Darrow an "agnostic," but the attorney-general wouldn't
make the sodality so catholic as that.

The judge's moment had come. He called on Richard Beamish,
chairman of the investigating committee of reporters. Beamish,
a veteran with the Philadelphia *Inquirer,* had the manner and the
voice of a bishop. His ample stomach was emphasized by his short
black coat and white waistcoat. He wore pince-nez glasses on a
flowing black ribbon. Judge Raulston, engaged in eating a bag of
unhulled peanuts, was cracking the hulls with his teeth.

Beamish reported that the offending newsman had not gotten
his information from the court stenographer or in any other improper way. The committee recommended that the incident be
forgotten.

The judge was not to be put off so lightly. He would show
them that he was no backwoods fool. How, he demanded to
know, had the reporter found out in advance about the decision?

Then the devastating words: "we find that the information
came from the court."

The judge blew out his surprise in a single word: "Well!" The
only person more astonished was Hutchinson, who thought that
he had successfully compounded his hoax, and now realized that
he had been victimized himself.

Beamish recited the facts: how Hutchinson on Tuesday had
inveigled the judge into saying that he would rule in the afternoon
on the motion to quash and that court would then adjourn until
Wednesday. Hutchinson had simply deduced, said Beamish, that
if the motion to quash were granted, the trial would end immediately and there would be no occasion for an adjournment. So the
judge must intend to uphold the constitutionality of the Butler
Act.

Raulston was ruffled. He summoned Hutchinson before the
bench and lectured him to the effect that reporters should not trick

judges. He dared do nothing more. Everybody but Raulston knew that he had stultified himself by his conceit; he had learned nothing, and would do it again before the day ended. "The heart is deceitful above all things, and desperately wicked: who can know it?" (Jeremiah xvii:9).

Darrow buffaloed to his feet and said that he didn't care a bit what Stewart had called him—"of course," he said indulgently, "the weather is warm." To him, Stewart's label was not an insult but a compliment. "I do not pretend to know where many ignorant men are sure; that is all agnosticism means." But he did hope that if Stewart felt it necessary to refer again to the subject, he would do it in such a way as not to prejudice the jury.

An abashed Stewart said that he was ready, if the opposition would join him, to try the rest of the case as lawyers. So the pledge was taken, only to prove as frail as many obtained by the Women's Christian Temperance Union.

The judge announced that he would now read his opinion on the motion to quash, and he would expect absolute quiet during the event. He turned to the photographers: "If you gentlemen want my picture, make it now." The resulting laughter in the courtroom did not deter the most eminent son of Gizzards Cove from posing for nearly five minutes. The photographers were to one side of him, tier on tier like a small mountain, first a row kneeling, then standing, then standing on chairs, then standing on tables. John T. Raulston faced them resolutely, leaning back in his chair and holding the opinion in his left hand. He knew the classic pose.

The judge read in an unattractive singsong voice, failing to pause when a sentence ended, running right along from one sentence to the next so that the 6,000 words took him only an hour. The content of the decision was little more than a paraphrase of Attorney-General Stewart's argument on Monday. On every point, the defense motion was denied. If any teacher's conscience required him to teach evolution, read the judge, he could teach it in the private schools or elsewhere. There was no law requiring anybody to teach in the public schools, and the Butler Act did not enjoin any religious beliefs on anybody. In meeting the charge that the law and the indictment were too vague and uncertain, Raulston ruled that the indictment was valid because it described the offense in the words of the law—and then he ignored the objection that the law itself was invalid.

The judge paused several times to wipe his face. Finally the sheriff took a revolving electric fan from the defense table and aimed it at Raulston's dripping brow. William Jennings Bryan listened intently, swaying back and forth in his chair, occasionally waving his palm leaf fan. Darrow got up and wandered around the room. Other defense lawyers were drinking soda pop from bottles. The judge conceded that the relevant parts of the decision in *Meyer* v. *Nebraska* were dicta and therefore questionable at best; nonetheless, that decision plus *Pierce* v. *Society of Sisters* and the *Leeper* case were sufficient answer to the allegation that the Butler Act violated the federal Fourteenth Amendment.

When the judge finished, John Neal said that he assumed the same rulings applied to the demurrer, which contained exactly the same points as the motion to quash the indictment.

Judge Raulston acknowledged that he had gotten the demurrer on the preceding day. But he had misplaced it. Rummaging through the papers on the bench, he said, "I've got so many papers and telegrams and other things here, I'm afraid it's got all mixed up."

Although the time was only 11:13, the judge said that court would adjourn until 1 P.M. Malone, thinking of all the fees he was losing by each day's absence from New York, protested. Hays joined him to ask whether court could not run past the usual time for adjournment. The judge would not be hurried. Court adjourned until 1 P.M.

III

The Scopes trial was to last eight days, but less than half a day was allocated to witnesses. After lunch on that Wednesday, July

15, the court heard the only testimony that became part of the record of the case.

Members of the cast also developed their roles. Arthur Garfield Hays, as befitted a man named after three Presidents, was charged with keeping the formal record in shape for review by higher courts. When the judge refused to dismiss the indictment, Hays entered an exception to the ruling. The defense demurred; Raulston overruled it; exception. And thus it went throughout the trial. Hays was the man who repeatedly jumped up to question, in proper style, the judge's rulings.

Ben McKenzie was official jester, a role that went well with his rotund body, quivering jowls, and buffoonery. When a newsman asked if the court could not provide chairs for the reporters, McKenzie asked if Raulston would not also tell the spectators to stop carrying away the chairs for the lawyers. "We are a necessary evil in the courtroom, supposed to be a part of it." Later in the day, when Dudley Field Malone questioned the Creation story, McKenzie would comment: "The only mistake the good Lord made is that he did not withhold completion of the job until he could have got a conference with you."

But not all the jokes came from McKenzie. The afternoon began ludicrously; when the prosecution read the names of its witnesses and asked them to assemble at the sheriff's office, there was no response. Stewart, remembering how witnesses had fled to the woods rather than appear before the grand jury, said whimsically: "Colonel Darrow, we may have to get you to agree to what we can prove if we cannot find the witnesses." Darrow got a good laugh by saying: "We might round them up later in the day."

After a plea of Not Guilty was made for Scopes, the attorney-general stated in a hundred words that the defendant had violated the Butler Act by teaching that man had descended from a lower order of animals.

Just here was another main issue in the case. It was not enough, said Malone in presenting the defense theory, for the state to show that Scopes had taught the theory of evolution; the state must show in addition that Scopes had "also, and at the same time, denied the theory of creation as set forth in the Bible." In brief, what did the Butler Act forbid: Teaching that man had descended from a lower order of animals? Teaching a story of human origins that conflicted with Genesis? Or both? The state held to the first construction of the law; the defense, to the third. They wrangled about it throughout the trial—and beyond.

Malone, in his opening statement for the defense, conceded that the theory of evolution contradicted the tales of Creation set forth in Genesis. But, he added, these tales contradict each other, and millions of people believed in both evolution and Genesis. Although admitting that Darwinism might conflict with "the peculiar ideas of Christianity which are held by Mr. Bryan as the evangelical leader of the prosecution," Malone denied that Christianity and Darwinism needed to conflict. He sought support from a thesis urged by the political and religious liberals: "We maintain that science and religion embrace two separate and distinct fields of thought and learning. We remember that Jesus said: 'Render unto Caesar the things that are Caesar's, and unto God the things that are God's.'"

Malone quoted at length from an introduction that Bryan had written to Jefferson's "Statute of Religious Freedom," in which Bryan had endorsed Jefferson's argument that truth could vanquish error in an equal combat. Stewart objected to these references to Bryan. Malone replied that he did not think Bryan minded.

The moment had come. For the first time in the trial William Jennings Bryan rose to speak. How would he answer Malone? He said,

"Not a bit."

And added that he needed no protection from the court: "when the proper time comes, I shall be able to show the gentlemen that I stand today just where I did . . ." The audience clapped wildly. But there was great disappointment that Bryan was content with one brief paragraph; the crowd wanted a speech that would scorch the heathens. Bryan, however, was saving himself. (For months he had been working up a speech. He would give it, at exactly the right moment, and once again he would sweep up the liberty-loving God-fearing people in a joyous tumultuous army, as he had done in Chicago on that day in 1896, and lead them to Armageddon.)

At last, at long last, the jury was sworn, and Walter White, county superintendent of schools and signer of the complaint against Scopes, was called as the first witness. By White's testimony, Scopes had said on May 5 that he had reviewed in class the entire book, Hunter's *Civic Biology,* and also that he could not teach the book without teaching evolution. After White had told the early history of the case, the attorney-general rose. He offered in evidence a King James Bible.

Hays objected. The statute referred merely to "the Bible." Which Bible? The King James version, published at London in 1611? The Catholic version, with an Old Testament published by the English college at Douai, France, in 1609, and a New Testament published by the English college at Rheims in 1582? All of these, Hays explained, were translations of Greek and Latin texts that themselves were supposedly translations from the original texts in Hebrew, Aramaic, and Greek. The oldest known manuscript in Greek of the Bible dated from the fourth and fifth centuries; the earliest known copy of the Old Testament in Hebrew dated from the 11th century. The Douai version contained six whole books, and parts of other books, not in the King James version. What, Hays asked again, was the Bible?

At the press table, John Washington Butler's head was whirling. More than one kind of Bible! He could scarcely believe it.

John T. Raulston could cope with surprises. He was satisfied to receive in evidence the Bible Stewart offered. Hays again objected. There were, he said, a Hebrew Bible of 39 books, a Protestant one of 66 books, a Catholic one of 80 books, a King James version differing from its own revision in some 30,000 respects.

But not all his statistics could shake the judge, who knew a Bible when he saw one.

Walter White took the stand again, to testify about the offensive passages in Hunter's book. On the cross-examination, Darrow drew from him several facts favorable to Scopes. *Civic Biology* had been in use in Tennessee schools since 1909. It had been officially adopted by the state textbook commission in 1919; when the five-year contract expired on August 31, 1924, the commission had not adopted any substitute text. Official textbooks were bought by students from certain depositories in the state; in Dayton, from the drugstore of F. E. Robinson. White admitted that, prior to May 4, he had not warned Scopes or any other teacher against teaching from Hunter's book. Nor had anybody protested about it until Rappelyea signed the complaint against Scopes.

Next came Howard Morgan, a 14-year-old student of Scopes at Central High School. Wide-eyed with excitement, he wore a white shirt open at the collar, and his tie was pulled down and off-center. He said that Scopes, teaching from Lewis Elhuff's *General Science,* had said that man was a mammal like cats and dogs, cows, horses, monkeys, lions. Stewart asked: "Did he explain what a mammal was?" The question shocked many, who thought the attorney-general indelicate to touch such objects in a courtroom crowded with ladies. One woman stuffed her fingers in her ears. Some children were hurriedly prodded from their seats and ejected from the room by parents; the children rushed downstairs to the lawn, where loudspeakers were blaring all of the salacious details.

Darrow began the cross-examination in a pureed voice:

Q—"He didn't say a cat was the same as a man?"

A—"No, sir; he said man had a reasoning power; that these animals did not."

Q—"There is some doubt about that, but that is what he said, is it?"

Morgan could not recall the definition of a mammal. Darrow asked: "Well, did he tell you anything else that was wicked?" The witness shot a quick glance at Scopes and grinned. Several specta-

tors from the surrounding hills now chuckled, while the townspeople, who knew Scopes as an upright church-going young man,
laughed heartily. The judge and the attorney-general smiled.
Bryan's rigidity cracked slightly. Repeatedly Darrow got the audience to laugh; he was a sure hand at leading spectators to the emotional hilltop he wanted them to watch from.

Harry Shelton, 17 years old, testified that Scopes had reviewed
in class all of Hunter's book up to and including the offensive passage on pages 194-195. Darrow wanted to know whether Shelton
had belonged to a church both before and after studying with
Scopes. Yes, he had. "You didn't leave church," Darrow asked,
"when he told you all forms of life began with a single cell?"
No, not at all. Darrow asked: "Did Mr. Scopes teach you that
man came from the monkey?" Spectators hunched forward. A
hush spread over the room.

A shriek from outside the building ripped through the silence. The piercing sound startled the uninformed; it may have
seemed an assertion of ancestry to those who recognized its
source: it originated with a monkey from the Hippodrome in
New York, being exercised by its master on the courthouse lawn.
In the turmoil, young Shelton's reply to Darrow was lost. Not
that it mattered much.

F. E. Robinson, the next witness, told how Scopes and Rappelyea had discussed the Butler Act in his drugstore. Scopes, he
said, had admitted teaching the evolutionary tree on page 194 of
Hunter's book. The defendant also had said, according to Robinson, that nobody could teach biology from any of the existing
books without violating the law.

The situation was made to order for Darrow. He began prob-
ing into Robinson's relation to Hunter's *Civic Biology*.

Q—"You were selling them, were you not?"

A—"Yes, sir."

Q—"And you were a member of the school board?"

A—"Yes, sir."

There was much laughter. Darrow trained a jocular eye on the constitutional ban on compulsory self-incrimination: "I think someone ought to advise you that you are not bound to answer these questions." Stewart caught the spirit, and got a bigger laugh, by saying: "The law says 'teach,' not 'sell.'" Robinson compounded the irony by admitting that he, the head of the school board, had a monopoly in Dayton on Hunter's book, and that he obtained copies of this criminal textbook from the official depository for the county at Chattanooga.

Darrow read to the jury the questionable passage on page 194, saying that there were 518,000 species of animals, including 3,500 species of mammals. From the next page, he read the reasons for classifying man with the vertebrates, then with the mammals, then with the apelike mammals.

Stewart was not to be outdone. In the swift cadence of a Southern exhorter, emphasizing points with urgent jabs of his hands, he read the first two chapters of Genesis. A smile benigned the face of William Jennings Bryan except when he stared at Darrow, slouched at the nearby table.

Stewart said that he had another witness, Morris Sout, to testify substantially the same as Morgan; and Charles Hagley, about the same as Shelton. Darrow indifferently agreed that this should be part of the trial record.

And that was the state's case. This was the whole of the evidence against the defendant. Arthur Hays bobbed up to move that the case be dismissed. Motion denied. Exception.

Now it was Darrow's turn to call the first defense witness. When the stout man with rimless glasses had no more than identified himself as Maynard M. Metcalf, the attorney-general interrupted. Stewart explained that, in Tennessee, a defendant had to be the first witness in his own behalf or he could not testify at all. Darrow said lightly that the mistake had already been made. The judge offered to let Darrow withdraw Metcalf and call Scopes. No, said Darrow, everything said against Scopes was true, so there would be no point in his taking the stand.

Dr. Metcalf seemed bent on being the stereotype of an absent-minded professor. When asked his age, he said: "58—no, 57, I think that is right." He had begun studying zoology when he was a 14-year-old student at Oberlin College, and had taught there until he retired in 1914 to work full-time at his own research. In July, 1925, he had just finished a year as chief of the Division of Biology and Agriculture of the National Research Commission, which had been set up by executive order of President Wilson right after the war to study scientific problems of importance to the country in peacetime. He had been president of the American Society of Naturalists and of the zoological section of the American Association for the Advancement of Science. He was also a member of the Congregationalist Church. Was he, Darrow asked, an evolutionist?

Metcalf said, "Surely under certain circumstances, that question would be an insult; under these circumstances I do not regard it as such."

Then came a crucial question in the defense effort to show that the Butler Act was so unreasonable and arbitrary that it could not be regarded as a valid exercise of the police power. Darrow asked: "Do you know any scientific man that is not an evolutionist?"

Stewart objected. The judge ruled out the question and all variants of it. Hearsay. Finally Raulston agreed that the witness could privately tell the court reporter what his answer would be if the question were permitted. Metcalf said he knew practically all of the important zoologists, botanists, and geologists of the United States. He was sure that every one of these men regarded evolution as a fact, "but I doubt very much if any two of them agree as to the exact method by which evolution has been brought about . . ." The judge cautioned the court reporters not to give this part of the testimony to the newspapers.

The attorney-general was still unsatisfied. He said the state would object to any expert testimony as to the meaning of evolution; such testimony, he said, would invade the "province of the court and jury." Darrow was waspish as he commented on the requirement that a jury "only one of whom had ever read about evolution, is forced to say what evolution is." He said nothing now about the judge—that would come later.

Judge Raulston was reminded by this exchange that the jury was present. He excused them, with a warning not to linger in the courthouse yard near those loudspeakers.

Metcalf was a cautious man. He turned some questions aside, answered others tentatively. Inorganic evolution, he said, was a matter for the astronomers and geologists. Nor would he testify as to the number of years since the Cambrian age, but he did say that such matters as the relation of uranium to lead were beginning to yield data on the age of the earth. In a cursory way, he told how the first organic matter must have been unicellular plants in the sea—where the water contained all of the minerals they needed for food and where they were also exposed to sunlight, their source of energy—and how it was an advantage to these plants to remain unicellular.

When Metcalf spoke of life existing 600,000,000 years earlier, spectators laughed incredulously. People whispered in disbelief. The judge gasped and took a long drink of water. A voice said: "He is about as authoritative as an evening breeze." It was nearly 5 o'clock; departures thinned the crowd rapidly and left patches of blank seats, as Darrow asked Metcalf about mammals. Metcalf refused to define the word but began listing characteristics: have hair, suckle their young, are vertebrates, have shoulder and hip girdles, and so on. He concluded: "I might, if I stopped to think up my lesson, tell you fifty points that are characteristic of the order of mammals in distinction from other organisms."

How would Metcalf classify man? As a primate, along with the lemurs, apes, baboons, monkeys. Asked for the chief evidence that man had evolved from lower forms of life, Metcalf cited the entire panorama of evolution extending through all the universe. The presumption against Homo sapiens having been an exception to this method of origin was "tremendously reinforced" by a single fact: with human kind, as with lower animals, the less developed varieties were found in the earlier geological strata.

After court adjourned, an enterprising reporter went to interview the mothers of the two youthful witnesses against Scopes. Mrs. Luke Morgan, whose husband worked at the Dayton Bank and Trust Company, said that she wanted her son to learn more about everything, including evolution. He was as keen a student of the Bible as of biology. She was sure his morals hadn't been damaged by reading Hunter's *Civic Biology*. Mrs. William R. Shelton said she would not mind if they taught evolution to her son "every day in the year. I can see no harm in it whatever." When young Harry Shelton was asked to testify against Scopes, he had to get his book out and bone up; he had forgotten the lesson.

But columnists like H. L. Mencken and most reporters were not interested in signs of enlightenment in Tennessee. Much better copy could be written about the Holy Rollers, who were regarded in Dayton, scarcely less than in New York, as a lunatic fringe. Groups of reporters went from Dayton into the neighboring hills to watch the nocturnal revivals of old-time religion. It was worth the trip. Even intellectual journals like the *Nation* printed sensual accounts:

> Rough wooden benches semi-circled the elms. And crude teapots with fat white wicks crammed into their snouts blew opal flame into the silver of the moonlight night. Night things all about. The screech of the bobcat. The wail of the whippoorwill. A whir of bats' wings, and the staccato of insects. . . .
>
> Testifying began. An old woman of seventy, her gray hair straggling over her lean, semi-bronzed face. Hands at her hips, she twisted her sharp-boned old body into gyrations, touched the ground, shrieked and moaned. Ma Ferguson "speaks with tongues" and testifies with strange and stirring words.
>
> "We cain't repine on no flowery beds of ease," said Ma Ferguson. "We gotta save the daughters and gotta save their bodies—gotta stop fornycation."

This effort was not wholly successful, according to Mencken, who reported of one revival meeting: "Now and then a couple at the ringside would step out and vanish into the black night. After a while some came back, the males looking somewhat sheepish."

In his dispatches to the Baltimore *Sun,* Mencken daily referred to the people of Rhea County as "morons" and "hillbillies" and "peasants." He wrote about "degraded nonsense which country preachers are ramming and hammering into yokel skulls." These insults were not swallowed easily. Chief Commissioner Haggard reported that late one night he had come upon a score of mountain men who had determined to ride Mencken out of town on a rail. Haggard persuaded them to disperse.

But if Dayton had been tense and militant when the trial opened, its general tone had relaxed considerably during the next five days. A reporter who assumed that the crowds on the courthouse lawn talked only of religion heard instead:

"Well, who ever married your sisters?"

"Well, Sid Smith, he married one; and Bob Holt, he married one; and John Green, he married one; and Judd Spivey, he married one; and Ed Rawls, he married one; and Gus . . ."

Chapter 7
The Sin

They had better go back to their
homes, the seats of thugs, thieves,
and Haymarket rioters and educate their criminals than to try to
proselyte here in the South . . .

General Ben G. McKenzie, speech
at Chattanooga, Tennessee, July 22,
1925

I

Attorney-General Stewart saw no need to pussyfoot; he had
just received a telegram from Governor Peay saying, "It is a poor
cause that runs from prayer. You are handling the case like a veteran and I am proud of you." When Darrow tried to open the
morning session of court on Thursday by asking a few more
questions of Metcalf, Stewart objected. Darrow tried to point out
that the Butler Act did not define "evolution" or "theory of divine
creation as taught in the Bible." He contended that the defense
had every right to show that the Bible, if construed literally, contradicted itself, but that an intelligent interpretation of the Bible
was compatible with the theory of evolution. The argument was
joined in earnest, and Metcalf was thrust aside.

Did the defense have the right to prove, by scientific witnesses, that the Butler Act was so unreasonable that it was not a
valid exercise of the police power? Or should the state be upheld
in its motion to exclude all expert testimony bearing on the meaning of evolution, its truth or falsity, and the permissible interpre-

tations of the Bible? The resolution of this procedural point would determine the future course of events in the courtroom.

And here occurred another in that chain of adverse rulings by Raulston which would ultimately provoke Clarence Darrow into a nasty outburst. The present issue, like many of the others, was minor but far from negligible. It involved a right of which any trial lawyer is jealous, the right to make the opening and closing arguments on a motion. Stewart contended that, since the state had made the motion to exclude the scientific testimony, it should open and close the argument. Instantly Hays leaped up to complain, saying that the defense attorneys, who had originally planned to move the admission of the scientific evidence, would never have agreed to let the state move to exclude it if they had suspected that by the change they would lose the chance to open and close.

Raulston was annoyingly pompous. He said that he was so impartial, so single-minded in his quest for "truth and light," that it made no difference which side spoke first and last. Therefore the state could do so.

Bryan, Jr., rose to speak. In manner and in matter he distinguished himself from his father. He spoke so softly that John Neal asked him to talk up. And he argued law, with numerous references to precedent. The expert testimony, he said, would be mere opinion rather than fact. All that any expert could say in this case was that the theory of evolution, as he understood it, did not conflict with the Bible as he understood it. A long line of precedents agreed on the dangers of this sort of opinion testimony, including the impossibility of preventing the expert from perjuring himself. Hadn't Darrow in the Loeb-Leopold trial accused one of the state's experts of lying? Finally, the one issue in this trial was whether the material that Scopes had taught was a violation of the law, and that was the issue on which the defense wanted to offer expert testimony. But the one place where expert testimony was never admissible was when it dealt with the issue which the jury had to determine.

Not so, said Arthur Hays in the first argument for the defense. "Is there anything in Anglo-Saxon law that insists that the determination of either court or jury must be made in ignorance? Somebody once said that God has bountifully provided expert witnesses on both sides of every case. But, in this case, I believe all our expert witnesses, all the scientists in the country, are only on one side of the question; and they are not here, your Honor, to give opinions; they are here to state facts." It was impossible to escape from the need to construe the Butler Act. The word "evolution" could mean either the fact of progressive development, on which scientists agreed, or the principle of natural selection, on which they did not agree. Or take the statute's words, "teach instead that man descended from a lower order of animals." If the word "order" were given its scientific meaning, man and monkeys belonged to the same "order"—neither belonged to a lower "order" than the other.

Sue Hicks, who followed, tried to stay on well-worn paths, but he strayed from them often. He not only said that the theory of evolution was unproven; he added that Maynard Metcalf could not be called an expert on evolution at all: "he has qualified in only one line, and that is in the line of biology." When he finished, Darrow impatiently asked if the motion could not be ruled on quickly by the court, out of consideration for the witnesses who had come from great distances and had been kept sitting idly for a week. Raulston replied: "I think it highly improbable the court will not pass on this question today—I don't know."

Darrow said, "I think you ought to pass on it immediately, even if you pass on it wrong. It is a very great hardship for these men to wait here. Some of them have to go."

The judge turned to Ben McKenzie and said, "I will hear you, General."

McKenzie's argument was half buffoonery, and all spread-eagle oratory. The judge had ruled the law constitutional, McKenzie said: "We have done crossed the Rubicon." The sole remaining issue was whether Scopes had violated the act.

Raulston broke in. Was this, he asked, the state's position: If Scopes had taught that man had descended from a lower order of animals, he had inevitably, by implication, denied the Creation story of the Bible? Yes, said McKenzie, that is our position. Warming to his subject, he accused the defense of trying to substitute another theory for the Bible's statement that God had created man in His own image: "they want to put words into God's mouth, and have Him say that He issued some sort of protoplasm, or soft dish rag, and put it in the ocean and said, 'Old boy, if you wait around about 6,000 years, I will make something out of you.' "

II

After lunch, William Jennings Bryan made his first speech of the trial. He said that he had not felt competent to speak in the early stages, when the disputes concerned Tennessee law and Tennessee procedure. But there were other matters at stake; in the next hour, he ran the full roster.

Referring to a recent New York law that had repealed the state enforcement of prohibition, Bryan asked what the newspapers would have said if Tennessee had sent experts to New York to testify that prohibition was really a good thing. But New Yorkers had not hesitated to impose their views on Tennessee. And what doctrine were these invaders teaching? What was the issue? It was simple: "the Christian believes that man came from above; but the evolutionist believes he must have come from below." (Bryan mistakenly thought the loud laughter was all with him.) He took up the evolutionary tree on page 194 of Hunter's book, which showed the number of species in each class of animals: 518,000 species in all—8,000 of protozoa, Bryan pointed out, 360,000 of insects, 13,000 of fishes, 3,500 of reptiles, 13,000 of birds. "And then we have mammals, 3,500, and there is a little circle and man is in the circle." Bryan challenged his audience: "Find him. Find him."

He was enraged. "Talk about putting Daniel in the lion's den.

How dared those scientists put man in a little ring like that with lions and tigers and everything that is bad!"

At this point his judgment faltered. He had begun his speech with jaw set and figure erect, his massive body and magnificent stance suited to the great orator, a man confident that he stood with the forces of righteousness. But now, speaking of helpless men locked in that circle with 3,499 other species of mammals, he feigned terror at the sight. Perhaps he sensed that his act was failing, for he switched to a tone of indignation as he described the effects on school children of the theory of evolution: "Why, my friends, if they believe it, they go back to scoff at the religion of their parents! And the parents have a right to say that no teacher paid by their money shall rob their children of faith in God and send them back to their homes, skeptical, infidels or agnostics or atheists."

(Wherever the verbal garment is thin, wherever the skeleton shows, there the old theme, the autochthonous itch: Parents live forever in their descendants; whoever steals your children steals one of your claims to eternal life.)

A reporter commented that, by Darrow's definition of "mammal," Bryan was right in denying that he was one: clearly Bryan did not have hair or suckle his young.

Bryan upbraided the defense for getting weaselly about Darwin. The distinction just made by Arthur Hays between evolution and Darwin's theory of natural selection had never been mentioned until "the absurdities of Darwin had made his explanations the laughing stock." But the disavowal of Darwin was just trickery; all of the evolutionists still accepted his idea that life had begun with a single cell and developed into man. But they had no valid evidence: "today there is not a scientist in the world who can trace one single species to any other, and yet they call us ignoramuses and bigots because we do not throw away our Bible . . ." Shaking his fist and smiling satirically, he argued that the scientists did not try to explain the origins of life, did not try to deal with the problems of life: "and yet they would undermine the faith of these little children in that God who stands back of everything and whose promise we have that we shall live with Him forever bye and bye."

The doctrine of evolution not only destroyed belief in a Savior and in heaven; it also destroyed all moral standards. This vile doctrine had produced men like Nietzsche. Why, Darrow himself had said that the professors who taught Nietzsche's creed to Nathan Leopold were as responsible as Leopold for the death of Bobby Frank.

Darrow objected that he had said no such thing. Besides (he spidered out the web): "was there a word of criticism of the theological colleges when that clergyman in southern Illinois killed his wife in order to marry someone else."

Bryan persisted in reading a paragraph from Darrow's argument in the Loeb-Leopold case, in which Darrow had said that Nathan Leopold could not be blamed if he had "fashioned his life" on a philosophy taught him at the University of Chicago.

Darrow grabbed the chance to disrupt the tone of Bryan's speech. When Bryan finished reading, Darrow asked for the copy of his Loeb-Leopold argument. Bryan replied that he wanted it back. Darrow said that he would get an autographed copy for Bryan. The audience laughed. Darrow objected to Raulston about the injection of the Loeb-Leopold trial into this case. The judge said it would not prejudice him. Darrow said sardonically: "Then it does not do any good." The audience laughed and applauded.

Bryan worked to win the audience back to a serious mood. Recalling that eleven jurors were church members, he said that "more of the jurors are experts on what the Bible is than any Bible expert who does not subscribe to the true spiritual influences or spiritual discernments of what our Bible says."

"Amen," shouted a voice in the audience.

Bryan became passionate: "The Bible, the record of the Son of God, the Savior of the world, born of the Virgin Mary, crucified and risen again—that Bible is not going to be driven out of this court by experts who come hundreds of miles to testify that they can reconcile evolution, with its ancestor in the jungle, with man made by God in His image, and put here for His purposes as part of a divine plan."

As he surged into his final hymn to "the Word of God as revealed," the audience clapped and cheered. Several voices shouted "Amen." Now at last Bryan's role was clear. He had not come to Dayton merely to wear a pith helmet and chew a palm-leaf fan. He had come as high priest to pronounce the proper words with the proper dignity, to intone the cabalistic incantations, to denounce the minions of darkness, to serve as midwife at the rebirth of the faithful.

But the applause was disappointing. Polite approval and little more. Even with this partisan audience, Bryan's speech did not arouse thunderous affirmation. It had lacked the impassioned certainty of the revivalist. His manner had been querulous. He had called the head of the school board "Mr. Robertson" (Imagine anybody not knowing that it's *Robinson's* drugstore), and he had blundered into false starts like "We have little— What is the Morgan boy's first name?" He had let the bickering with Darrow kill the momentum of his oration. And that embarrassing time when he tried to act scared (Imagine a grown man—a man who had run for President at that—being scared at a picture in a book).

But after a brief recess, he really met a barrage. Darrow and Malone ruthlessly drove through the openings that Bryan had created for them. First Darrow insisted on his right to read the paragraph in his Loeb-Leopold argument following the one Bryan had read. It was in his best I-respect-you-too-much-to-lie-to-you manner, and his diaphanous voice revealed the truth of human existence, a truth that rebuked Bryan's weak-minded optimism.

As Darrow began to read, there was an enormous crash near the judge's bench.

An officer of the court announced: "Just a picture machine fallen over."

Darrow went on reading:

Even for the sake of saving the lives of my clients, I do not want to be dishonest, and tell the court something I do not honestly think in this case. I do not believe that the universities are to blame. I do not think that they should be held responsible. I do think, however, that they are too large, and that they should keep a closer watch, if possible, upon the individual. But you cannot destroy thought because, forsooth, some brain may be deranged by thought. It is the duty of the university, as I conceive it, to be the great storehouse of the wisdom of the ages, and to let students go there, and learn, and choose. I have no doubt but that it has meant the death of many; that we cannot help. Every changed idea in the world has had its consequences. Every new religious doctrine has created its victims. Every new philosophy has caused suffering and death. Every new machine has carved up men while it served the world. No railroad can be built without the destruction of human life. No great building can be erected but that unfortunate workmen fall to the earth and die. No great movement that does not bear its toll of life and death; no great ideal but does good and harm, and we cannot stop because it may do harm.

Dudley Field Malone pressed the pursuit of Bryan. He got up to begin his argument, this belligerent immaculate divorce lawyer, and he looked at Bryan, and he said: "We have been told that this was not a religious question. I defy anybody, after Mr. Bryan's speech, to believe that this was not a religious question." But Bryan and General McKenzie were not the only defenders of the Bible. "There are other people in this country who have given their whole lives to God. Mr. Bryan, to my knowledge, . . . has given most of his life to politics."

The applause encouraged a pejorative tone. Malone accused the prosecution of saying: "Destroy science, but keep our Bible." The defense replied that no such choice was necessary. And why did Bryan talk so much about protecting children? What did adults have to be proud of—hadn't the recent war claimed 25 million dead? How could the rising generation do worse than that? The least that adults could do was "to give the next generation all the facts, all the available data, all the information that learning, that study, that observation had produced. . . . Make the distinction between science and theology. Let them have both."

Bryan was visibly fretful. He sipped occasionally from a three-gallon graniteware jug of water. The prickly heat on his nose was becoming worse by the minute.

Malone capped his plea for educational freedom by calling for fair play, and he seized on Bryan's flatulent rhetoric to imply that Bryan was no Christian. Bryan had called the trial a "duel to the death." Malone replied:

> I don't know anything about dueling, your honor. It is against the law of God. It is against the church. It is against the law of Tennessee. But does the opposition mean by "duel" that our defendant shall be strapped to a board and that they alone shall carry the sword? Is our only weapon—the witnesses who shall testify to the accuracy of our theory—Is our only weapon to be taken from us, so that the duel will be entirely one-sided?

The clapping was louder than it had been after Bryan's speech. A bailiff pounded on a table with a policeman's club. The Chattanooga chief of police asked him why he didn't applaud. The bailiff replied excitedly: "What do you think I was doing, rapping for order?"

Joseph Wood Krutch heard Mencken's exuberant voice: "Tennessee only needs fifteen minutes of free speech to become educated."

Scores of people crowded around Malone to congratulate him. Here came Mencken down the aisle. Malone eagerly awaited his praise. "Dudley," said Mencken, wiping his brow, "that was the loudest speech I ever heard."

The judge began to question Malone about the defense views of the Bible. Darrow got up to reply. The Bible said only that all animals had been created from "the dust of the earth"; it didn't say whether this had been done by evolution or in some other way. Genesis was entirely silent on the process by which God had created man. Darrow ended his heuristic flourish by saying that when God made man, it was not necessarily the same as a carpenter making a table.

Judge Raulston asked: "Does your theory of evolution speak at all on the question of immortality?"

Darrow said: "Evolution, as a theory, is concerned with the origins of man. Like chemistry and geology, evolution does not speak of immortality and hasn't anything to do with it." He archly added that many evolutionists believed in immortality.

By this time, probably not a score of spectators remembered that the question in dispute was the legal one of the admissibility of scientific testimony. To make matters worse, the day was Malone's. Attorney-General Stewart tried to repair this situation by his closing speech for the defense.

He began by talking about the principles of construing statutes in Tennessee, where a long line of decisions held that the ruling consideration was the intention of the legislature. Everybody knew that the legislature had meant to say in the Butler Act that the doctrine that man had descended from a lower order of animals was in contradiction of the Biblical account of Creation. Therefore no scientific testimony on whether they conflicted could be relevant.

Arthur Hays started another legal wrangle. Under Stewart's construction, would the Butler Act mean the same thing if the phrase "to teach any theory that denies the story of the Divine Creation of man as taught in the Bible" were omitted entirely? Yes, said Stewart, so far as evidence is concerned, the requirements for conviction would be exactly the same if that phrase were omitted.

But wasn't it a rule in Tennessee, said Hays, that every word in a statute was to be given weight in construing it? Stewart replied: "No, sir. The court has a right, under our rules of construction, to leave out the words that do not express the intention of the legislature."

A train whistled.

Hays said that the defense planned to move that the law be invalidated because it was not a reasonable exercise of the police power. Didn't Stewart agree that the defense had a right to introduce evidence to show that the law was unreasonable?

Stewart said: "No, sir; I absolutely do not."

He resumed his argument, which gained speed and lost control until at length he drew himself erect, and he flung his arms up to heaven, and his tall athletic body shook with emotion as he cried out against the insidious doctrines of the defense. If this trial were a conflict of science and religion, he shouted: "I want to serve notice now, in the name of the great God, that I am on the side of religion. . . . I stand with religion because I want to know beyond this world that there may be an eternal happiness for me and for all."

He almost wept just thinking about Darrow: "He is the greatest criminal lawyer in America today. His courtesy is noticeable—his ability is known—and it is a shame, in my mind, in the sight of the great God, that a mentality like his has strayed so far from the natural goal that it should follow—" He was overcome with anguish as he shouted: "Great God, the good that a man of his ability could have done if he had aligned himself with the forces of right instead of aligning himself with that which strikes its fangs at the very bosom of Christianity!"

This from a man who had begun his argument, an hour earlier, by calling for "a purely legal discussion." When he finished and court adjourned, Dudley Malone quipped: "He is a good talker."

It seemed that day as if Dayton's influential men were hardening in their fundamentalism. Plans were announced to found Bryan University, a fundamentalist college at Dayton, which had been proposed by Walter White. F. E. Robinson and a wholesale grocer had subscribed $1,000 each, and the principal of Grayville high school had offered 20 acres of land. The big gift, $10,000, had come from George F. Washburn of Massachusetts and Florida, a real-estate millionaire who was to become the sugar-daddy of fundamentalism.

And George W. Rappelyea, for the third time since the trial started, was arrested for speeding. He said that he was a victim of persecution, and that he was the most careful driver in Rhea County.

But with the populace it was different. Scopes had been liked right along. Now the initial hostility to the defense lawyers had been dissipated, and they were treated cordially everywhere. Dudley Malone's speech was a sturdy bridge between the infidel raiders and many a Southern heart. His homily to human freedom had been emotional enough, and empty enough, to stamp him as the right sort of orating lawyer. It was even forgotten that he and his wife, a leading suffragette, had registered for a double room at the Aqua Hotel as Doris Stevens and Dudley Field Malone.

III

The farmers and laborers of Tennessee had come to the Scopes trial because they were curious about evolution or because they wanted fervid pageantry. Instead of a scientific lecture or a revival meeting, they had gotten mainly confusing wrangles about dull questions of legal procedure. Caring little about the outcome of the trial, they had no reason to stay. The speeches on Thursday afternoon, the expectation that Judge Raulston would rule the next morning on the propriety of scientific evidence, were not enough to hold them. On Friday the former swirling commotion on the courthouse lawn dwindled to a few small groups of bystanders.

In court, prayer, and Judge Raulston began to read his opinion. He summarized fairly the conflicting interpretations of the Butler Act. Then he said: "It is not within the province of the court under these issues to decide and determine which is true, the story of divine creation as taught in the Bible, or the story of the creation of man as taught by evolution." The impartial surface did not cover his rejection of the defense argument that both stories could, in different senses, be true. He then repeated the gist of Stewart's statement on the principles of construing statutes.

The intent of the legislature, said the judge, was defined by the last clause of the law. Why then call experts? Anybody could understand the words: "descended from a lower order of animals." Raulston added that he thought the evolutionists "should at least do man the consideration to substitute the word 'ascend' for 'descend.'" He upheld the state's motion to exclude all scientific testimony.

Turmoil. The fundamentalists aglow; Scopes' friends downcast. The spectators pressed forward, jumped on chairs, alerted ears and eyes.

Hays at once took an exception to the ruling. He pointed out that the court would have to rule whether the law was reasonable or not. For the judge to do so without hearing evidence was for him to assume full knowledge on a subject that scientists had been studying for generations.

Now Stewart leaped up to exclaim that Hays' remark was "a reflection upon the Court."

The judge said: "Well, it don't hurt this Court."

Darrow rasped out: "There is no danger of it hurting us."

Stewart shot back: "No, you are already hurt as much as you can be hurt."

The retort was true enough. The defense was left with no defense at all. Judge Raulston had upheld the constitutionality of the law. Now he had refused to hear evidence about the meaning of evolution, the evidence of its reality, or interpretations of the Bible. Darrow, his mouth raw from repeated curbing, jumped under Stewart's rowel.

"Don't you worry about us. The state of Tennessee don't rule the world yet." He hulked his shoulders upward, he pointedly ignored the judge. "With the hope of enlightening the court as a whole, I want to say that the scientists probably will not correct the words 'descent of man' and I want to explain what 'descent' means, as starting with a low form of life and finally reaching man." He turned to Raulston and said in a tone that would have corroded metal: "We will submit your Honor's request to the Association of Scientists."

Hays hastily moved that the judge, in the absence of the jury, should hear evidence on whether the Butler Act was reasonable. Stewart objected that such a procedure would make "a farce" of the ruling the judge had just made.

Dudley Malone was annoyed. He insisted that Stewart should withdraw the word "farce." He added, prophetically: "We haven't really provided any low comedy here so far."

The low comedy came at once. Stewart said that the defense should simply submit affidavits stating what they would try to prove by the witnesses they were offering. In that way, the higher courts would be able to determine whether Judge Raulston had ruled correctly in excluding testimony by the scientists.

Bryan got up. The doughty warrior had abandoned his collarless shirt for a neat madras and a bow tie. He asked: If the defense presents its witnesses to say what they would testify to if they were allowed to testify, will we be allowed to cross-examine them?

The judge said: "You will, if they go on the stand."

It was more than Darrow could bear. He pointed out that the only purpose of the witnesses would be to state "what we want to prove." The state had absolutely no right to cross-examine them under these circumstances. If the judge, after hearing this preliminary offer of proof, decided to admit the testimony, the state could then cross-examine the witnesses on their testimony itself. But not now. If the summary statements by scientists of their intended testimony did not enlighten the court, "cross-examination by Mr. Bryan would not enlighten the court."

The spectators laughed.

Bryan began to speak, but Darrow chopped him off to say that he and his colleagues "well know what the judgment and verdict in this case will be." All they wanted was to present their case to another court. And the state had no right whatever to cross-examine when the defense was trying merely to state what they wanted an opportunity to prove.

Judge Raulston, rankling, asked if the purpose of the cross-examination was not to arrive at the truth.

No, Darrow replied, in this instance the only purpose of cross-examination would be to create prejudice. He asked: "Has there been any effort to ascertain the truth in this case? Why not bring the jury and let us prove it?"

Judge Raulston began: "Courts are a mockery—"

Darrow interrupted: "They are often that, Your Honor."

The judge went on: "—when they permit cross-examination for the purpose of creating prejudice." Up on his feet, his right hand holding the gavel, he said that Darrow should "always expect this court to rule correctly."

"No, sir, we do not." The crowd laughed. Darrow rose to tiptoe, glaring back at the judge, daring him. Darrow continued the baiting:

"We expect to protect our rights in some other court. Now," he urged his propaedeutic, "that is plain enough, isn't it?"

The judge refused the bait. Darrow asked if the defense lawyers could have the rest of the day to draft their statements of what they would hope to prove by scientific testimony.

Raulston began to speak.

Darrow interrupted to say—sneeringly—that the judge had taken a half day "to write an opinion."

Raulston started to deny it.

Darrow interrupted again. "I do not understand why every request of the state and every suggestion of the prosecution should meet with an endless waste of time, and a bare suggestion of anything that is perfectly competent on our part should be immediately overruled."

Raulston exclaimed: "I hope you do not mean to reflect on the Court."

Darrow hitched up his suspender and said, very slowly: "Well, Your Honor has the right to hope."

Raulston flushed. He said ominously: "I have a right to do something else, perhaps."

The spectators were no longer amused. They were nervous, expectant. Many reporters thought Darrow would be sent to jail instanter for contempt.

And still Darrow scorned: "All right, all right"—with a smile that was more insulting than the words. He folded his arms across his chest, rocked back and forth on his heels, and waited.

The crowd waited. Nothing happened.

Judge Raulston adjourned court until Monday so that the defense could prepare its affidavits about the burden of the scientific testimony.

The judge called out to ask Dudley Field Malone if he, Darrow, and Hays would step over to pose with Bryan and John T. Raulston.

Malone smiled nunnishly and said: "I think it would be more satisfactory all around if Your Honor were photographed with counsel for the prosecution alone."

Darrow, less fecund, told a reporter: "We are now interested in two things: That a higher court shall pass upon this case, and that in other states those who wish to pursue the truth will be left free to think and investigate and teach and learn."

Even John Washington Butler had his doubts about the judge's exclusion of scientific testimony. When it had been announced, he had differed from most fundamentalists by remaining in his seat, silent, impassive. After adjournment he explained: "I'd like to have heard the evidence. It would have been right smart of an education to hear those fellows who have studied the subject."

To another reporter he said that anybody who had played baseball, as he had, likes "to see things done fair." Why not let Darrow present his experts; then let Bryan cross-examine them and present his own experts? "That," said Butler, "would have been fair to *everybody*." But he still felt that, if he had to make the decision again, he would introduce the Butler Act in the legislature.

The concessionaires also were displeased by the judge's ruling. They complained that now the trial would not last long enough for them to recover their outlays in renting the sites and putting up the stands. It was widely believed that the trial was over. Mencken wrote that nothing remained to be done except "the formal business of bumping off the defendant," and that Genesis was "completely triumphant." Some of Dayton's businessmen had been so irritated by Mencken's columns that they had formed a committee to invite him to leave town; he missed the fun by going home to Baltimore on Saturday without knowing of the movement against him.

The one apparent prospect of excitement arose from Darrow's contumacy. Would the judge punish him on Monday? Why hadn't he done so immediately? The Chattanooga *News* explained that the pawky lawyer had thrust a dilemma upon the judge: If he sent Darrow to jail for contempt, the lawyer would be thought a martyr, the judge a Pilate; but if he did not, the people of Tennessee would think him a poltroon. Although the *News* had opposed passage of the Butler Act and still favored repeal, it saw Darrow's actions as an illustration of "the fell designs and sinister endeavors of the defense against our state."

Rumor also had the Chattanooga Bar Association planning action to disbar Darrow from practicing in the courts of Tennessee. And Chattanooga's Beth-El Temple decided that Rabbi Jerome Mark, who had been attending the Scopes trial, should not lecture on his impressions of it until the entire membership had granted sanction.

But the defense was not humiliated. Nine scientists in Dayton wrote to Michael Pupin of their respect for Darrow's "ability, high purposes, integrity, moral sensitiveness and idealism." Arthur Garfield Hays told the newspapers that "the case did rightfully belong to the Tennessee bar." But the lawyers of the state had not taken any initiative to defend Scopes, probably, said Hays, because they were waiting for somebody to offer them a fee; therefore the out-of-state lawyers had volunteered their services to defend the "vital principles" involved.

Darrow, Scopes, Malone, and several of the scientists spent the week-end in Chattanooga at the invitation of the president of the Chamber of Commerce. On Sunday afternoon Darrow lectured to 2,000 people at the Tivoli Theater about Tolstoi. It was a set-piece that he had been delivering for 20 years and he stayed pretty close to the subject, but Frank L. Carden, a prominent local attorney who introduced him, was not so irenic. He ripped into Governor Peay: "He is an honest governor; he has stolen none of our gold, he has only deprived us of a few of our liberties." And into Judge Raulston. Carden said that "any number of Tennessee lawyers" would have been willing to handle the defense in a test case of the Butler Act "if Judge Raulston had not made a deliberate attempt to secure the case. . . . so great was the haste of this judge that he indicted the professor with a grand jury whose term had already expired. They talk about lawyers who make unethical attempts at securing lawsuits; what may one think of a judge who engaged in this practice?"

Bryan, at Pikeville in the Sequatchie Valley, told an open-air meeting that the Scopes trial had uncovered "a gigantic conspiracy among the atheists and agnostics against the Christian religion."

From a quiescent Dayton, 20 miles away, the New York *Times* reported a lesser conspiracy: "it is not altogether improbable that the defense may call to the stand the chief of the prosecution, Mr. Bryan." The objective had been hinted on Friday in Darrow's comment that he was amazed that henceforth Bryan was to be "the one and only judge of what the Bible and Christianity mean."

Darrow's mapped route for the trial had reached dead end—

in a legal and educational dump. He had argued that the Butler Act violated freedom of speech and religion. The judge had overruled him. He had planned to show that the Act was too vague to be valid because the theory of evolution and the Bible both required interpretation. He had also planned to show that the Act was not a reasonable exercise of the police power because the evidence of evolution was overpowering. The judge had blocked both those roads. So Darrow sought to by-pass the road blocks by opening a new road. He bulldozed it, ruthlessly. Arthur Hays later implied that the events of Monday, July 20, were unpremeditated. Actually Darrow had written the script in his 55 questions about Genesis, addressed to Bryan and printed in the Chicago *Tribune* on July 4, 1923.

And on Sunday evening, July 19, 1925, in the dilapidated Mansion a mile from Dayton, Clarence Darrow held rehearsal. His accomplice, Kirtley Mather, was not only chairman of the geology department at Harvard, but also an ardent Baptist. Only two days earlier, as he passed through Chattanooga en route to Dayton, Mather had explained that he was mainly concerned with the effects of the Scopes trial on religion. "When men are offered their choice between science, with its confident and unanimous acceptance of the evolutionary principle on the one hand, and religion, with its necessary appeal to things unseen and unprovable on the other, they are much more likely to abandon religion than to abandon science. . . . Fortunately, such a choice is absolutely unnecessary."

That Sunday evening, Darrow and Hays took Mather into a separate room, and sat him down in a chair. They told him that he was Bryan, that he should answer each question as he thought Bryan would answer it. For two hours they had a hilarious time. Mather asked how they planned to get Bryan on the witness stand. They said smugly that they had ways.

Chapter 8
The Indulgence

> At last gleams of light have come, and I am almost convinced (quite contrary to the opinion I started with) that species are not (it is like confessing a murder) immutable.
>
> Charles Darwin to Sir Joseph Dalton Hooker, January 11, 1844, in *The Life and Letters of Charles Darwin,* ed. Francis Darwin (New York: D. Appleton and Company, 1887), Vol. I, p. 384

I

John T. Raulston stalked into the courtroom on Monday morning. His face remained grim and determined during the prayer. "Sometimes," the minister prayed, "we have been stupid enough to match our human minds with revelations of the infinite and eternal."

The judge declared that "contempt and insult" had been expressed in court on Friday. He then read the record of his colloquy with Darrow. The judge said that it was his policy to be courteous to visiting counsel. This courtesy must be reciprocated. Darrow's actions were an insult to the court and to the people of Tennessee, "one of the greatest states in the Union," a state that, by its kinetic patriotism in wars, had "justly won for itself the title of the Volunteer State." Such contumely could not be ignored. Darrow was cited to appear in court the next morning to show cause why he should not be punished for contempt. He was instructed to post bond of $5,000.

Darrow had listened quietly, showing no reaction at all. He said that he was not sure he could get a bondsman, but Frank Spurlock of Chattanooga volunteered, and the bond was arranged.

A court officer reminded the spectators that the proceedings were "not a circus."

Arthur Hays was then allowed to read Governor Peay's message approving the Butler Act. Those telltale phrases: "I can find nothing of consequence in the books now being taught in our schools with which this bill will interfere in the slightest degree. . . . Probably the law will never be applied." Stewart objected. Hays replied that, since the governor's signature was requisite to the law, his intention was certainly relevant to its interpretation. Judge Raulston said the message was "of no consequence at all in the court," and he excluded it from the record.

Hays read from the new textbook just adopted by the state commission, *Biology and Human Welfare* by Peabody and Hunt. This book called *The Origin of Species* "one of the epoch-making books of all time," and declared that the primates other than man had "evolved (developed) along special lines of their own, and none of them are to be thought of as the source or origin of the human species." These extracts were evidence, said Hays, that nobody could teach biology without teaching evolution. Raulston provisionally admitted the passages into the record, saying that he could always knock them out later.

Another quarrel over procedure. Hays had learned, by conferring over the week-end with prominent Tennessee lawyers, that an offer of proof could be made in any of three ways: by testimony of witnesses, by affidavit of counsel, or by oral statement of counsel to the court. He wanted to present the statements of the scientists orally, both as an offer of proof and in hope of persuading Judge Raulston that the Butler Act was unreasonable.

Stewart objected. He wanted the statements to be simply entered in the record for purposes of the appeal. For the defense to read them in court could have no purpose except "furthering its educational campaign, as they call it, or spreading propaganda, as I call it." He gibed: "The crowd is not going to try the lawsuit."

Malone replied: "We are not talking to the crowd. We are talking to His Honor."

When Stewart complained that the defense was trying to turn the courtroom into a chautauqua, Hays took the chance to again deride Bryan: "No one on this side of the table talks on the chautauqua."

Raulston was puzzled. He explained that he had not previously had "a big case like this." He would have to consult the precedents.

Bryan again asked if the state could cross-examine the scientific witnesses. Darrow was venomous: "I don't suppose there is any dispute between us lawyers on it, but you may differ, Mr. Bryan." He said the defense wanted to protect the record for the appeal by reading some of the statements orally; the others could be simply entered in the record.

The judge ruled that the defense could have an hour to read some of the statements. "I want to be fair to both sides and it occurs to me that that is fair." By the time of adjournment for lunch, Hays had read statements by five expert witnesses of the gist of their proposed testimony.

When court convened at 1:30, Attorney-General Stewart rose. He said that he had conferred during the noon hour with some of the defense lawyers, especially with Darrow, who wished to make a statement.

Darrow lumbered to his feet, his entire manner speaking the bluff but humble man. Arthur Hays had persuaded him to apologize, but he found his own way of doing it. On Friday, he said, word had chased word out of his mouth like a school of fishes. He had not realized what he had said until, after court adjourned, he read the transcript. Instantly he had resolved to apologize to the court on Monday morning. But over the week-end the newspapers had said that he was trying to make the judge punish him for contempt. Then, slyly: "I was at a loss what to do, but I knew Your Honor wanted to be heard first."

He explained how law-abiding and moderate he was. For 47 years he had been practicing law. In many of his cases he had been forced to do "what I have been doing here—fighting the public opinion of the people in the community where I was trying the case—even in my own town." But never once in those 47 years had any judge criticized him for his actions in court.

He became contrite. "I do think, however, Your Honor, that I went further than I should have gone." But his sin had not been willful: "So far as its having been premeditated or made for the purpose of insult to the court, I had not the slightest thought of that." He was not the only sinner: "One thing snapped out after another—as other lawyers have done in this case." He loved the people of Tennessee: even though he had never been in any community where his religious views differed so widely from the majority opinions, "I have not found upon anybody's part, any citizen here in this town or outside, the slightest discourtesy."

His conclusion explained, evaded, blandished, and, finally, apologized. "I haven't the slightest fault to find with the court. Personally, I don't think it constitutes a contempt, but I am quite certain that the remark [as if there had been only one] should not have been made and the court could not help taking notice of it and I am sorry that I made it ever since I got time to read it and I want to apologize to the court for it."

The spectators did more than applaud. They cheered. He cozened them, and they loved him for it. He not only slipped the hook; he caught the fisherman, for he cozened Judge Raulston too. Kirtley Mather knew, at that moment, that Clarence Darrow could have made a fortune on the stage.

The irony of it is strong enough to delight the tongue. The judge, Bryan, Stewart—they had all tried to make the trial into a religious ritual. Darrow had burlesqued their every deed. Now he had appropriated a sacerdotal rite and manipulated it for his pagan purposes. No rite is more widespread than the confessional: the Aztecs were practicing it before the first Spaniards arrived in Mexico. None is more ancient: the Jewish prophets had found in repentance the key to divine grace. How could it be that the Jews were Yahweh's chosen people; had they not been enslaved repeatedly? This paradox arises, said the prophets, because the Jews have offended against Yahweh's law. If they repent and return to the prescribed ways, Yahweh will forgive them and restore them to prosperity.

Darrow, by his confessional, forced Judge Raulston to become surrogate of the merciful Christ. "If we confess our sins, He is faithful and just to forgive us our sins, and to cleanse us from all unrighteousness" (I John i:9). The judge slipped easily into the role:

"My friends and Colonel Darrow, the Man that I believe came into the world to save man from sin, the Man that died on the cross that man might be redeemed, taught that it was godly to forgive, and were it not for the forgiving nature of Himself I would fear for man. The Savior died on the cross pleading with God for the men who crucified Him. I believe in that Christ. I believe in these principles. I accept Colonel Darrow's apology."

The judge's remarks were punctuated by clapping and cheers. "Verily, verily, I say unto thee, Except a man be born again, he cannot see the kingdom of God" (John iii:3).

Judge Raulston announced that cracks had developed in the ceiling of the room below the courtroom. He feared that the large crowds might collapse the floor. Therefore court would convene outdoors on the courthouse lawn. It did so, and Hays resumed reading the scientific statements.

II

Under the cloud-flecked sky, the crowd, despite the distractions of the outdoors, was fairly attentive. Ever since the Scopes case began on May 7, books on evolution had been in heavy demand at public libraries (even at school libraries) in Tennessee.

This was better than any book. Judge Raulston, it is true, had prevented a full-scale statement of evolution, and rejoinder by its opponents. But still, Hays was reading statements, prepared especially for the uninitiated—prepared, that is, for the court—about the meaning of evolution, examples of the evidence for it, its relation to religion.

And the statements were by reputable scientists. Besides Maynard Metcalf, the only one actually allowed to be a witness, summaries of their proposed testimony were submitted by seven scientists:

Wilbur A. Nelson, state geologist of Tennessee, president of the American Association of State Geologists, former president of the Tennessee Academy of Science.

Kirtley F. Mather, chairman of the geology department at Harvard University.

Jacob G. Lipman, director of the New Jersey Agricultural Experiment Station at New Brunswick since 1911, director of the College of Agriculture of the State University since 1915, editor-in-chief of *Soil Science*.

Fay-Cooper Cole, professor of anthropology at the University of Chicago.

Charles Hubbard Judd, director of the School of Education of the University of Chicago for 16 years, president in 1909 of the American Psychological Association.

Winterton C. Curtis, chairman of the zoology department of the University of Missouri, specialist in invertebrate zoology and parasitology.

Horatio Hackett Newman, dean of the College of Science of the University of Chicago, specialist in experimental embryology.

These men explained that soil, and plants, and animals, must necessarily have evolved in a certain order. The early forms of life included bacteria capable of developing in a purely mineral medium—capable of obtaining the energy for their life processes by oxidizing various gases. Some of them could manufacture nitrogen compounds out of the simple nitrogen in the air, thus supplying material from which the protoplasm in plants could be made. The plants died and became soil. After bacteria had converted rocks and gases into soil, simple plant forms could sustain themselves. These evolved into more complex plants. Plants had to develop in both quantity and quality before there was sufficient food for animal life.*

The surface configurations of the earth had changed immensely. At one time the mouth of the Mississippi River had been near Cairo, Illinois. The present-day deposits of China clay in western Tennessee had been laid down in shallow water when tropical plants flourished in that region. East of Dayton, the well-exposed Cambrian rocks dated from the age of the early invertebrates. Several techniques existed for estimating when geological events had occurred. For instance, you could count the light-colored and dark-colored bands of clay which had been deposited, as the glaciers retreated northward, by the melting of the ice sheet in the fresh-water lakes; each dark layer was laid down during one winter, each light layer during one summer.

The older the rocks, the simpler the fossil forms found in them. The oldest rocks yet discovered, formed at least 100 million years ago in the Archeozoic era, showed no trace whatever of any animal or plant life. Then fossils of a group of plants called algae appear. Proterozoic rocks hold a few simple fossils of shell-bearing animals. Rocks from the early Paleozoic Era, which began at least 50 million years ago, contain no fossils of animals with backbones, but the later Paleozoic has yielded very scanty and fragmentary remains of primitive fishes, as well as the oldest known forest. Toward the end of this period there were amphibians and reptiles, "the first animals with a backbone which could breathe air by means of lungs." **

---

* This sequence would now be considered misleading in important respects: for instance, soil was not involved in the origin of plants.

** Since 1925 scientists have devised much more rigorous techniques of geological dating, based on the new knowledge of the disintegration of radioactive materials. The result has been a great stretching of the past. The age of the earth is now

The Mesozoic era, which began at least 25 million years ago, was the age of reptiles, cold-blooded animals with scales, back-bones, and four limbs. Fossils have been found of the transitional form between reptiles and birds; these animals had enough feathers to fly, yet they had claws on their forelimbs and teeth in their jaws. From this period we have also a very few fragments of primitive mammals. The first flowering plants appeared in mid-Mesozoic times.

But not until the early Cenozoic, 5-10 million years ago (by 1957 reckoning, some 70 million years ago), did grasses, herbs, nut- and fruit-bearing trees become plentiful; only then did the earth's population of mammals grow rapidly and shoulder the reptiles aside. The scientists explained that fairly complete pedigrees had been worked out for some present-day species. The modern horse, for instance, could be traced through a number of intermediate forms from Eohippus, which lived in North America in the early Eocene epoch. This creature was 11 inches high at the shoulder and had four hoofed toes of nearly equal size in the front feet but only three toes in the hind feet.

The fossil record of man was less complete than that of horse or elephant, camel or rhinoceros, but it showed many of the main developments. Java man, of the same family (Hominidae) as modern man but of a different genus (Pithecanthropus), was intermediate in body structure between ape and man: intermediate in brain capacity, with receding forehead and a ridge of bone above the eyes, but with leg-bones showing that he had walked on his hind legs. In the first interglacial period lived Heidelberg man of the genus Paleanthropus; he had teeth like modern man, but in his lack of chin and in other features of the skull he resembled apes.

Neanderthal man, about 200,000 years ago, of the genus Homo like man, was a different species. His brain capacity was

---

estimated, with great confidence, at 4.5 billion years. The Paleozoic era is now thought to have begun, not 50 million years ago, but 500 million; the Mesozoic to have begun, not 25 million years ago, but 200 million.

nearly equal to that of the most primitive present-day tribes;* and his chin development was midway between Heidelberg man and modern man, but his forehead receded and the bony ridge above his eyes, while less than that of Java man, was nonetheless present. Finally, some 40,000 or 50,000 years ago in the last glacial age, a member of Homo sapiens appeared in southern Europe. This was Cro-Magnon man, with a large brain capacity, prominent chin, high forehead, and with eyebrow ridges similar to those of modern man.

The scientists also spoke of a fossil find announced only a few months earlier, in February, 1925. Dr. Raymond A. Dart, professor of anatomy at Wilwatersrand University in Johannesburg, South Africa, had found "the skull of an animal well developed beyond modern anthropoids in just those characteristics, facial and cerebral, which are to be expected in a form intermediate between man and the anthropoids." Was this perhaps the "missing link" that the opposition had repeatedly demanded that the scientists should produce?

The evidence of evolution did not consist merely in the fossil records; the theory could also be tested experimentally by many laboratory sciences. This was true because, as Newman put it, "the entire fabric of evolutionary evidence is woven about a single broad assumption": that structural resemblance arises from kinship. The point can be illustrated at the familial level by monozygotic twins, who show the closest possible resemblance and also the most intimate of all kinships, since they are products of the early division of a single zygote. For instance, the nine-banded armadillo, a mammal, almost always gives birth to four young at a time. These four young are 93 per cent identical with each other. A study of their embryonic history shows that they are derived from a single normally fertilized egg.

The principle of homology is crucial: homologous structures

---

* The implication that "primitive" modern men have small brains (in relation to body size) is not in general true, and the average Neanderthal had as large a brain as modern man.

have the same embryonic origin and the same relation to other structures, but they are superficially quite different in appearance and they play different functional roles. The human arm is homologous with the foreleg of a horse, the wing of a bird, the flipper of a whale. The whale's flipper is "apparently without digits, wrist, forearm, or upper arm, but on close examination it is seen to possess all of these structures in a condition homologous, almost bone for bone and muscle for muscle, with those of the human arm."

Vestigial structures spoke powerfully of evolution. How could those who believed in the special creation of each species explain the hind limbs of the whale? Some species of whale had a handful of ridiculous small bones, with no muscular connections and no function, entirely buried in the thick cushion of blubber in the pelvic region. Even those species of whale that lacked these vestiges as adults yet had, in the early embryonic period, limb buds that atrophied later.

Homo sapiens had at least 180 vestigial structures: the vermiform appendix, the abbreviated tail with its set of caudal muscles, muscles like those used by other species for moving their ears, scalp muscles like those used by some animals for erecting the hair, miniature third eyelids (the nictitating membranes) that were functional in all reptiles and birds but were greatly reduced or vestigial in all mammals, a complete set of embryonic down or hair (the lanugo) that disappears long before birth and serves no purpose while it lasts. The vestigial structures in man were evidence that he had descended from ancestors in whom these structures were functional.

If one group of animals had descended from another, we would expect to find present-day species that were intermediate forms. And we do. The lung fishes, for instance, have gills like fishes; they also have lungs homologous to those of land vertebrates.

The scientists described the taxonomy contained in the evolutionary tree, with phyla branching into subphyla, into classes, into orders, into families, into genera, into species, into varieties. Within many species there was an enormous amount of variation; a species is not a fixed and definite assemblage of characteristics as one would expect if it had been specially created on some master plan.

Man's relation to other animals was indisputable. Mather, who had worked in vertebrate morphology, concluded: "Comparing the body structure of monkeys, apes, and man, it is apparent that they are all constructed upon the same general plan; with only trivial exceptions every bone in the body of one has its counterpart in the body of the others." Newman amplified this comparison: "If a man is a creature apart from all animals it is extremely difficult to understand the significance of the fact that he is constructed along lines so closely similar to those of certain animals; that his processes of reproduction are exactly like those of other animals; that in his development he shows the closest parallelism step for step to the apes, that his modes of nutrition, respiration, excretion, involve the same chemical processes . . ."

On the basis of comparative anatomy and the fossil record, hypotheses had been formed about the relations of man to other species. Now serology provided an entirely independent means of testing these hypotheses. To determine what animals are most like man in blood composition, human blood is drawn and allowed to clot. The liquid serum is then injected at two-day intervals into a rabbit, which will develop an anti-human serum. When this serum is mixed with human blood, a definite white precipitate forms immediately. When the anti-human serum is mixed with anthropoid blood, the precipitate is obvious, but less abundant and slower to appear. The reaction with Old World monkeys is less prompt and less abundant, with New World monkeys still less so, with lemurs there is no reaction at all. These results are a dramatic confirmation of the degrees of kinship postulated on the basis of morphology and taxonomy. But different techniques of study do not always produce results that are perfectly parallel; perfect parallels cannot be expected since different characteristics of any species evolve at different rates.

Embryology, another extension of comparative anatomy, also has yielded important evidence on evolution. The principle that ontogeny recapitulates phylogeny is far from precise—many embryonic organs have developed to serve the needs of the embryo itself; but the theorem is still useful if applied intelligently. The human circulatory system is an example. It grows embryonically through a series of stages that resemble the adult condition of a series of ascending vertebrate classes. Take the human heart. At one stage a single tube differentiates lengthwise into two cavities, auricle and ventricle (adult fish). Then the auricle divides into two chambers (adult amphibian). Then the ventricle divides, resulting in the four-chamber heart characteristic of mammals. Or take the gill slits of the human embryo. These structures exist in the embryo because of inheritance from man's early aquatic ancestry, but their lack of function in the human adult caused their disappearance in favor of more useful structures. Comparing the human embryo to the anthropoid embryo, there are specific differences at every stage, but still "the embryology of man and that of any of the anthropoid apes show the closest of resemblances at every stage and diverge sharply only in the late stages of prenatal life."

Consider even the most marked characteristic of Homo sapiens: the extraordinary specialization of his nervous system. Even here, the fundamental psychological processes of man are similar in kind to those of lower animals. Much can be learned about human learning by studying the learning processes of animals, and it is "quite impossible" to study the mental development of children without taking account of facts derived from the study of animal psychology.

Such were the conclusions about evolution that the scientists were ready to offer in evidence. Such were the facts, drawn from a wide range of sciences, available to support those conclusions. But the scientists did not rest there.

Newman challenged the opposition: "Think what a sensation in the scientific world might be created if some one were to discover even one well-authenticated fact that could not be reconciled with the principle of evolution. If the enemies of evolution are ever to make any real headway in their campaign they should devote their energies toward the discovery of such a fact."

Curtis exposed the opposition, which had seized on a speech before the American Association for the Advancement of Science at Toronto in 1922 by William Bateson, the noted British geneticist. In this speech, so Bryan and his colleagues had contended, Bateson had expressed his doubts about evolution. Not true, said Curtis, and he read the speech and a letter from Bateson to prove his point. Curtis emphasized the need to distinguish between the causes and processes of evolution, about which much was still unknown, and the fact of evolution, which was established beyond dispute.* "The campaign against the teaching of evolution," Bateson had written to Curtis, "is a terrible example of the way in which truth can be perverted by the ignorant."

Curtis had also entered upon a public relations campaign by appealing to the nonscientific authority of Woodrow Wilson. Wilson had replied: "of course, like every other man of intelligence and education, I do believe in organic evolution. It surprises me that at this late date such questions should be raised."

("Must be a forgery. Woodrow Wilson was a Democrat," whispered the fundamentalist Democrats of Dayton.)

---

* In the last three decades, due chiefly to the advances in our understanding of genetics and to recognition of differential reproduction as the chief element in natural selection, it has become possible to formulate the general forces of evolution, and the resultant process, with considerable assurance. To quote a recent summary: "The evolutionary materials involved in this complex process are the genetical systems existing in the population and the mutations arising in these. The interacting forces producing evolutionary changes from these materials are their shuffling in the process of reproduction, the incidence of mutations (their nature and rate) and natural selection." George Gaylord Simpson, *The Meaning of Evolution,* rev. (New York: New American Library, 1951), p. 98.

Finally, the scientists emphasized the overwhelming practicality of the theory of evolution. Not only has evolution occurred in the past, it is still occurring. And man, by applying the natural laws discovered by science, can influence its direction. If a farmer wants a better vegetable or plant, he can order it from a plant breeder and, within limits, it can be produced for him within a few years. (The old farmer who was foreman of the grand jury had said it already: "the razor back hog looked like a hound dog. Stand it beside our current Poland China—then ask me if I believe in evolution.")

III

The defense also was prepared with testimony about the Bible, its interpretation, and the relations of science to religion. Besides the natural scientists who expatiated on these topics—Metcalf, Mather, and Curtis—four linguists or theologians stood ready:

Rabbi Herman Rosenwasser of San Francisco could speak fluently in English, German, Yiddish, Hungarian, and Hebrew; in addition he could read or translate Latin, Greek, Chaldaic, French, and Italian.

The Reverend Walter C. Whitaker, rector of St. John's Episcopal Church of Knoxville, was chairman of the Episcopal committee that passed on the competency of new ministers for the United States.

Shailer Mathews was dean of the Divinity School of the University of Chicago.

Dr. Herbert E. Murkett was pastor of the First Methodist Church of Chattanooga.

To understand the Bible, said Rosenwasser, one must know Hebrew, but in 1611, when the King James translation was made, little was known of that language—scientific study of it did not begin until 1753. Therefore much of the King James translation was inaccurate. For instance the word *bara,* rendered as *create,* should be *to set in motion.* Even more striking, the word *Adam* means *any living organism containing blood*. Thus the statement that we are descended from Adam could mean that we are descended from lower orders of animals. Wherever the Hebrew Bible wishes to refer to the spiritual and intellectual side of man, it uses *Gever* or *Ish*, not *Adam*.

We cannot escape the need to construe the Bible if we would find its "higher and truer meaning." The entire Bible teaches the fundamental difference between body and soul. God is the father of spirits and not the father of flesh. Therefore it is man's soul only that is the Son of God and is in the image of God. Genesis gives four separate accounts of the creation of the human body, and the only way to reconcile them is to recognize that the Bible says only that God created the human body and the material that he used, but says nothing of the method that he used.

Natural science, the theory of evolution, has discovered the method by which God brought the human body into being. As Shailer Mathews put it, "Genesis and evolution are complementary to each other, Genesis emphasizing the divine first cause, and science the details of the process through which God works." The theories of evolution held by most scientists do not contradict Genesis, said Kirtley Mather; "rather they affirm that story and give it larger and more profound meaning."

Mather did not hold with the view, expressed by Henry Fairfield Osborn and others, that science proved the validity of religion. Nor did he agree with Osborn that evolution had been Purposive. He did believe, however, that the more knowledge science gives us about material realities, the more likely we are to see deeply and truly into the *essence* of any object. And it is this search for essences that marks religion, while science is a search for material processes: "Evolution is not a power or a force; it is a process, a method. God is a power, a force; he necessarily uses processes and methods in displaying His power and exerting force." Science tells us nothing about the origin of matter. It deals with immediate causes, not with ultimate causes. "For science there is no be-

ginning and no ending; all acceptable theories of the earth's origin
are theories of rejuvenation rather than of creation from nothing."

Mather sharply denied that a belief in evolution involved the
Christian in a moral dilemma. It is true that the law of Christ is
Love, but it is not true that survival of the fittest implies survival
of the cruellest or the most aggressive. "Survival values at different times have been measured in different terms. . . . Especially in the strain that leads to man can we note the increasing
spread of habits of co-operation, of unselfishness, of love. . . .
Even in evolution it is true that he who would save his life must
lose it."

Curtis pointed out that the Bible may be read as the record of
evolution: the evolution of man's religious and moral conceptions.
The earlier Old Testament offers the concept of a "barbarous
and vengeful Jehovah." The later prophets preach of a "God of
righteousness and justice." Finally, Jesus of Nazareth comes to us
as a symbol of a compassionate and forgiving Father who gave
His only begotten son that man might find salvation.

Here, then, were the outlines of the case that the defense
sought to present. It argued that the evidence of evolution was so
overwhelming that any law banning its teaching was not a legitimate
exercise of the police power. It argued that the meaning of Genesis was so obscure and contradictory that no law could be valid which
banned the teaching of any theory conflicting with the Bible. It
argued that, if the Bible and the theory of evolution were properly
understood, they did not conflict at all. Although Judge Raulston
prevented the defense from presenting this case to the jury in Dayton, he did not prevent them from submitting it to the American
people: the statements by the expert witnesses were printed verbatim by newspapers in all parts of the United States, including the
South.

When Arthur Hays finished reading the statements, the judge
directed that the jury should return to the jury-box. But no. Dar-

row got up. He had a request to make before the jury returned. He called attention to the sign on the wall of the courthouse: "Read Your Bible." It was ten feet long, and contained a huge hand pointing to the words. He wanted the sign removed.

Ben McKenzie objected. (This was as bad as the caviling at prayer.) Judge Raulston said to the General, "Of course, you know I stand for the Bible." The General's son, Gordon McKenzie, said, "I believe in the Bible as strong as anybody else here," but he agreed that the sign might come down. Malone said placatingly that the defense merely wanted to remove anything that might prejudice the jury.

This enraged the General's son. He withdrew his suggestion that the sign should come down. He said: "I have never seen the time in the history of this country when any man should be afraid to be reminded of the fact that he should read his Bible, and if they should represent a force that is aligned with the devil and his satellites—"

Now Malone objected. Gordon McKenzie continued: "—Finally I say when that time comes then it is time for us to tear up all the Bibles, throw them in the fire and let the country go to hell."

Amid great confusion the judge ruled that "satellites of the devil" should be expunged from the record. That affable bailiff, Kelso Rice, rapped for order and shouted: "People, this is no circus. There are no monkeys up here."

Maybe they were all inebriated with the outdoor air. The spectators were feeling like spectators at a ball game. Court in session or not, boys selling soda pop circulated through the huge crowd. The warm air carried the scent of sweet gum. Adventurous onlookers were leaning out of the windows of the courthouse; others were sitting on the roofs of cars parked just outside the iron fence that enclosed the courtyard.

The argument continued until Judge Raulston finally ruled that the sign should be removed from the courthouse wall.

Arthur Hays was on his feet again. He was just cleaning up

the technical details now. He routinely offered in evidence a Catholic Bible, a Hebrew Bible. Then, with no preparation, he sprung the trap.

"The defense desires to call Mr. Bryan as a witness—" Ben McKenzie objected that it was improper. Bryan was startled. His palm-leaf fan beat the air with a quicker tempo. He had no desire to take the witness stand, but he was afraid not to. There he was, surrounded by 2,000 people on a courthouse lawn in a little town in Tennessee. It was like an old-fashioned Southern camp meeting. Bryan, year after year, had been telling people like these what the Bible meant. He had written countless screeds on the need to do battle for the true faith. He had assured them all along that he knew what the true faith was. Now his opponents were calling on him to give expert testimony about the Bible. He could not refuse.

Judge Raulston could have saved him. But he did not. If the judge had not actually connived at the event, he certainly welcomed it. John T. Raulston lusted for headlines as others lust for harlots or for Heaven, and already, in this brief trial, he had vented his lust in ways more meretricious than this.

Bryan futilely sought to delay by saying: "I insist that Mr. Darrow can be put on the stand, and Mr. Malone and Mr. Hays."

The judge said: "Call anybody you desire."

Bryan said: "Then, we will call all three of them."

Darrow chided: "Not at once?"

There was no escape. Bryan, coatless, still carrying his palm-leaf fan, walked to the witness stand. He may have sensed that he was walking toward the abyss; he may even have sensed that he had dug it himself. It comes to most men at times, even to men like Bryan—the crippling recognition that you have come face to face with fate.

Chapter 9

The Stillborn Miracle

> It is almost impossible to secure a verdict which runs counter to the settled convictions of the community.
>
> G. Louis Joughin and Edmund M Morgan, *The Legacy of Sacco and Vanzetti* (New York: Harcourt, Brace and Company, 1948), p. 196

I

Sitting on hard wooden benches under the maple trees, spectators; sitting cross-legged in the grass, spectators; pressing close around the wooden platform where Judge Raulston sat at an informal table, where Bryan sat in the witness stand, where Darrow negligently rested one hand on a table, his right foot on a chair, and toyed with his gold-rimmed spectacles, spectators; perched in the branches of the trees, small boys absorbed by the spectacle —they all watched while Darrow plucked the protective feathers from William Jennings Bryan, and twisted the head off his prestige, and flung him flopping to his onetime admirers.

Darrow began quietly, asking if Bryan had not "given considerable study to the Bible." Bryan admitted it. Then Darrow began his ruthless efforts to make Bryan admit that the Bible could not always be taken literally, that it was sometimes vague, that the Butler Act was fatally indefinite when it forbade the teachings of "any theory that denies the story of the Divine Creation of man as taught in the Bible."

Did Bryan think that Jonah had remained three days in a whale's belly?

167

Bryan replied: "I believe in a God who can make a whale and can make a man and make both do what he pleases."

Was this whale just an ordinary big fish, or had God created him especially for this purpose?

The Bible does not say, said Bryan; therefore I do not know." *

"But," Darrow persisted, "do you believe He made them—that He made such a fish and that it was big enough to swallow Jonah?"

"Yes, sir," said Bryan stoutly. "Let me add: One miracle is just as easy to believe as another."

"It is for me," said Darrow caustically.

And Bryan, stinging already, hotly replied in Darrow's exact words.

Darrow began asking whether Joshua had really made the sun stand still. Did the sun go around the earth, as the Bible implied?

Attorney-General Stewart, who had worked so hard to limit the trial to narrow factual issues, now strove to maintain that barrier. He objected to any further questioning of Bryan, and he asked that the prior questions be stricken from the record.

But Judge Raulston was enjoying himself. He said: "I will hear Mr. Bryan."

Darrow's febricant questions began again. Is there any conceivable way that a day could be lengthened unless the earth stood still? What would happen to the earth if it suddenly stopped? Wouldn't it become a molten mass?

Bryan was increasingly ruffled. His palm-leaf fan, which had formerly beat vigorously, now paused, flickered, scratched in nervous ineffectuality. He flushed at some questions, fleered at Darrow because of others.

Darrow had never faced a more difficult witness: he could seldom get Bryan to answer any question directly. Bryan backpedalled and parried; Darrow continued to probe. The Tennessee

---

* A. Powell Davies, *The Ten Commandments* (New York: New American Library, 1956), pp. 101-3, analyzes the story of Jonah and the whale as a parable satirizing the Judaic prophecies of doom for all gentiles.

sun ate into them, and Darrow's efforts brought sweat through his shirt, and he tugged repeatedly at his suspenders and twirled his glasses in his hand and despised Bryan's tight hard smile.

Doubtless Darrow's original intent in getting Bryan onto the witness stand had been mixed: the legal shrewdness of forcing a leader of the prosecution to admit that the Bible must be interpreted, the glee to be found in exposing a. fanatic, the exquisite pleasure that any craftsman finds in using his tools. But in the heat of the deed all of these motives coalesced into a dominant emotion: anger.

Bryan testified for an hour and a half. Throughout that time he tried to evade. The more he did so, the more angry Darrow became. During the trial he had found repeated frustration. Judge Raulston had stopped him from examining the scientific witnesses, and had repeatedly ruled against him on points large and small. This had led to Darrow's outburst at Raulston—a double-edged episode: Darrow's success at gulling his oppressor may have mitigated but could not erase his coerced apology. Now Bryan was trying to escape, and Darrow's pent-up resentment drove him in pursuit. Relentlessly, viciously, he brought Bryan to bay.

When, asked Darrow, did the flood occur? Bryan would "not attempt to fix the date."

But didn't every printed Bible say that the flood had happened about 4004 B.C.?

Yes, that was the estimate given.

How was the estimate arrived at?

Bryan: "I never made a calculation."

Darrow: "A calculation from what?"

Bryan: "I could not say."

Darrow: "From the generations of man?"

Bryan: "I would not want to say that."

Darrow: "What do you think?"

Bryan: "I do not think about things I don't think about."

Darrow: "Do you think about things you do think about?"

Bryan: "Well, sometimes."

The laughter, with Judge Raulston an eager participant, marked the end of conflict, the beginning of rout.

Again Stewart, joined now by McKenzie, tried to rescue him. But Bryan was grievously hurt, and he would not be rescued. Turning to the audience, he indicated the defense lawyers: "These gentlemen have not had much chance—they did not come here to try this case. They came to try revealed religion. I am here to defend it, and they can ask me any question they please."

There was loud clapping.

Darrow said: "Great applause from the bleachers."

Bryan: "From those whom you call 'yokels.' "

Darrow: "I have never called them 'yokels.' "

They wrangled on. Bryan said: "Those are the people whom you insult."

Darrow: "You insult every man of science and learning in the world because he does not believe in your fool religion."

Now Judge Raulston protested: "I will not stand for that."

Darrow: "For what he is doing?"

The effrontery of it startled the judge into saying: "I am talking to both of you."

Again Stewart tried to halt the questioning (a Southern reporter called his efforts "pathetic"). Again Raulston said: "To stop it now would not be just to Mr. Bryan. He wants to ask the other gentleman questions along the same line."

Darrow kept worrying at the witness about the dates that Bishop Ussher, calculating from the ages of the various prophets, had assigned to Scriptural episodes. The Bishop had computed the date of Creation as 4004 B.C. He had been even more specific: this happy event had occurred on October 23 at 9 A.M.

A voice in the audience added: "Eastern Standard Time."

Bryan wriggled and writhed, but Darrow kept pressing him. And eventually Bryan gave answers.

Did Bryan believe that all of the species on the earth had come into being in the 4,200 years, by the Bishop's dating, since the Flood occurred? Yes, said Bryan finally, he did believe it.

Didn't Bryan know that many civilizations had existed for more than 5,000 years? Said Bryan: "I have never felt a great deal of interest in the effort that has been made to dispute the Bible by the speculations of men, or the investigations of men."

Didn't Bryan know that many old religions described a Flood? No, he had "never felt it necessary to look up some competing religions."

Had Bryan ever read Tylor's *Primitive Culture,* or Boas? Had he ever tried to find out about the other peoples of the earth and how old their civilizations are? Said Bryan: "No, sir, I have been so well satisfied with the Christian religion that I have spent no time trying to find arguments against it."

He went further yet: "I have all the information I want to live by and to die by."

Darrow: "And that's all you are interested in?"

Bryan: "I am not looking for any more on religion."

Now Bryan, condoned by Raulston, began a series of discursive speeches about other religions. It was mainly hearsay: what he had been told by some anonymous man in Rangoon, what he had learned about Buddhism from an Englishman converted to that religion, and so on. (Dudley Field Malone surreptitiously bought his wife a bottle of soda pop.)

Did Bryan know how old the earth was? No, he didn't. Wasn't there some scientist that he respected? He named George M. Price and "a man named Wright, who taught at Oberlin." Darrow called them mountebanks.

By this time Bryan's self-esteem was suppurating, and his wits entirely deserted him. Having discredited himself with everybody who did not believe in the literal truth of the Bible, he now destroyed himself with those who did. It took one deft question by Darrow, and a six-word reply.

Darrow asked: "Do you think the earth was made in six days?"

Bryan: "Not six days of twenty-four hours."

(Sitting under a tree at the fringes of the crowd, surrounded by fundamentalists, Kirtley Mather heard the startled gasps. His neighbors were aghast. "What does he want to say that for?" they demanded of each other.)

Stewart again tried to stop it. "What," he asked, "is the purpose of this examination?"

Not even waiting for the judge to answer, Bryan said that the defense lawyers had "no other purpose than ridiculing every Christian who believes in the Bible."

Darrow said directly to Bryan: "We have the purpose of preventing bigots and ignoramuses from controlling the education of the United States and you know it—and that is all."

Dudley Malone observed that Bryan seemed to be trying to get into the trial record some evidence to disprove the scientists' statements.

A porcine-eyed Bryan leaped to his feet and shouted to the crowd in the courtyard: "I am not trying to get anything into the record. I am simply trying to protect the word of God against the greatest atheist or agnostic in the United States!"

The applause was thunderous and prolonged. When it died down, Darrow said:

"I wish I could get a picture of these clackers."

And again Stewart protested against any continuance of the examination. They argued and argued. Judge Raulston said that of course the questions would not be proper testimony before a jury, but that he was permitting them for purposes of the record on the appeal.

Not so, said Bryan, he was not talking for the benefit of any appellate court. He was talking for only one reason: "I want the Christian world to know that any atheist, agnostic, unbeliever, can question me any time as to my belief in God, and I will answer him." They argued and argued, and the questions went on.

Darrow read the passage from Genesis: "The morning and the evening were the first day." He asked if Bryan also believed that the sun was created on the fourth day. Yes, Bryan did.

Darrow asked how there could have been a morning and evening without any sun. Bryan had no answer.

Those "days" in Genesis, Darrow asked, they might have been long periods? Yes, said Bryan, the Creation might have lasted for "millions of years." He squirmed vigorously. He did not want to commit himself, and Darrow forced the choice upon him. So far as the "days" are concerned, said Bryan, "My impression is that they were periods, but I would not attempt to argue against anybody who wanted to believe in literal days."

Darrow began to ask about Eve and the serpent. The Bible said that God had punished the serpent for having tempted Eve. Darrow asked:

"Do you think that is why the serpent is compelled to crawl upon its belly?"

Bryan: "I believe that."

Darrow: "Have you any idea how the snake went before that time?"

Bryan: "No, sir."

Darrow: "Do you know whether he walked on his tail or not?"

Bryan: "No, sir, I have no way to know."

They laughed. The crowd laughed. Now Bryan's nervous condition was eloquent. His hands trembled, his lips were quivering, his face was suffused and dark. He broke completely. He said:

"Your Honor, I think I can shorten this testimony." He would answer the question. Yes, he would. And he jumped to his feet and turned to the people with outstretched hands and he shouted at an almost hysterical pitch:

"I want the world to know that this man, who does not believe in a God, is trying to use a court in Tennessee—"

Darrow: "I object to that."

Bryan: "—to slur at it—"

Darrow: "I object to your statement. I am examining you on your fool ideas that no intelligent Christian on earth believes."

And the judge adjourned court for the day.

Darrow's admirers swarmed around him, laughing and shaking his hand.

Bryan stood almost alone, deserted, a tired expression on his sagging face. It had been a long afternoon, and the twilight was closing in.

(Kirtley Mather heard the fundamentalists around him planning a group visit to Bryan that night to tell him, to his face, how much they disapproved of the concessions he had made. "I do not think they were twenty-four-hour days." The Judas.)

Indeed a long day: the judge's citation of Darrow for contempt, the reading of the scientific statements by Hays, Darrow's mock apology, more scientific statements, the examination of Bryan. A day of reversals: at noontime, Darrow vulnerable and Bryan vicariously regal; four hours later, Darrow ascendant and Bryan a maunderer.

"The words of a wise man's mouth are gracious, but the lips of a fool will swallow up himself. The beginning of the words of his mouth is foolishness; and the end of his talk is mischievous madness" (Ecclesiastes x:12-13).

II

Darrow's manhandling of Bryan had a shattering impact. To the detached onlookers, it was hilarious burlesque. To Darrow's friends, it was masterly trial tactics. But to many Southerners— the very people that the defense had been trying to win over—it was deeply offensive. Typical of this group was George Fort Milton of the Chattanooga *News,* one of the outstanding editors in the South. Milton had been rather equivocal about the Scopes case. He had opposed passage of the Butler Act, and he favored its repeal. But he was a Southern chauvinist who fiercely denounced the Yankee invasion. He was also a Democrat who had long idolized Bryan. Now he was not equivocal about Darrow's inquisition; it had been, said Milton, "a thing of immense cruelty."

In order to offset such indictments, the defense that evening issued a statement saying that it had been actuated, not by a desire to humiliate Bryan, but solely by legal reasoning as to the best way to frame its appeal to higher courts.

The situation was even more disturbing to the prosecution. The jousting of Darrow and Bryan had swept the trial far outside the strait limits set for it by Tom Stewart. It introduced a vast uncertainty, and no prosecuting attorney enjoys uncertainty. Stewart now saw William Jennings Bryan as a major clog in the machine of justice. That night Stewart went to Bryan and told him that he would not be allowed to return to the witness stand the next morning. Bryan protested bitterly; he wanted to recoup himself with his admirers. The two men quarrelled vehemently and long. But Stewart held the trump cards: he was the official chief of the prosecution, and he knew John T. Raulston, and logic was on his side. And thus did Tom Stewart finish the job that Clarence Darrow had begun. The Bryan who went to court on Tuesday, July 21, was an exhausted and broken man.

The trial resumed inside the courtroom, driven back indoors by a drizzling rain. Judge Raulston opened by saying that his excessive zeal to be fair had led him into error on the previous day. All questions had already been eliminated from the trial except the one issue: "whether or not . . . this defendant taught that man descended from a lower order of animals." The judge did not see how Bryan's testimony could help the higher courts in deciding that question, and therefore he ordered it expunged from the record.

Darrow got up. "Of course," he said, "I am not at all sure that Mr. Bryan's testimony would aid the supreme court or any other human being, but he testified by the hour there and I haven't got through with him yet." He took an exception to the court's action. He then explained that in view of the court's statement that only the one issue remained to be decided, the defense had no case to present: it could not deny the state's case, it had no witnesses and no proof to offer. He concluded:

"I think in order to save time we will ask the court to bring in the jury and instruct the jury to find the defendant guilty."

Stewart agreed, and then Hays made several motions to make sure that the record was in proper shape for the appeal. Bryan saw the lid coming down on his coffin, and he writhed a little before dying, saying that he had not reached the point, in his testimony the previous day, where he could answer the charges as to his ignorance and bigotry, saying further that he could not answer them in court since the judge had ruled as he had, saying that he would give his replies to the press and appealing to the newspapers to print his replies fairly and to print also the questions that he would have asked the defense lawyers if the court had permitted it.

Darrow said sardonically: "I think it would be better, Mr. Bryan, for you to take us out also with the press and ask us the questions and then the press will have both the questions and the answers." After they hasseled about it some, the jury was brought into the courtroom for the first time in days, and the opposing lawyers went to the bench for a conference with the judge.

With jury and spectators ever so curious but unable to hear, Darrow said he wanted a guilty verdict as quickly as possible. Stewart agreed and promised to do what he could to ensure that the case would get to the state supreme court at its term beginning the first Monday in September at Knoxville; if they missed that date they would have to wait a full year because the court had only one term a year.

Judge Raulston's charge to the jury had three points of interest:

1. If the facts showed that Scopes had taught that man had descended from a lower order of animals, he should be found guilty. This latter clause in the Butler Act showed the intention of the legislature and interpreted the preceding—"to teach any theory that denies the story of the Divine Creation of man as taught in the Bible . . ."

2. The defendant's failure to testify could not be considered in any way in determining whether he was guilty.

3. If the jury thought that Scopes' offense deserved a fine of

more than $100, it should impose a fine not to exceed $500. "But if you are content with a $100 fine, then you may simply find the defendant guilty and leave the punishment to the court."

Darrow got up to speak to the jury. He was brief. This case, he said, can only be settled by higher courts, "and it cannot get to a higher court unless you bring in a verdict." He did not want a divided jury. In view of the judge's charge, he did not see how the jury could find Scopes not guilty. Darrow said he wanted only to get to a higher court in order to determine whether the Butler Act was valid and whether Judge Raulston should have allowed the scientific testimony.

Stewart got up to question Judge Raulston about the portion of his charge to the jury which dealt with the technique of imposing the fine. Should not the jury fix the amount of the fine?

No, said Judge Raulston, the court could impose the minimum fine allowed by any statute. At least that was the practice in bootlegging cases, where the minimum fine was also $100.

Stewart said to Darrow: "We have more of that kind than any other."

Darrow said: "That is encouraging."

"How is that?" the judge asked.

Darrow said regretfully: "I have not even seen a cause for a case since I got down here."

But about this fine. Stewart said: what about the general statute governing the imposition of fines? Raulston explained that it prescribed that any fine exceeding $50 had to be set by the jury. But, said Raulston, that is not the common procedure. Darrow said he didn't care who imposed the fine and that the defense would not take any exception on that score—all they wanted was a ruling on the statute.

Thus occurred the technical defect, in the setting of the fine, that the state supreme court would finally use to dispose of the Scopes case. But who can know whether any of the participants in the trial consciously preserved the defect as a way for the appellate tribunal to escape embarrassment?

Stewart's summation to the jury was even briefer than Darrow's. And blunter. He said: "What Mr. Darrow wanted to say to you was that he wanted you to find his client guilty, but did not want to be in the position of pleading guilty because that would destroy his rights in the appellate court."

Darrow said nothing, and the jury left the courtroom at 11:14 A.M., retired to the west side of the courthouse lawn, lit cigarettes or took good-sized chews of tobacco, whispered together, and nine minutes later they were back in the jury box. Guilty.

Raulston asked if they had fixed the amount of the fine. No, they had left it to the court.

Scopes was standing. Raulston asked him to step before the bench and imposed upon him a fine of $100. Then he asked, belatedly, if Scopes had anything to say.

The defendant looked rather tired. He was stooped, coatless. He stepped away from his lawyers and looked squarely at the judge for a moment. He showed a flicker of emotion but stifled it at once, and he said simply:

"Your Honor, I feel that I have been convicted of violating an unjust statute. I will continue in the future as I have in the past, to oppose this law in any way I can. Any other action would be in violation of my ideal of academic freedom—that is, to teach the truth—as guaranteed in our constitution, of personal and religious freedom. I think the fine is unjust."

Raulston again imposed the fine, and the Baltimore *Sun,* Menken's paper, posted the bond of $500. The judge explained the requirements of the appeal, saying that in Tennessee the bill of exceptions consisted merely of a copy of the evidence and the proceedings and the judge's charge to the jury.

Hays was back on his feet moving for a stay of judgment, moving for a new trial, and the judge denied everything except the leave to appeal, and Hays took his exceptions in good form. And there was no more business.

They all made valedictories. Bryan predicted that the trial would "stimulate investigation," and the crowd clapped. Darrow thanked the judge, "who might have sent me to jail, but did not," and the crowd laughed. Hays offered to send the judge a copy of *The Origin of Species,* and a spectator shouted that Judge Raulston should send Hays a Bible. The trial was over.

The crowd, mostly fundamentalists, rushed to Darrow to congratulate him, and they held their children up to shake his hand. His yellow face softened. (Not until later did the crowd seek out Bryan.) Darrow shook hands heartily with the jurors who had convicted his client. "We wanted you folks to do just what you did," he exclaimed. He revealed that the defense fears of a hung jury had prompted his unusual summation. "The state won ten of the jurors but I won the two others to conviction," he claimed. "There is no doubt but that the jury would have disagreed if it had been allowed to decide on the merits of the case."

This claim wins credence from the statements made by the foreman of the jury, Captain Jack Thompson: "Personally, I have always had an open mind on the subject of evolution. And I will always have. What I want now is information on that important topic. Along with the other jurors, I feel a deep disappointment that the scientific witnesses were not allowed to testify. It would have been an opportunity to find out something about how we came into the world." Thompson was resentful that the judge had so often excluded the jury from the courtroom, and he was glad the trial was over: "the peach crop will be coming in."

William Jennings Bryan said in a public statement that Darrow was "the finished product of evolution . . . He embodies all that is cruel, heartless and destructive in evolution." Darrow replied: "Mr. Bryan is not a product of evolution, but comes under the classification of those who revert to type." He could not say whether he felt more love of mankind than did Bryan, and added: "I fancy no one in need of a friend or help would have any uncontrollable impulse to fly to him."

John Thomas Scopes, a convicted sinner, was troubled. As he was driving around Dayton that afternoon in a borrowed roadster he saw a friendly newspaperman. He insisted that the man go for a ride with him. Scopes drove out to the edge of town and parked the car. He said that he had been worried about something all through the trial. The fact was that he had not violated the law.

The reporter expressed confusion. Scopes explained that he had missed several hours of class, and the evolution lesson had been one of them. The boys who had testified against him could not remember whether they had studied evolution or not. And he had been afraid since the trial began that he might be put on the witness stand, where he would have had to admit his innocence. He hated to think of the consequences if he had snatched away from Dayton its hour of fame.

The reporter said: "Well, you're safe now."

All of the reporters loved Dayton and the kind of hospitality that had been shown them. To vent their gratitude they hired the village dance hall, imported a band from Chattanooga, and invited the town. The town came. Darrow danced with the high-school girls and smoked cigarettes with their boyfriends. He waltzed with the wife of Dudley Field Malone while the entire crowd applauded them. Malone pointed to Darrow's purple suspenders and quipped: "Not only were they the sole support of Mr. Darrow's trousers, but at times they were the principal support of our case."

III

Six weeks before the Scopes trial opened, the newspapers reported that William Jennings Bryan was writing a speech to deliver in the courtroom. But Darrow, Stewart, and Judge Raulston deprived him of that forum. The trial collapsed so precipitously on the final day that only Darrow and Stewart made summations to the jury. Eight days after the trial ended, Bryan's proposed jury argument was released through the Associated Press. As an added irony, Bryan had planned to speak for at least an hour and a half; actually Darrow spoke only a few minutes, Stewart even less.

Always the encomiast of popular rule and rural America,

Bryan keyed in by contrasting "the disturbing noises of a great city with the calm serenity of the country," and he rejoiced that the issues of this case would be decided by "a jury made up largely of the yeomanry of the state." He then reviewed the legal aspects, contending that the only issue was the right of a state to control its employees in their public duties. He denounced the "little irresponsible oligarchy of self-styled 'intellectuals'" who were trying to force irreligion on the children of Tennessee. The meaning of the Butler Act was clear, and the evidence proved that Scopes had violated the law.

Bryan next discussed evolution's claims to be scientific. If men were paid in proportion to their service to society, it would be impossible to reckon our debt to the men who had mastered steam and electricity, invented better farm implements, conquered typhoid, yellow fever, diphtheria, and pneumonia. But evolution, in contrast, is nothing but "millions of guesses strung together." The refutation of evolution is conclusive. In chemistry, each of the 92 original elements is separate, distinct, and unchanging. Second, it is absurd to argue that structural resemblance shows kinship: "There is no more reason to believe that man has descended from a small, inferior animal than there is to believe that a stately mansion has descended from a small cottage." Third, evolution assumes a "pushing power" within each organism which drives it to modify in certain ways. No such power exists. But, said Bryan, "there is a lifting power that any child can understand. . . . There is a spiritual gravitation that draws all souls toward heaven, just as surely as there is a physical force that draws all matter on the surface of the earth toward the earth's center. Christ is our drawing power . . ."

Having disproved evolution, Bryan spent the last three quarters of his speech on the religious and moral implications of evolution. This false doctrine degrades man by putting his "immortal soul in the same circle with the wolf, the hyena, and the skunk." It shakes our faith in God as a beginning by putting Creation so far away from us. It also creates doubt of the existence of Heaven.

By disputing the Scriptural account of man's Creation, evolution shakes faith in the Bible as the word of God. And the Bible contains "the only evidence that we have of Christ's existence, mission, teaching, crucifixion, and resurrection." Consider the example of Darwin himself: in 1820-31 believing in the literal truth of the Bible, by 1879 denying "that there ever has been any revelation" and skeptical about "a future life."

Although we know the consequences of evolution for man's life on this earth, we cannot calculate its effect on his immortal soul. Bryan urged a quarantine: "The bodies of our people are so valuable that druggists and physicians must be careful to properly label all poisons; why not be as careful to protect the spiritual life of our people from the poisons that kill the soul?" There could be no doubt that "bad doctrines" corrupt morals, and as a case in point he again commented on lengthy extracts from Darrow's plea for Loeb and Leopold.

Evolution diverts our energies from urgent social problems to "trifling speculation" about the characteristics of ancient worms. College graduates especially need to have education "entwined" with religion so that their hearts will be "aflame with love of God and love of fellowmen"; this will prepare them "to lead in the altruistic work that the world so sorely needs." But evolution, by emphasizing that changes take place over enormous stretches of time, paralyzes the hope of reform. It has no program for human betterment except "scientific breeding."

"Evolution, disputing the miracle and ignoring the spiritual in life, has no place for the regeneration of the individual. It recognizes no cry of repentance and scoffs at the doctrine that one can be born again." Against this lethal prognosis Christianity poses the story of the Prodigal Son. Here is the sublime truth: "A heart can be changed in the twinkling of an eye, and a change in the life follows a change in the heart. If one heart can be changed, it is possible that many hearts can be changed, and if many hearts can be changed, it is possible that all hearts can be changed—that a world can be born in a day."

Finally, if evolution is accepted as a philosophy of life it will "carry man back to a struggle of tooth and claw." Science can improve our machinery, but it cannot prevent the misuse of machinery. Science has made war ever more terrible; the only force that can prevent the utter wreckage of civilization is Love, the Love preached by Jesus of Nazareth. But evolution seeks to degrade the name of Christ, "for, carried to its logical conclusion, it robs Christ of the story of the virgin birth, of the majesty of His deity and mission, and of the triumph of His resurrection." Evolution even—the ultimate crime—"disputes the doctrine of the atonement."

The issue in the Scopes trial was identical, said Bryan, with the issue in Pilate's court: "Again force and love meet face to face . . . A bloody, brutal doctrine—Evolution—demands, as the rabble did 1900 years ago, that He be crucified. That cannot be the answer of this jury representing a Christian state and sworn to uphold the laws of Tennessee."

IV

Bryan's undelivered speech was no mere lallation. If the content resembles dozens of his other speeches and articles, the occasion does not. Here is a supposed summation to a jury, begun long before he had heard the evidence or investigated the law, and disposing of those topics hastily. This peculiarity raises again the question asked by the Tennessee attorney on the eve of the trial: What business did Bryan have in that Dayton courtroom? What did he want to accomplish by his remarkable speech?

A miracle. His aim was to demonstrate "that all hearts can be changed—that a world can be born in a day." The final words of his speech were a reminder to the jury that their verdict was "eagerly awaited by a praying multitude." True, perhaps Bryan was not expecting so sweeping a consummation from one speech; his ritual oration was meant rather to prompt a sign, that is, a minor miracle that augurs major miracles to come.

A miracle, Raglan writes, "is not any wonder, but a particular kind of wonder—that is, a ritual wonder," that can be produced on fitting occasions. Its characteristics are three: The person performing it must possess superhuman powers, and Bryan began his speech by stressing the propriety of prayer "to the Ruler of the universe for wisdom to guide us in the performance of our several parts in this historic trial." By these words he tapped, so to speak, the pipeline of infused grace. Second, the goal of the miracle must be fitting for superhuman power, and the aim of changing "all hearts" seems to meet this test. Third, the ritual must be an authoritative procedure for invoking divine action, and Bryan was complying with the formulae of an established ritual —the revival meeting.

The opposition to revival meetings outraged Bryan. It is exactly this issue, he contended, that distinguishes "the destructive higher critic" of the Bible from true believers. The higher critic, said Bryan, "understands how one can have a spasm of anger and become a murderer, or a spasm of passion and ruin a life, or a spasm of dishonesty and rob a bank, but he cannot understand how one can be convicted of sin, and, in a spasm of repentance, be born again." Bryan hoped to effect such a "spasm of repentance"—and this he could do only with God's direct intervention.

Bryan repeatedly asserted his belief that God, in answer to prayer, exerts His divine power to tamper with natural processes and human hearts. This belief he shared with Governor Peay (or the Governor thought that enough Tennessee voters shared it with Bryan to make it expedient for a politician to profess belief also): in September, 1926, when a hurricane swept across Florida, Governor Peay saw retribution in the disaster; he declared that the people of Florida had forgotten God and He had sent them a forcible token of His watchfulness.

The Scopes trial was, on one level, an effort to ward off a similar fate for Tennessee. Scopes had offended against the daddy-worship of the South by giving shelter to a new idea and an incompatible mode of thought; he had also run the risk of offending God by casting doubt on His revelation. Such reckless impiety exposed to danger not Scopes merely, but the entire community. In these circumstances, toleration in itself was a mortal sin. "When the street statues of Hermes were mutilated," Walter Bagehot writes, "all the Athenians were frightened and furious; they thought they should *all* be ruined because some *one* had mutilated a god's image, and so offended him." If, as seems likely, only a small minority of Tennesseans believed that retribution was imminent, many others were mildly uneasy and thought that precautions could do no harm.

But the expiatory ritual, which was prompted largely by a sense of offense against the received forms, could be effective only if it was carried out according to the received forms. So Bryan's speech is like all of his speeches; they exude Scriptural passages and stock phrases from the rhetoric of other evangelists. In the revival meeting, originality of phrase is no virtue.

The matter runs further. Ritual is an acting out of myth, just as myth is a verbalizing of ritual. On Christmas Day every year, Jesus is born again, to suffer for mankind, to be crucified, and to arise. The myth exists, not in time, but outside time, independent of time, and the mythical past is made present by the ritual. The actual events of the historical past are trivial beside the mythical events celebrated in the ritual. A myth, says Raglan, "is a description of what should be done by a king (priest, chief, or magician) in order to secure and maintain the prosperity of his people, told in the form of a narrative of what a hero—that is, an ideal king, etc.—once did." And Bryan's undelivered speech pivots inevitably on the story of the Prodigal Son. He would save Tennessee and the world by presiding at a rebirth. But earthly prosperity is as dust beside immortality, and he sought, not simple rebirth, but rebirth into eternal life.

In going to Dayton, Bryan remained in part the defeated but aspiring politician. In part he projected himself into the revered father who had summoned a small son into his office each day at noon to instruct him in Proverbs. "The bond with the father," said Thomas Mann, "the imitation of the father, the game of be-

ing the father, and the transference to father-substitute pictures
of a higher and more developed type—how these infantile traits
work upon the life of the individual to mark and shape it!" Even
so, and Bryan's deepest failures came from his inability to create
for himself "father-substitute pictures of a higher and more developed type"; he remained cramped by the father-image that had
molded him in childhood and that isolated him from discordant
and maturing experiences. To harden the fardel there stood, behind Silas Lillard Bryan, the ecclesiastical prototype of the Apostles, who had summoned the people to repent of their sins and
elect the Word of God.

The revival meeting is an outgrowth of at least 6,000 years of
rebirth rituals. In the ancient Near East, the chief rite for protecting the community was an annual event in which the king was
killed, only to be immediately reborn in the person of his succes-
sor. Later the death and resurrection of the king were symbolic
only, and simultaneously involved the death of the old world and
the creation of a new. The creation myths began as descriptions
of this ritual. In many of these agricultural countries the liveli-
hood of the people was dependent on the annual flood of a river,
and the flood myths probably began here. The ritual settled, until
the following year, the destinies of the community, and this implied that a necessity conditioned all events; if man played his role
in the prescribed and authoritative fashion, the universe and the
gods must likewise follow the established forms.

In Judaism, the priestly and prophetic strains modified this ritual pattern in differing ways. The repeated conquests of the He-
brews and their other contacts with gentiles exposed them to false
gods. To fend off this threat, the priestly code emphasized the
formal and precise observance of elaborate sacraments. In contrast, the transformation worked by the prophets was wondrously
deep and rich: they found a magical rite and made it into a profound ethic. The competing strains in Judaism are both found
in Genesis, of which the priestly first chapter resembles the Babylonian creation myth, while the prophetic second chapter meets

head-on the problem of explaining the origin of evil in the world. In doing so, the prophets borrowed freely.

Stories similar to the Fall of Man occur in many religions, and usually, as in Genesis, the Fall involves man's infringement of some divine interdiction. The Garden of Eden is clearly Babylonian: in the Babylonian language *edinu* means a pleasant plain. One of the two rivers in the Garden is called the Euphrates, the other is the Hidekkel (unquestionably the Tigris) which is said to run "toward the East of Assyria."

The Old Testament is filled with episodes and personalities on loan from gentile rituals. By studying the careers of many mythical heroes, Raglan formulated a standard plot-pattern of 22 points; the hero's father is a king, his mother a divine virgin, and so on. Of these 22 points, the story of Moses contains 20, of Joseph 12, of Elijah 7. But Raglan was unable to find a single man known to have been a historical figure whose career contained more than six, "or perhaps seven in the case of Alexander the Great." The mythical heroes, including many Scriptural personages, were, it seems not real men at all but actors in ritual dramas. The myth often became detached from the ritual, spread to new areas and cultures, was copied and transformed, all the while keeping its spurious historicity. Thus the story of David and Uriah has parallels in the Iliad and elsewhere, and David's conquest of Goliath seems less remarkable after we hear that Cuchulain of Ulster, when only a "little lad," killed one of the fiercest champions of Ireland by striking him on the forehead with an iron ball.

We probably owe the Devil to some such source. The prototype in a ritual drama was a character who wore the horns of a bull or goat, such as the king in his role as promoter of fecundity. Then the horns became identified with the old king, the opponent in the ritual conflict of the new king (and of the rebirth that the new king symbolized), and so "the Horned Man became the antagonist of the Hero. Eventually," Raglan writes, "he stepped out of the ritual into real life, and became, what to millions he still is, a figure far more real than any historical character has ever been to anyone."

Of the Christian sacraments, some are nonrepetitive climaxes that are chiefly initiation rites: baptism, confirmation, marriage, the taking of holy orders. But Christianity is not without its re-birth rituals. One is the confessional, whether whispered to the discreet ear of a priest, shrieked in unison to the accompaniment of muscular jerks, or staged as painless therapy at Madison Square Garden where droves shuffle forward to declare for Christ. An-other is the Eucharist. Many primitive religions share the belief that the personal qualities of a dead warrior can be ingested by eating his heart. In the Greek mystery cults, man could entirely fuse with the divine by eating the god. The benefits to a Christian of the Eucharist are not limited to rebirth on earth; since the body of Christ was resurrected into eternity, the Christian gains im-mortality by partaking of it.

Not just rebirth, but immortality—this major innovation in the ritual pattern was made by the Hebrew prophets. The ancient cycle of birth, life, death, and rebirth bursts out of its closed cir-cle and becomes a spiral. God does not die but lives forever, and by his justice he creates an orderly world that man can understand and flourish in. Man can even flourish out of this world into the next, but only by incessantly warring against temptation and the evil in his own soul. And the prophets came to ultimate paradoxes. God is good, but evil exists, and it is only by struggle against darkness and death that man can win his way to light and life. God guides man unerringly to salvation, but man must by his own choice lose himself in God if he would find himself. Man must win salva-tion by his own works, but God is merciful and exercises divine grace and even the worst sinner can be reborn into faith and gain immortality.

"The dead men shall live, together with my dead body shall they arise. Awake and sing, ye that dwell in dust: for thy dew is as the dew of herbs, and the earth shall cast out the dead" (Isaiah xxvi:19). "He that findeth his life shall lose it; and he that loseth his life for my sake shall find it" (Matthew x:39). "I am the resurrection and the life: he that believeth on me, though he die, yet shall he live: and whosoever liveth and believeth on me shall never die" (John xi:25-6).

From the time when Isaiah predicted the Savior to the time when William Jennings Bryan called the people to the Way of the Lord, the notion of spiritual rebirth has moved the hearts of men. It resounds exultant in the 14th-century Easter song of Guillaume de Machaut, "Ma fin est mon commencement." It speaks with sweet delight in Spenser's Easter sonnet:

> This joyous day, deare Lord, with joy begin,
> And grant that we for whom thou diddest die,
> Beeing with thy deare blood cleane washt from sin,
> May live for ever in felicitie.

Chapter 10

To the Loser Belong the Spoils

> If you have no God what is the
> meaning of crime?
>
> Father Zossima, in Fyodor Dos-
> toyevsky's *The Brothers Karamazov*,
> trans. C. Garnett (Modern Library),
> p. 391

I

The day after the trial ended, the newspapers printed Bryan's questions to Darrow, and the replies. The terse, direct exchange was in marked contrast to the examination of Bryan by Darrow.

Q—Do you believe in the existence of God as described in the Bible?

A—I do not know of any description of God in the Bible. . . . Mr. Bryan said in effect that God is like a man and is fashioned in the image of man. I do not believe in this kind of God. As to the origin of the universe and who or what is back of it, I do not pretend to know.

Q—Do you believe that the Bible is the revealed will of God, inspired and trustworthy?

A—. . . . I believe that it should be taken like every other kind of book and that the portions that are sublime are like other such portions of any great book—as much inspired as, say, *In His Image*.*

Q—Do you believe in the supernatural Christ . . . ?

A—. . . I believe that the Christ prophesied in the Old Testament was a great Jew who should deliver his people from their physical bondage and nothing else.

* A book of theology by Bryan, published in 1922.

Q—Do you believe in the miracles recorded in the Old and New Testaments?

A—I do not believe in miracles. I believe the universe acts and has always acted in accordance with an immutable law . . .

Q—Do you believe in the immortality of the soul?

A—I have been searching for proof of this all my life, with the same desire to find it that is incident to every living thing, and I have never found any evidence on the subject.

The same morning the town of Dayton was trying to puzzle out whether the trial had brought it more good than harm. Certainly it had gotten publicity: an average daily press file of 165,000 words from Dayton, a total of 2 million words by telegraph alone. But one resident commented: "We didn't get the kind of publicity we expected out of it and I can't see that the kind we got did Dayton any good." Another said: "Well, I'm glad it's over, it didn't do Dayton much good any way."

If the rejuvenation of Dayton was deferred, not so with that of John Thomas Scopes. Fred E. Robinson, the head of the school board, said that Scopes could have his old job back if he would adhere "to the spirit of the evolution law," but Scopes asked that he not be considered. The scientific witnesses at the trial had formed a committee, with Watson Davis of Science Service as secretary, to raise funds to send the defendant to graduate school. Scopes hoped to enter an Eastern university in the autumn.

As to who had won the trial, in the South there was disagreement. An Oklahoma paper declared: "Mr. Bryan came out more than victorious. He made a monkey out of the defense counsel and left them gasping." But the Little Rock, Arkansas, *Gazette* said: "For the state of Tennessee the Scopes trial has been a moral disaster. It will plague the citizen of Tennessee wherever he may go." Dudley Malone, back in New York, went to the Ziegfeld Follies one night and Will Rogers hailed him onto the stage. Malone said the trial had been a "victorious defeat."

Bryan was claiming unsullied victory. Determined not to be thwarted by the unforeseen end of the trial, he arranged with George Fort Milton of the Chattanooga *News* for publication of his undelivered speech. He then spent four days revising and expanding it. This speech might still be the irresistible summons to a new crusade: it would win support for his anti-evolution amendment to the Constitution of the United States; it might even lead to formation of a new political party.

On Saturday, July 25, Bryan was scheduled to speak at Winchester, the home of both Judge Raulston and Tom Stewart. En route there by automobile from Chattanooga, he tried excerpts from his jury speech on a crowd of 2,000 people at Jasper. They adored it. A man living in the mountains ten miles away from Dayton presented the Bryans with a box of apples, and said: "I have nine boys, and I'm for you, and if they take the Bible away from us there isn't anything left." Stirred by this response Bryan went on to Winchester, where he repeated his speech to crowds that had been gathering since early morning. Finally back to Chattanooga, where he spent the evening working on the proofs of his speech. Since morning he had given two lengthy speeches, and had ridden 200 miles in his car.

Why this feverish activity? It bespeaks desperation, a frore presentiment that the current of fundamentalist adulation was about to dump him on some exposed and arid mud flat. George Fort Milton, who talked with him at some length four days after the trial ended, found him still "quivering with hurt" at the harsh names he had been called. "He was," wrote Milton, "a crushed and broken man."

In these bitter circumstances Bryan did the most effective thing possible to regain his fundamentalist support—he died. On Sunday, July 26, he drove from Chattanooga to Dayton, where he led the congregation in prayer at the Methodist Church, South. After a hearty mid-day dinner at the private home where he and Mrs. Bryan were staying, he went upstairs to take a nap. He died of apoplexy in his sleep.

The response was galvanic. Hundreds of men, women, and children trooped through the private home to see the Great Commoner for the last time. Men brought their babies to gaze upon the remains of the champion of Christianity. While an honor guard of servicemen ringed the house, the mourners sang, "Nearer, My God to Thee." The Reverend Charles R. Jones, pastor of the church where Bryan had made his last public utterance, conducted the services. "Behold, I shew you a mystery; We shall not all sleep, but we shall all be changed, In a moment, in the twinkling of an eye, at the last trump: for the trumpet shall sound, and the dead shall be raised incorruptible, and we shall be changed. For this corruptible must put on incorruption, and this mortal must put on immortality" (I Corinthians xv:51-53).

Even Darrow, vacationing in the Smoky Mountains, toadied to the politic by making a stilted expression of regret. Eugene Debs scorned such a course and said: "The cause of human progress sustains no loss in the death of Mr. Bryan." H. L. Mencken began his obituary column in the Baltimore *Sun* by writing: "Has it been duly marked by historians that William Jennings Bryan's last secular act on this globe of sin was to catch flies?"

But the folks around Dayton, wrote George Fort Milton, regarded Bryan's death as "martyrdom, a death from an ordeal of faith." To many fundamentalists, Bryan had walked the stony road to Calvary, and there had ascended the Cross. Alive, he had suffered death at the hands of Clarence Darrow; dead, he became a stamen once more. Nor was this the final irony.

II

From the first involvement of the American Civil Liberties Union in the Scopes case, many leaders of the organization rued their lack of control over policy, and rued especially Darrow's prominence in the situation. After Scopes' conviction this restiveness increased, spurred by strident attacks on the ACLU itself. On July 10, the first day of the trial, a leading Chattanooga minister had published in the local *Times* an extract from the report of the Lusk Committee of the New York legislature: "The American Civil Liberties Union, in the last analysis, is a supporter of all subversive movements and its propaganda is detrimental to the best interests of the state. It attempts not only to protect crime, but also to encourage attacks upon our institutions in every form." The Knoxville *Journal* reprinted these charges and added that the ACLU owed its existence "to the notorious pacifist organizations of war-time fame which were presumably financed by German agents in this country."

The events of the trial stimulated a similar hostile tone in some liberal publications. Under the heading, "The Baiting of Judge Raulston," the *New Republic* asserted that the defense had cheapened the trial by subordinating the issue involved "to the exigencies of theatrical newspaper publicity." Although the Butler Act was "barbarous," the Tennessee legislature had undoubted authority to pass such a law. The editorial, cognizant of the recent spate of court decisions outlawing social legislation, said that for any court to restrict legislative discretion in this instance would extend further a judicial power already far too great. The desirability of the Butler Act, like all policy questions, should be decided by the people acting through the legislature.

In a letter to the publication, Walter Nelles, a lawyer high in the ACLU, replied that the real question was: How many minds were opened by the conduct of the trial? By that standard he thought the defense tactics were quite successful. The *New Republic* dissented. It insisted that Scopes' lawyers should have eschewed propaganda and used the trial to teach the American people to think scientifically. It also prescribed what should have been done for Scopes: local attorneys; no real effort to deny his legal guilt; a committee, mainly of Tennesseans, in his behalf, with its chief effort to expose the irrationality of the Butler Act in order to build support for its repeal.*

The pressure told. In early August, Forrest Bailey, now co-director of the ACLU, wrote John Randolph Neal that he should

---

* Unquestionably wise; also impossible, as the history of the episode showed.

be more prominent, Darrow less so, when the case went to the state supreme court—this even though Darrow had just been chosen to the national board of the organization, and even though Bailey complained in the same letter of Neal's failure to keep in touch with him.

Neal's lack of incisiveness soon manifested itself again. He filed a petition in the federal court at Chattanooga seeking a temporary order, in Scopes' behalf, to halt state officials from further enforcement of the Butler Act. The petition alleged two violations of the Fourteenth Amendment: denial of equal protection of the laws, and invasion of Scopes' property rights without due process of law. But it had already been announced that Scopes planned to leave the state anyway, so further enforcement of the Butler Act could hardly damage him financially. While Fred E. Robinson announced that a Nashville reporter, after passing a rigid test of his fundamentalism, had been hired to fill Scopes' place, Neal frantically claimed that Scopes wanted his old job back.

Neal and Darrow also filed a petition at Knoxville for a federal restraining order in behalf of a taxpayer of Rhea Springs, father of five children, who claimed that he could not educate them properly under Tennessee law and thus was being deprived of liberty and property without due process.

At this juncture Governor Peay returned from six weeks of rest at Battle Creek and took command of the fundamentalist forces. The "reckless teaching of evolution," he declared, had been converting adolescents to agnosticism "in shocking numbers." This country has always been "a Christian nation," but if it embraces infidelity "its doom is sealed." Another Tennessean, George Rappelyea, was moved to write Forrest Bailey his ardent praise of John Neal and his conviction that the raucous Darrow was unfit to argue before the state supreme court. Bryan's death, he said, had utterly wiped out any gains that had been made with the people of Tennessee; Rappelyea proclaimed himself the only "modernist" left in Dayton.

The public attacks on Darrow were frequent, and his replies were mordant. In response to criticism by John Raulston, Darrow said: "Judge Raulston was elected on a fluke and is now campaigning for re-election this fall. The trial was part of his campaign." At a public meeting in Dayton of the Bryan Memorial Association, Raulston denied the allegations, and Tom Stewart denounced Darrow as "the greatest menace present-day civilization has to deal with." The Association, formed to build a fundamentalist college in honor of Bryan, announced its plans to raise a $5 million endowment. It seemed that Bryan himself might provide posthumously a good start toward this goal: a quarter of his estate, provisionally estimated at $500,000, had been willed to educational purposes.

John Roach Straton, the Brooklyn fundamentalist, fumed that Darrow had told a group of young men in Knoxville how he had made his first money by playing poker. C. T. Marshall, chief justice of the Ohio Supreme Court, called Darrow an "unethical practitioner." The law of the Scopes trial, said the judge, was plain. The Butler Act had nothing to do with evolution. Yet Darrow had tried to bullyrag Judge Raulston into admitting expert testimony on this irrelevant topic. Darrow replied that Marshall should read the Butler Act before giving speeches about it.

The mere thought of Darrow in the Tennessee supreme court, wrote Bailey to Rappelyea, was distressing, so much so that he planned to write Felix Frankfurter and ask him to appeal to Darrow. Much depended on Neal, who at that moment was en route to New York. But while Bailey was waiting for Neal in New York, Neal was sending Bailey a telegram from Annapolis, saying that he had been called out of New York unexpectedly and was going back to Tennessee at once. Bailey was bewildered. Neal told Rappelyea that his hasty flight from New York without seeing Bailey had been due to the serious illness of a niece. But Rappelyea thought that Neal just could not face the prospect of a fight with Arthur Garfield Hays, who was determined that Darrow should continue in the case.

Refusing to give up, Bailey wrote to Charles H. Strong, New York lawyer and president of the Unitarian Laymen's League, saying that many protests had been received about Darrow. If Strong felt that way too, would he write to Darrow or Neal expressing his views, but being sure it seemed that he was writing on his own initiative? Strong replied that he was hesitant to do so because he had agreed to write an *amicus curiae* brief for the state supreme court, and he did not want it to appear that he was trying to replace Darrow. But he was sorry that Darrow was in the case; it should be Charles Evans Hughes or John W. Davis.

Darrow let it be known that he had gotten wind of these machinations, and Bailey sent him a long explanation. The executive committee of the ACLU, he wrote, was deeply appreciative of the contribution Darrow had made, but it had received many criticisms of the conduct of the trial at Dayton, and it was concerned about the effect on future events of this hostile reaction. It had communicated these sentiments to Neal, while assuring him that he was in charge of the case and should act as he saw fit. Darrow replied jocularly that he was accustomed to criticism, and added: "I know perfectly well that the case was handled in the proper way and I doubt whether many people could have brought the attention of the country to it as we did, and after all, this is the main thing." And Darrow began his own manipulations. Neal, he said, was a professor and not a lawyer. The defense must have a competent Tennessee attorney, and Darrow suggested Frank Spurlock of Chattanooga or Robert Keebler of Memphis. He closed by asking Bailey not to tell Neal about the letter.

With all factions of the defense unhappy, each for its own reasons, Charles Evans Hughes heartened them all on September 9 by his speech at the convention of the American Bar Association. Without mentioning the events in Tennessee, Hughes stated his concern at "the growth of an intolerant spirit," and denied the wisdom of efforts "to control public instruction in the interest of any religious creed or dogma."

Walter Nelles was stimulated to make a new proposal for sidetracking Darrow: Let entire control of the appeal be placed in the hands of a committee of scientists, which could then seek to engage respectable lawyers such as Hughes, or Roscoe Pound and Thomas Reed Powell of Harvard. Bailey was enthusiastic. But Arthur Hays was not. He wrote Nelles that he felt sure the decision would be reversed on appeal (but admitted that perhaps he had been over-persuaded by the brief he had just written). This victory had been won by Darrow and Malone, and they should get the credit. He continued:

> I am quite willing to have conservative lawyers handle any case if that would be helpful. I am not willing to have conservative lawyers and conservative organizations reap the benefit of work done by liberals or radicals. I think the whole idea is wrong. I never yet found any conservative lawyer who, at the beginning, wanted to undertake a case which *might* reflect discredit upon him. When it turns out differently and there seems to be some publicity or honor to be had, then offers of assistance come in from all over the country. If, under such circumstances, the conservatives are going to be favored, I don't know how you are going to get men who are really interested in the thing itself to undertake these matters.

Nor did Hays think that the mere prominence of an attorney would influence the court. "If Hughes has a good case, he wins it, and he usually chooses good cases; if he has a bad case, he loses it." Hays' letter to Nelles concluded: "P.S. Forrest tells me that you feel the case should be brought into the realms of respectability. Why?"

Nelles wrote Hays to explain his position. From the beginning, he had agreed with Felix Frankfurter that, from the viewpoint of final success in the courts, the case needed a lawyer like Hughes. But he had thought that in the trial court the legal aspects were less important than the possibilities for educating the public. Now the situation had changed: the appellate courts offered limited chance for popular education. Of course lawyers with big names were handicaps more often than they were assets. But victory in this case depended on getting a lawyer who could symbolize that portion of the community whose approval the appellate judges would appreciate. Darrow could not be such a symbol.

The pressure on Bailey continued. John A. Ryan, director of the National Catholic Welfare Conference, declined to serve on the ACLU committee because he would not endorse the position that teachers had a right to expound anti-religious doctrines. D. Brewer Eddy, of the Congregationalists' American Board for Foreign Missions, wrote from Boston that in the building where he worked not one of the liberal Christians had a good word to say for Darrow's tactics. Eddy estimated that not 5 per cent of the Congregationalist clergy or membership would endorse Darrow's conduct. Bailey replied that the presence of Darrow and Malone in the case had indeed been unfortunate. He added that if the defense had been allowed to offer its witnesses, the viewpoint of liberal Christianity would have been heard.

And now Bailey sent to Darrow a copy of Nelles' letter to Hays. In a covering note, he assured Darrow that the idea for a committee of lawyers to handle the case was merely an effort to capitalize on Hughes' speech and did not indicate any dissatisfaction with the lawyers who had handled the trial. Bailey also complained to Darrow that he could get no information at all from John Neal, and asked if they should not pressure Neal to hire other Tennessee lawyers, such as Spurlock or Keebler. Darrow sent the suggestions to Arthur Hays and urged him to go down to Tennessee and see that another local lawyer was hired. Neal, wrote Darrow, was "absolutely hopeless." Two weeks later, on October 5, Bailey remembered that the case had a defendant. He wrote to Scopes, now studying at the University of Chicago, and urged him to go to Tennessee and force Neal to hire another lawyer. Scopes replied that he was too busy with his studies to make the trip. For his part, he reported, he had not heard anything from Neal since leaving Tennessee.

While these plots and counter-plots continued to abort, the attorney-general of Tennessee filed a motion with the supreme court to strike out the bill of exceptions. The grounds?—Neal had not filed the bill of exceptions within the 30 days allowed by Judge Raulston.

The facts were these. On the last day of the trial, Raulston had explained that he could allow up to 60 days to perfect an appeal. He preferred not to allow that much time because it would carry them past the next session of the supreme court. Finally he granted 30 days, but with the clear intimation that he would give the defense more time if necessary. Now the attorney-general claimed that somebody had tampered with the record of the trial by striking out "30" and inserting "60" days.

Raulston had also explained that "in Tennessee the bill of exceptions is just a copy of the evidence and proceedings and the judge's charge." So if the bill of exceptions were thrown out by the supreme court, the defense would no longer be able to challenge a single one of Judge Raulston's rulings during the trial: his ruling that court should open with prayer, that the scientific testimony was not proper, that Governor Peay's message approving the Butler Act was not pertinent. All of those times that Arthur Hays had gotten up to say "Exception" would go for nothing—because John Neal had not filed some papers on time.

While the defense anxiously awaited the court's decision on the bill of exceptions, it did make some progress. Spurlock agreed to help argue the case in the supreme court. Scopes wrote Bailey that perhaps the reason why the court had deferred the actual hearing on the appeal until after the election was because the judges planned to declare the Butler Act unconstitutional but would not risk losing their seats on the bench.

Less than two weeks before the election, the court threw out the bill of exceptions (152 Tenn. 424, 178 SW 57). The sole issue remaining for the appeal was the validity of the statute. This prompted Bailey to renew his efforts. He wrote Scopes that perhaps Spurlock and Neal should handle the case alone. Scopes replied that he was unable to get in touch with Darrow, who was now in Detroit in connection with the impending trial of twelve Negroes who had allegedly committed murder while defending their home against a white mob.

A month later, Neal was again expected in New York. Bailey went to meet him. Again Neal did not appear. This time he wired Bailey from Washington that he was forced to return at once to Tennessee to rescue the water of the state from the power trust. Simultaneously the Tennessee newspapers reported that the supreme court was about to throw Scopes' appeal out entirely because the assignment of errors had not been filed on time. With Neal, anything seemed possible. But this rumor proved false. The court had allowed until January 10, 1926, for filing the required papers and briefs. The prescribed deeds were done, and the case lapsed into quiescence until the hearings before the Tennessee supreme court in June, nearly a year after the trial.

Everything was quiet, that is, except fund-raising. Here was a major source of the ACLU anxiety. In 1925, the Tennessee Evolution Case Defense Fund had received as contributions only $2,075.53. It had a little income from other sources. But it had spent nearly $7,000, even though Darrow and the other attorneys had served without fee and had paid their own expenses. Two thirds of the expenditures had gone to pay court costs, fees of Tennessee lawyers, and the expenses of the expert witnesses who had been assembled from distant spots.

In June, 1925, before the trial, the ACLU had estimated that the case would require $10,000 even if it did not go to the United States Supreme Court. By August, Bailey was writing Charles Strong that the organization was endangering its general activities by tapping its customary sources for this special purpose; his appeal for Strong to suggest possible angels doubtless made him especially sensitive to Strong's criticism. In September Nelles suggested that the ACLU committee on the case needed to add some names redolent of money before it approached any big-name lawyers. Roger Baldwin made persistent efforts to enlist Raymond B.

Fosdick, a New York attorney who was close to Rockefeller, and was doubtless affected when Fosdick finally admitted that he would not serve on the committee because of the way the trial had been conducted by Scopes' attorneys. Likewise D. Brewer Eddy, Charles Nagel, a St. Louis lawyer, and a professor at Elmira College all implied that they would contribute, and raise, a lot more money if only Darrow were not running things.

The money did dribble in. Dudley Malone raised $1,350 himself by the time of the trial. The Slovenian National Benefit Society sent in $502 in September, 1925. But in 1926 the ACLU appealed to the members of the American Association for the Advancement of Science. A single mailing changed the former deficit into a substantial surplus. If churchmen and lawyers were upset by Darrow's tactics, evidently many scientists were not.

III

The brief submitted to the supreme court by the petitioner, Scopes, was largely a repetition of the points raised during the trial by the motion to quash the indictment: the Butler Act was invalid because it violated religious equality, violated the due-process and equal-protection clauses, was too vague and indefinite, was too arbitrary to be a valid police measure. The brief also sought to raise again the propriety of Judge Raulston's exclusion of the scientific testimony.

The defense did not challenge the right of the legislature to control the public schools, even to the extent of dropping biology from the curriculum, but denied that it could compel the teaching of false biology. To the contention that the case did not involve a religious question, the brief quoted from Governor Peay's message that the Butler Act upheld "faith in man's divine creation and the soul's immortality." The law not only gave a preference to the Protestant Bible over all others; it also favored the literalist sects over other Protestants. In *Watson* v. *Jones* (80 US 679, 728), the Supreme Court had said: "The law knows no heresy and is committed to the support of no dogma, the establishment of no sect."

A Tennessee law of 1915 required that ten verses from the Bible be read in class on each day of school. This meant that pupils would hear the Scriptural account of Creation. The Butler Act was a proscription of a conflicting account. This discrimination amounted to a "religious preference" established by law, in violation of the state constitution.

Pierce v. *Society of Sisters* (268 US 510) in 1925 had held: "Rights guaranteed by the Constitution may not be abridged by legislation which has no reasonable relation to some purpose within the competency of the State." The Butler Act was too fanciful to be related to any legitimate public purpose, and it clearly deprived Scopes of his rights to liberty and property. And who knew what it meant? The Bible gave various stories of Creation. The word "teach" could mean many things. If the word "order" were given its scientific meaning, man and monkeys belonged to the same order of animals, so who could tell what "lower order" intended?

These arguments for Scopes were castigated by the state's brief as "the fustian and specious pleading of our adversaries," "captious and quibbling criticism," "superficial and incomplete." This country, said the state, is a Christian nation, and proved it with a lengthy quotation from *Holy Trinity Church* v. *U. S.* (143 US 457). But the Butler Act did not raise any religious issue at all, since no religion taught that man had descended from a lower order of animals. Moreover, there is no valid evidence in support of evolution, which "now finds its chief protagonists in the realm of the *pseudo*-scientist and the disbelievers in continuing organized government."

The state's basic contention was simple: The Butler Act is one of a special class of laws governing the terms on which employees of the state shall render service to it. As such, it cannot be reviewed at all by any court. The leading case is *Atkin* v. *Kansas*

(191 US 207) which held: "it belongs to the State, as the guardian and trustee for its people, . . . to prescribe the conditions upon which it will permit public work to be done in its behalf . . . No Court has authority to review its actions in that respect." To the same effect were many other federal and state decisions.

Even if the Butler Act were not one of this special class of laws, it would still be a valid exercise of the police power. The state constitution withheld the right to public office from anybody who denied God or immortality. Only in 1895 had such disbelievers been given the right to testify in court, and some states still disqualified atheists in this regard. If the legislature could reasonably find that evolutionary doctrine "had some *tendency*" to make disbelievers of students, the court should sustain the law.

The views of education advanced by Scopes' attorneys were outrageous. Imagine saying that teachers did not have an obligation to explain to their students what "the *truth*" was. If this view were adopted, the public schools would be opened to "the doctrine of communism, . . . of Bolshevism, of 'Free Love' or 'Free Thought' or 'Free Property.'" The defense brief had even dared to cite J. B. Bury's *History of the Freedom of Thought,* in which was made the "perverted and repulsive statement" that true education depends on reasoning from evidence rather than acceptance of authority. The state's brief was particularly exercised by Bury's conclusion that "in this sense it might be said that 'Distrust thy father and mother' is the first commandment with promise." To show the heinous effects of atheistic education, the state quoted those passages of Bryan's undelivered speech that had quoted and commented on Darrow's argument in the Loeb-Leopold case.

The only novel argument advanced in the brief for Scopes had been a contention that the Butler Act "impaired the obligation of contracts," contrary to the federal Constitution, Art. I, Sec. 10. Under the federal Hatch Act, Congress appropriated funds to each state for agricultural experiment stations that would "permit scientific investigation and experiment respecting the principles and applications of agricultural science." Acceptance of these funds by the Tennessee legislature had finalized a contract. As evidence that the Butler Act infringed Tennessee's obligation, the petitioner cited the testimony proffered at the trial by Jacob Lipman. The state brief replied to this argument by saying that Congress, in the Morrill Act of 1862, had specified that the legislature of each state should determine the "manner" of teaching the prescribed subjects.

The *amicus curiae* briefs that opposed the Butler Act added little to the main brief for Scopes. The one prepared by Charles H. Strong for the Unitarian Laymen's League was diffuse and meandering. More significant was the one for the Tennessee Academy of Science: significant for its contents (parallel to those advanced by petitioner), for its authors (four Tennessee attorneys), for its sponsorship, and for its list of "leading ministers of this State," including two Episcopal bishops and the dean of Vanderbilt's school of religion, who had condemned the Butler Act. Counsel for Scopes also filed a supplemental brief, which amounted less to a rebuttal of the state's arguments than to a repetition of their own.

Thus matters stood when the oral argument was had in Nashville on June 1, 1926. Nearly a year had passed since the trial, and several Tennessee lawyers now rallied to Scopes' side. In their arguments before the supreme court, the local attorneys especially emphasized the vagueness of the statute—a ground that was regarded as convenient for the court if it wished to invalidate the statute while avoiding offense to fundamentalist sentiment.

Even the atmosphere of the state capitol could not impose utter dignity. Counsel for the state cited the attacks on the ACLU in the report of the Lusk Committee, and ironically it was Darrow who defended the ACLU and said the Committee "was intensely partisan and thoroughly discredited." E. T. Seay, special counsel for the state, told of a certain father who had been grievously hurt when his small son came home from school questioning the story of Creation, and it was Darrow who quipped: "It is seldom

that a railroad lawyer makes me cry in that way." Then Darrow
became serious. He felt sorry, he said, for any father who
learned that science disproved the "ancient legends" that he believed.

> But what of it? I am sorry for the poor Chinese
> father whose religion and whose feelings the missionaries
> ignore when they go to China and teach the children
> that their religion is a fable . . .
> But life is full of awakenings, and the life of a
> child is nothing but learning and finding out. It is get-
> ting rid of illusions and delusions from whatever source
> they come . . . It may be that a little learning is a
> dangerous thing and a great deal of learning is fatal, but
> in spite of that, as long as man has an inquiring mind he
> will seek to know and to find out. He is bound to do it.
> And every child ought to be more intelligent than
> his parents.

Darrow ranged over all the arguments against the Butler Act. He
analyzed the main precedents used by the state, contending that
a law banning evolution was much different from a law prohibiting public contractors from working their men more than eight
hours a day. Of course a state has the right to regulate its employees, but the regulations cannot be capricious.

He was sportive with the Supreme Court's decision in the
Trinity Church case. An act of Congress prohibited American
employers from making contracts about conditions of work with
workingmen who were still residing abroad. Trinity Church had
contracted with a preacher in England to come to this country.
Did the contract-labor law ban this transaction? "If I had been
on the Court," said Darrow, "I would have taken judicial notice
that it didn't because I think a preacher is not a workingman . . ."

The tone of Darrow's argument did nothing to reduce the
misgivings of the ACLU leaders. As the state supreme court took
the case under advisement, Baldwin and Bailey faced the possibility of an appeal to the Supreme Court of the United States.

They were dismayed by the thought of Darrow there. Baldwin objected vehemently to raising money for a case that was being handled in a disagreeable way. He would see Darrow, but only if it were decided definitely who had the right to select counsel for any further appeal.

The decision ultimately was up to Scopes, who was spending the summer in southern Illinois doing research on glacial geology for the state geological survey. Early in August he visited Chicago and saw Darrow. He then wrote Bailey a note that must have chilled the recipient's soul. From the very beginning of the case, wrote Scopes, we have been trying to get a conservative lawyer. Isn't this, he asked, rather cowardly? Any radical program is best prosecuted by radicals. The right thing to do is to state your position candidly, as had been done at Dayton. For his part, wrote Scopes, he hoped that matters would continue in the same way, even if a change of personnel was made.

The ACLU leaders had been persistently oblivious to the nature of the man they were dealing with. This was no blue-eyed stripling. During the trial he had impressed everybody by his moderation, his dignity, his humor. The enormous publicity had not inflated his ego a whit. He had turned down all sorts of offers—cash offers—to succumb to sensationalism; instead he had chosen to attend graduate school and work for the geological survey.

As with Clarence Darrow and William Jennings Bryan, so with Scopes: he was the son of his father. Thomas Scopes, 65 years old, had grown up in London a Presbyterian. After migration to the United States he became a railroad mechanic, working for a time at Lincoln's town (and Bryan's) of Salem, Illinois. He joined in the Pullman strike of 1894, and was blacklisted for it. This last sequence, reported his son, was repeated several times. Thomas Scopes became a socialist, an admirer of Eugene Debs. He said in 1925 that he didn't know anything about Heaven-and-Hell Christianity. "But I do believe what Christ taught—that God is love and love is God," he said. "That's how I try to live."

These facts had been used to denounce the defendant even

before the trial opened, but the ACLU leaders did not draw any implications. They continued their efforts to get Darrow and Hays to withdraw, and the weeks of waiting became months, and still no decision by the state supreme court. It was finally announced on January 14, 1927, more than seven months after oral argument. And when it came, it was bewildering.

Of the five justices, one was new to the bench and did not take part in the decision. Chief Justice Green, for himself and *one* justice, upheld the Butler Act, construing it precisely as had Stewart and Judge Raulston at the trial. The statute was sufficiently clear; so was the indictment. Since the law was one of the special class of laws prescribing the terms on which service should be rendered to the state, due-process provisions did not apply. The clause of the state constitution requiring the legislature "to cherish literature and science" was merely directory and too vague for a court to enforce. (But the Butler Act was clear enough.) The statute did not give a religious preference, since "so far as we know, there is no religious establishment or organized body that has in its creed or confession of faith any article denying or affirming" that man had descended from a lower order of animals. (An amazing statement: the *amicus* brief of the Tennessee Academy of Science had quoted a resolution adopted by the Southern Baptist Convention at Houston in 1926 which repudiated "as unscriptural and scientifically false every claim of evolution that declared or implies that man evolved to his present state from some lower order of life.") Moreover, while the law banned from the public schools all statements that man had descended from a lower order of life, the teaching of a contrary theory was not prescribed legally; the required Bible reading "could scarcely be said" to have that effect.

So much from 40 per cent of the court. Justice Chambliss, another 20 per cent, also upheld the Butler Act, but he straitly confined its meaning. Accepting the distinction between "theistic" and "materialistic" theories of evolution, he held that the law banned only the latter. So long as evolution did not deny that God had played *some* role in man's creation, it could legally be taught in the public schools. Not enough, said the dissenting Justice McKinney, who held that the entire Butler Act was "invalid for uncertainty of meaning."

It thus seemed that the court (or 40 per cent of it) had affirmed the banning of even theistic evolution from the public schools. This was rather confusing, but the court further compounded it. The three justices who had upheld the statute now focused on the fact that Judge Raulston had imposed the minimum fine of $100 allowed by the law. But the state constitution required that any fine of more than $50 must be imposed by the jury. So the judgment was reversed.

The reversal on this ground would, in itself, have outraged Scopes' lawyers; the question of who should impose the fine had been discussed at length during the trial, and they had agreed not to raise the issue on appeal, and indeed they had not done so. But the court went further yet. "We see nothing to be gained," said the chief justice's opinion, "by prolonging the life of this bizarre case." It was therefore suggested to the attorney-general that he should enter a *nolle prosequi,* that is, just drop the indictment and forget the whole thing, instead of bringing Scopes to trial again as would have been customary in these circumstances.

Scopes' lawyers bleated loudly. Some of them said the decision would be appealed to the United States Supreme Court. But the state supreme court had outflanked them completely. The statute was upheld, and the entry of a *nolle prosequi* would throw the case out of the courts entirely and would leave no way for Scopes to get back into the courts. Arthur Hays said with chagrined admiration: "We are dealing with astute church people in that case, and I guess we did not credit them with the astuteness that they really possessed." And so it happened that the state supreme court denied motions for a new hearing, and the *nolle prosequi* was entered, and the Scopes case had ended, and even the pompous yelps of John Randolph Neal could not revive it.

This ironic conclusion speaks of a lack of realism in those

who had wanted to handle the case as a strictly constitutional issue. If this approach had been used, all would have been lost and nothing gained. Darrow's broadside offensive, which he had pressed not in the ways he had chosen but in the ways Judge Raulston left open to him, had at least created a situation in which Arthur Hays could say: "Tennessee will never try to enforce that law again, because it is afraid of a test case. The anti-evolution law in that State is dead, and the people of the country learned more about evolution through the Dayton exhibition than they could have in any other way." Far less perceptive was the final statement of John Neal: "To me personally and the Civil Liberties Union, the case was neither a religious nor scientific controversy, but a fight for civil liberty." But of course it was all three, and the three were inseparable.

The same objection applies to the *New Republic*'s contention that the Butler Act was clearly unwise but clearly constitutional. The wisdom of the law and its constitutionality cannot be split so cleanly. The constitutional criterion, said Charles Evans Hughes in his speech to the American Bar Association, is whether a law regulating courses of instruction "has relation to a legitimate object within the State power and is not to be condemned as arbitrary and capricious." The *amicus* brief of the Tennessee Academy of Science urged exactly this objection: "The statute is unconstitutional because it is an unreasonable, arbitrary and capricious misuse by the legislature of the public funds."

To say this is not to say that the United States Supreme Court as it existed in 1927 would have invalidated the Butler Act. The record of Justices McReynolds, Sanford (both Tennesseans), Sutherland, Butler, and Van Devanter, and perhaps Chief Justice Taft, is ample to shatter any blithe presumption as to the outcome. It is also ample to expand the original proposition: Neither in logic nor in the actual decisions of courts can we sharply sever the constitutional from the wise.

IV

A recent student, Norman F. Furniss, has pointed to Bryan's death as an important cause of the decline of fundamentalism, since it left the movement without a nationally known figure to inspire and unify it. But the facts can be seen quite otherwise: Nothing hurt fundamentalism as much as Bryan's spiritual death at Darrow's hands, while his physical death acted to rejuvenate the movement by giving it a symbol of Christian martyrdom which could be used in appealing to the free-floating guilt of many Southerners. Certain it is that the anti-evolution campaign spurted ahead in some states right after Bryan's death.

In Texas, Governor Miriam Ferguson, as head of the state textbook commission, laid down the policy of selecting only those biology texts that contained no mention of evolution. The commission adopted Truman J. Moon's *Biology for Beginners*, but only on condition that three chapters dealing with evolution be eliminated; contracts permitting the deletion of offensive passages were arranged with such publishers as Henry Holt and Allyn and Bacon. The commission also threatened to dismiss any teacher using books that had not been approved.

The form of the fundamentalist upsurge after Bryan's death suggests again that the crusade against evolution consisted of a tiny but organized minority, playing on the vague fears of voters and the more specific fears of politicians. In January, 1926, the Supreme Kingdom was founded at Atlanta by Edgar Young Clark, once the highly successful membership director of the Ku Klux Klan—forced out by the Klan's moralists for good reason: indicted in 1922 for using the mails to defraud, then found to be living in sin with a colleague, arrested in 1923 for violating the Mann Act. Clark hired a former business manager for Billy Sunday to promote the organization, and he imported John Roach Straton from Brooklyn to give 60 lectures on evolution for a fee of $30,000 (not all the Yankee invaders of the South were agnostics). When the Macon *Telegraph* revealed that Clark was pocketing two thirds of every $12.50 initiation fee, the Supreme Kingdom disintegrated.

More successful were the Bible Crusaders of America, formed in November, 1925, with substantial financing from a friend of Bryan. George F. Washburn, although he made his winter home in Florida, was a Northern millionaire who had made his money in real estate and hotel operations. The Crusaders' director of campaigns was T. T. Martin, the wild-eyed white-haired man who looked a religious fanatic—but was not. Early in 1925, trying to win a $50 prize, he had entered an essay contest on the topic: "Why Evolution Should Be Taught in Our Schools Instead of the Book of Genesis." He entered his contribution under a false name, but was unmasked.

In February, 1926, when an anti-evolution bill seemed to be beaten in the Mississippi legislature, Martin hurried to Jackson to stimulate popular support, and drummed up so much that he was invited to address the legislature. The bill was passed by ample margins, signed by the governor, and the local papers credited this result to Martin. He then swept on to Louisiana, where a committee of the house had pigeonholed an anti-evolution measure. The bill was reported out, and the house passed it 52 to 43. But it was narrowly defeated in the senate, chiefly because the New Orleans *Times-Picayune* at the last minute bestirred itself to a sharp denunciation.

The other state to tardily adopt an anti-evolution law was Arkansas. A bill passed the house by 3 votes in 1927, but was tabled in the senate. Ben Bogard, a Baptist minister, then led a campaign for a referendum at the 1928 election. When the voters in November approved the bill by 108,000 to 63,000, the administrative officials in the public schools withdrew from use any textbook that might be offensive. But representatives of major student organizations at the University of Arkansas had publicly opposed the measure, saying: "We do not want to be laughed at, as are the graduates of the University of Tennessee, and practically boycotted by larger universities and medical schools when we seek to pursue our education further."

Isolated and transient victories were scored elsewhere during 1926 and 1927: Cleveland, Ohio; Mecklenburg County, North Carolina; Paducah, Kentucky; the public school system of Louisiana; Baylor University and Oklahoma Baptist. But important church groups emerged to attack the anti-evolution movement. In October, 1925, the Central Conference of American Rabbis called for complete freedom of scientific investigation. In 1927 the Education Association of the Southern Methodists almost unanimously opposed "all legislation that would interfere with the proper teaching of science in American schools and colleges," and even rejected an amendment disavowing "the agnostic Darrow."

Darrow had provided a major weapon against the fundamentalists—ridicule. Will Rogers, who was in Arkansas when the legislature was considering a bill in 1927, commented: "I don't know why some of these states want to have their ancestry established by law. There must be a suspicion of a doubt somewhere." An anti-evolution bill in Missouri in 1927 met with laughter in the legislature. A sponsor of the measure received a letter from one of his Ozarks constituents which read: "About all you are fit for is to hunt possums and coons. . . . You ought to slink back to Coon Hollow and not try to disgrace the State of Missouri with your ignorance." An anti-evolution bill in Kentucky met with a companion measure requiring that water in the state should run uphill.

By 1927, except for the anachronism in Arkansas, the tide had run out. Oklahoma, which had been in 1923 the first state to ban Darwinism, repealed its law in 1925 and the legislature defeated a bill two years later. Virginia in 1926, Florida, Delaware, West Virginia, California, North Dakota, Minnesota, New Hampshire, and Maine in 1927—all these states saw anti-evolution bills beaten easily. The World's Christian Fundamentals Association was in the doldrums. Alleged offenses by professors in 1927 were refreshingly various: at Winthrop College, South Carolina, one was fired for modernism; the State Normal College at West Chester, Pennsylvania, fired one for criticizing Coolidge's policy in Nicaragua; Northwestern dismissed a history instructor for his religious views; the University of Washington fired an instructor who read to his classes from Bertrand Russell's "What I Believe"; and Columbia was asked to fire Carlton J. H. Hayes for being unpatriotic. Market-oriented agitators like Gerald Winrod in Kansas began to spice their denunciations of evolution with attacks on Jews and Catholics. Subversion even penetrated to the heart of the temple: a newly chosen dean of the Bible Institute of Los Angeles, the stronghold of conservative theology on the West Coast, "delivered himself most unfortunately [wailed the *Christian Fundamentalist*] concerning the evolution controversy."

Certainly the events at Dayton do not alone account for the decline of the anti-evolution movement. In 1926, for instance, prohibition again became an issue, and many conservatives among the Southern Baptists and elsewhere diverted their energies to that cause. But many types of evidence suggest that the Scopes trial was crucial for rallying the opposition to fundamentalism and repression.

The financial facts are indicative. All told, the Tennessee Evolution Case Defense Fund expended $8,993.01. But contributions to it were $11,328.63. When the Fund was dissolved, $561.29 was returned to contributors, while the remaining surplus of $1,868.03 was transferred to the ACLU to be used in fighting other academic-freedom cases. (These figures fail, by slightly less than $100, to add up properly; the failure is inconsequential here.) In addition, the committee headed by David Starr Jordan, former president of Stanford, made a sizable grant to the graduate education of John Thomas Scopes.

Many contemporaries gave Darrow credit for arousing the public. Sir Arthur Keith, president in 1927 of the British Association for the Advancement of Science, called Darrow "a great defender of Liberty." Fay-Cooper Cole, one of the scientific witnesses at Dayton, said in April, 1927: "Mr. Darwin once wrote: 'It is my fondest hope to make people think.' Mr. Darrow has achieved Mr. Darwin's aim." Such papers as the Newark *News* said the Scopes trial had aroused much wider and more intense interest in evolution. In 1925 and 1926 Darrow lectured about evolution in many cities; at Erie, Pennsylvania, the local paper said that his audience was probably larger than had ever attended any lecture there.

More important was the 42-minute motion picture, "The Mystery of Life," distributed by Universal Pictures in 1931. Running over much of the same ground as the scientific testimony at Dayton, the film basically offered first-rate nature photography from this country and Europe. It was designed by H. M. Parshley, head of the zoology department at Smith College, to illustrate the theory of evolution, and Parshley and Darrow appeared in it as narrators. Whether for its visual impact, or for Darrow, or for the disgustingly lurid promotion by Universal, the movie was well received.

Many reviews in the daily press were enthusiastic. In New York, the *Times* called it "excellent in the way it presents its material," while the *Mirror* found it "neither stiff nor patronizing." In Baltimore it drew strong endorsements from the *Post* and the *Sun*. At the Alhambra Theater in Philadelphia it was "going strong" in its third week. At the Capital in Atlanta it did a "record week's business." It was greeted cordially at Knoxville, where the *Journal* said: "Many of the scenes were wonderfully portrayed, especially those that showed the development of the various forms of plant and animal life." The review urged everybody to see it, "whether evolutionists or fundamentalists." Of Darrow's performance the *Journal* reported: "He takes a few slaps at Tennessee and its evolution trial at Dayton, but the guests of yesterday were amused rather than offended." But when the film was booked by a Dayton theater in July, 1931, the local ministerial association called for a boycott of the "anti-Biblical and anti-Christian" picture. This resolution reflected the shift in social issues: it denounced Darrow as a "notorious agnostic and one openly advocating the breaking and defying of our national prohibition laws."

Darrow visited Dayton a few years after the trial, and when he got out of his automobile in front of the Aqua Hotel, the first thing he saw was a new church that had just been completed across the street. "I didn't do much good here after all!" he quipped. The Scopes case had little effect on religious views in Dayton. Scopes left town. A few months later Rappelyea moved to New Orleans, telling the ACLU: "I couldn't stay in Dayton after the trial. I would have been as lonely as the ark of truth on Mt. Sinai." Fred E. Robinson, druggist and head of the school board, said 25 years after the trial that Dayton had developed a greater interest in the outside world and in reading; but, he added, while folks read more science, they also read the Bible more, so that they were "more deeply religious than ever before."

Bryan University was started in 1930 in an abandoned high school. Five years later it began a building, but funds ran out after the stone and concrete foundation was set into a hilltop. Classes met in makeshift rooms in this basement. Tobacco and liquor were banned, and applicants for admission had to take a loyalty oath to literalism. In 1935 eleven students were expelled for drinking wine down in the cherry orchard. Of the 90 students enrolled in 1939-40, only 13 per cent were Tennesseans.*

In the state as a whole, religion declined after the Scopes trial, perhaps partly because of it. In May, 1926, for instance, the county school board at Chattanooga discontinued the Bible classes in the public schools, and also stopped giving academic credit for religious study. From 1926 to 1936, the membership of churches in Tennessee dropped more than 10 per cent. This decline was concentrated in the more evangelical denominations, the Methodists losing 60,000 members, the Baptists 40,000.

Darrow made friends even of eastern Tennesseans. Robert S. Keebler, who met Darrow during the trial and became one of Scopes' attorneys in the state supreme court, came to feel both

---

* Present enrollment is about 300.

respect and affection for Darrow. More amusing is the case of Ben McKenzie, who was writing fond notes to Darrow within two weeks after the trial ended. The following February, McKenzie was arrested in Spring City, Rhea County, for allegedly violating the liquor laws. Darrow promptly offered to defend him. McKenzie replied that it was all a frame-up because his son was running for county judge; besides, the liquid taken from him by the policeman was not an intoxicant at all.

Two months after the Scopes trial, a liberal at Bristol predicted that Governor Peay could be beaten for re-election because of the Butler Act and an unpopular tobacco tax. This prediction was awry; Peay was chosen to a third term in 1926. (He prevented further tests of his popularity by dying.) John T. Raulston, however, was beaten in his effort that year to remain on the bench. Tom Stewart had an eminent career, being elected to the United States Senate in 1938 by what was, wrote Virginius Dabney, "one of the rankest exhibitions of patronage jobbery the country has seen."

Over the years the Tennessee legislature repeatedly defeated efforts to repeal the Butler Act. In 1951, a repealer was introduced by the representative from Rhea County, but without success. The statute remains on the books. But, as Arthur Hays predicted, no further effort has ever been made to enforce it, and it has had little lasting effect on educational practice. Instructors of science soon bootlegged Darwinism back into their lectures, sometimes not as "evolution" but as "organic development." The Butler Act still stands, a sweeping gesture of mass expiation.

Chapter 11

Some Perspectives

> Evolution has no purpose; man
> must supply this for himself.
>
> George Gaylord Simpson, *The
> Meaning of Evolution*, rev. (New
> York: New American Library,
> 1951), p. 155

I

In considering the ritual aspects of the Scopes trial, we should know what elements of ritual are pertinent, and realize how they permeate human life from childhood to death.

The first element is fixity of pattern. Watch young boys at a film about cowboys and Indians. Every Saturday afternoon they go together, sit alike, clap simultaneously, while watching the inevitable sequence of evil men, wagon train, Indian attack, the circled wagons, the death of the evil men. Adults regard such films as incitements to aggressiveness, or as stereotyping Indians, or simply as dull because so predictable. But to alter the pattern would be like juggling with a High Mass. The boys are participating in a ritual victory of good over evil.

And they participate by acting together. Ritual needs physical gestures performed by all participants. Consider a sequence in E. M. Forster's *A Room with a View*. Two young English travelers, Lucy Honeychurch and George Emerson, witness a killing in the Piazza Signoria in Florence. They then walk along by the river, stop, each leans his elbows on the parapet and looks into the water. Forster comments: "There is at times a magic in identity of position; it is one of the things that have suggested to us eternal comradeship."

A function of ritual is to create this sense of joint commitment to a transcendent cause. But common performance of physical gestures is no guarantee that those gestures have a common meaning to all participants. To illustrate, a visitor to the construction site of a church asked several bricklayers what they were doing. So far as could be seen, all were doing exactly the same thing. Yet the first replied that he was laying bricks; the second said that he was earning his wages; the third claimed to be building a cathedral as a monument to God. We may surmise that the third man, who acted from the deeper meaning, found in his actions the deeper satisfaction.

So with the Scopes trial. The fundamentalist spectators were as similar as if they had all been kneeling in church. They applauded in unison. They were together, in eternal comradeship, worshipping God. Bryan even imagined that the trial could be held to a fixed pattern, not realizing how the ritual of the law would scramble the ritual of the revival. He anticipated the whole event as predestined; the witnesses would testify, he would give his exegesis, Scopes would be convicted. Perhaps Scopes would even repent; surely thousands of persons in the courtroom and outside would fling off the trammels of a living death and join the crusade to redeem the world. The air was scented with hopes of rebirth: the commercial rebirth of Dayton, the political rebirth of William Jennings Bryan, the spiritual rebirth of countless backsliders. The one rebirth that actually occurred was that of John Thomas Scopes—into a trained scientist.

The theme of rebirth is not limited to religious observances and the initiation rites of fraternal orders. It appears in criminal law in our provisions for parole. It occurs in civil law in the approval of bankruptcy and of bankruptcy's near relative, divorce. It is the core of the promise offered by psychoanalysis. The Christian promise to redeem the soul shares it with the socialist promise to redeem society.* It may be seen in the political slogans that have

---

* In 1949 I published a biography of Eugene Debs. It was called *The Bending Cross,* and the title page quoted his speech: "Let the people take heart and hope

swept three Presidents into the White House—the New Freedom, the New Deal, the Fair Deal.

The last two of these slogans, like their antecedent the Square Deal, would have been less appealing in the 19th century, when many fewer Americans would have agreed that life was a game of cards in which the ruling factor was Chance. But in the new world where nothing seems stable, where the terms of every situation are incessantly shifting, where the rule is frustration because the sequences that would lead to achievement cannot be found, in such a world men find it even more essential to sometimes participate together in a fixed pattern of actions leading to a foreseen end, and thus to renew their feeling of common emotions and common hopes. Ritual is a way to meet this need. A deeply felt ritual provides communion, and a feeling of communion brings sanity. William Jennings Bryan, by his inchoate perception of the need for ritual, pointed to a need of every society and of all individuals. Behavior and feeling flow into and through each other, and the feeling of our common humanity will not last long nor work deeply where there are no shared ways to express it. And in all except a few happy ages of history, the most gripping rituals are auguries of rebirth; typically the ordinary man is so tortured by his life that he hopes above all else to be born into a better one.

Since the Scopes trial was meant largely as a traditional ritual, the South was the fitting site. William Faulkner is only the most famous of the many Southern writers who have protested against the passing of the old order and the rise of the new. If his traditionalism, so fanged against the New South, is vague as to its grounds of attachment to the preceding society, John Crowe Ransom and other poets are coherent in their longing for the bygone kinship and for the rituals that expressed and sustained it. Modern man, while becoming isolated and atomized, has also lost his grace and his sense of the right way of doing things. Matter

---

everywhere, for the cross is bending, the midnight is passing, and joy cometh with the morning." A prominent socialist who is also a minister complained that the title was obscure.

and manner have dissolved together, for matter depends upon manner, upon manners.

In this, Bryan saw better than his modernist critics who have supposed that ritual is an incubus upon religion. Bryan's insight is stated, more cogently than Bryan stated it, in *The Magic Mountain* when Hans Castorp appraises the devout and the free-thinking ways of thought: "They both have their good sides; what I have against Settembrini's—the free-thinking line—is that he seems to imagine it has a corner in human dignity. That's exaggerated, I consider, because the other has its own kind of dignity too, and makes for a tremendous lot of decorum and correct bearing and uplifting ceremony; more, in fact, than the free-thinking, when you remember it has our human infirmity and proneness to err directly in mind, and thoughts of death and decay play such an important role in it."

Man should be devout toward life and toward other men, and he needs the ritual that pullulates from this sense of solidarity. Since the advent of capitalism this feeling for others has been so rare and sporadic that man has been unable to create any new rituals. The initiation rites of the thousands of so-called fraternal groups are a shabby pretense and do not fool, or satisfy, or rejuvenate, the participants in them. The existing rituals that touch large social groups date from at least the feudal era, and they cannot be indefinitely preserved. The meaning has gone out of them. Some expressed too narrow a kinship, as the Southern kinship was limited to respectable white folks, or as the rituals of patriotism are often manipulated for the cause of chauvinism. Others are laced through with beliefs that cannot stand against present knowledge. The modern mind is not the feudal mind, and Bryan's pathetic fate shows the folly of any attempt to pretend that it is.

II

The Butler Act rested on the belief that truth can be determined by taking a vote. Discussing this aspect of the affair in 1927, Walter Lippmann made a devastating attack on the premise.

Majority rule, he contended, is nothing more than a device for settling practical questions that must be settled, and it is preferable to other devices only because it is less disruptive of social order, only because it requires less coercion than do the alternatives.

But the contention of the fundamentalists was rooted in a century of the American democratic tradition. Even though Thomas Jefferson, not Andrew Jackson, founded the spoils system, he never doubted that the offices responsible for policy making should be filled by men whose careers and characters fitted them for exercising that responsibility wisely. Jefferson showed his beliefs in founding the Virginia Dynasty, which occupied the White House for 24 years as his lieutenants Madison and Monroe ascended through a fixed sequence of jobs to the Presidency. It was left for Jackson to proclaim, in his first annual message, "The duties of all public offices are . . . so plain and simple . . . No one man has any more intrinsic right to official station than another."

This view that one man's opinion is as good as another's on any topic came to be almost dogma among the more democratic American parties, the challenges of it coming from the conservatives. If Bryan propagated the Jacksonian bias, so did Clarence Darrow. Darrow repeatedly declared that colleges were worse than useless, since they destroyed compassion without imparting wisdom. In his memorial address for Altgeld, Darrow said that one reason for his hero's greatness was that he had never suffered the misfortune of being educated. The view that education counts for nothing persists to our own day, when we find the pro-segregation statement of 96 Southern Congressmen saying: "parents should not be deprived by Government of the right to direct the lives and education of their own children." Smart politics this is, but foolish doctrine: rare indeed are the parents competent to direct the education of their children in even one subject. The only worthy objective of the schools is to produce children who are better informed, and wiser, than their parents.

But the overwhelming pressure of society is against this.

Men must have a frame of orientation and devotion, and most men never question the frames that were taught them in childhood. Belief is much easier than disbelief, as Bagehot pointed out; rejection of an oft-heard idea requires more evidence, and more effort, than acceptance of it. Rejection is especially rare in closed societies like the rural South, where the frame was consistent and unvaried, where it was persistently hammered home, where competing frames were seldom heard. For most Southerners a suspension of judgment was almost impossible, and when they had judged they tended to become intolerant of other judgments. They wanted their children to think as they did.

Yet this needs a major qualification. Bagehot also saw that the average man wears his beliefs lightly, that he can cheer one opinion this minute and a conflicting opinion the next, that he is in fact *almost* indifferent to nearly every question.

Thus we reach other defects in the usual theory of majority rule. The voting records in American elections suggest on their face that a majority almost never exists, that most people are not concerned enough to vote. If we do not stop at counting heads, but seek to gauge the strength of feelings in the several hearts, the point becomes stronger. It seems possible that there has been no issue in our politics in this century, not even the decisions on entry into World Wars I and II, that moved a majority of the American people to clear-cut and deeply held convictions. The point becomes stronger yet if we realize that most people hold opinions that point to conflicting decisions on most questions. *Should we enter the war? Well, this country is the best there is, and I want it to be the strongest there is, and the price of corn would go up, and Germans are no good, but even Germans are human, and the Bible says thou shalt not kill, and my three sons would have to go in the Army, and I'd have a terrible time hiring hands, and gas for the truck would be hard to get.* These thoughts are all present in one man, all are relevant to the issue, but they are not all active. Which ones become active depends on the leadership he is subjected to.

We have been slow to admit this. When we seek to export democracy, the commodity we offer is the political system we like to pretend we have, not the one we do have. Meanwhile our practice has run ahead, and we are not without instruments for measuring the intensity of feeling on different sides of a question. But we are usually ashamed of such devices as the lobby and the filibuster. Democracy cannot function without lobbying groups, and the supposed objections to the filibuster are not directed against it at all. When a score of segregationist Senators are able to thwart the professed desires of a much larger number of integrationists, this merely shows that the minority can throw into the scales a greater quantum of dedication than the majority. The actual fault is not that the Senate rules allow filibusters, but is rather that the white supremacists are grossly overrepresented while the Negroes, who hold opposing views with equal or greater intensity, are grossly and illegally underrepresented.

In our urge to abstract and quantify we make each vote count as one, and we suppose that all fundamentalists were alike. They were not. As a corrective to Bryan there is Ben McKenzie, the easygoing buffoon. The Scopes trial, to him, was hardly an effort to enforce the will of God; it was more like an effort to expiate God, to copper a bet on Heaven, if indeed God cared about such matters as the teaching of Darwinism. The whole episode was a Sunday-go-to-meeting substitute for reform. McKenzie's emotional investment in the trial was trivial; even at the minimal task of going through the right motions, his lapses were frequent.

But common is the idea of a Solid South: solid in politics, on Negro-white relations, on religion. In this view the Butler Act was the product of a determined and deeply religious majority, who saw evolution as a threat to their religious and ethical views. The facts are recalcitrant. The Scopes case was begun mainly for commercial reasons, fostered partly for political ones. The foreman of the grand jury that indicted Scopes was an evolutionist. Most of the veniremen said they had never thought about evolution at all. The schoolboy witnesses were so reluctant to testify that they fled to the woods. Their mothers said that they wanted the boys to learn about evolution. John Washington Butler made the same statement about his children, and he was sorry that Judge Raulston would not let the scientists testify. Two of the jurors were reluctant to convict, and did so only on Darrow's urging. The state supreme court labelled the case "bizarre" and killed it. Since 1925 no indictment has been brought under the law.

A veteran Tennessee journalist, basing his conclusion on wide travel and interviews, said on the eve of the trial that almost half of the state's population wanted the Butler Act invalidated by the courts, while a slightly larger group wanted it sustained, including some evolutionists who wanted it repealed by the legislature but who thought the legislature had a right to pass it and who feared an extension of judicial power over legislative discretion. This seems a reasonable summary—if we add that few people on either side cared much. If the Butler Act was a majority measure at all, this was true only in the sense that most voters would have affirmed it in a referendum, and even here the result may have been different on a secret ballot from the one secured on voice votes in the legislature and the state supreme court.

No law moves a majority, and the minority excited about the Butler Act was very small. The great mischief done by Bryan and the fundamentalists was to raise the issue at all, to force people to choose between religion and science or else to find some way to reconcile the two. Even persons who had grown cool in their religious faith were likely to plunk for it if put to the test. Probably God did exist. Maybe there was to be a Last Judgment, an eternal state of rewards and punishments. At least it could do no harm to vote that way. The childhood training of most Tennesseans, the full thrust of their upbringing, their loyalty to the ways of their fathers, were in that direction. They had no similar loyalty to reason and science, which still are bloodless abstractions to the great majority of mankind. Bryan used the popular education of the parents to undermine and negate the education of the children.

Which is only to recognize how many men live in the spirit of Pascal's well-known wager that even skeptics should bet on God because it costs them nothing and may bring some benefits.

This is a sobering context in which to appraise the criticisms of Darrow's strategy. Perhaps negation of the Butler Act by the courts would have been neater and more dignified than the hurly-burly of popular agitation. But nobody could be sure in 1925 that the Supreme Court would invalidate the Butler Act. And should the court intervene in cases of this kind? Certainly one tenet of democracy is that issues of policy will be resolved by the electoral process and by elective officials, not by appointive judges. Even ignoring this, can the courts settle issues where two sizable groups of voters meet in head-on conflict? The legal rights of trade unionism were settled, not by a century of judicial interference, but by new laws and by changes in public opinion (and in union strength) that largely preceded the laws. Fifty years of Supreme Court decisions in favor of the separate-but-equal doctrine failed to settle the issue of Negro rights, and the Court's recent reversal of the doctrine will not be the chief element of a solution in many parts of the South. Court decisions may be influential, even vitally so, but that is no reason to rely on them exclusively. The Supreme Court itself is often reluctant to trespass in the area of policy; it recognizes that, by doing so, it may prejudice its authority in less controversial areas (as the recent decisions on segregation show vividly).

By this measure, Clarence Darrow was more realistic, and more democratic, than his constitutionalist and modernist critics. While he was not indifferent to judges, he cared more for popular opinion. He was frankly seeking converts to the cause of science and intellectual freedom. He never believed that he could enlist a majority of Southerners, nor did he think this necessary. From the beginning he regarded the Butler Act as the fruit of a noisome minority that had spiritually intimidated a vapid majority. Darrow ignored the majority. He concentrated on activating a minority that would equal in fervor the minority led by Bryan. Given a thousand persons in the state who opposed the Butler Act with the dedication and intelligence of John Thomas Scopes, the undignified and bizarre trial at Dayton might never have occurred at all.

Darrow has also been faulted on the score that, by ridiculing fundamentalism, he helped to "make compromise impossible." Presumably this means that, if you tell a man why his views are absurd, you only confirm him in them. Even if this were true, you might be able to keep him from imposing his absurd views on everybody else, which was the issue at Dayton. Although these critics of Darrow have not been at all specific about the grounds on which a compromise might have taken place, the criticism deserves a hearing. Most of its exponents were religious modernists, who prided themselves on avoiding the extremes of the agnostic Darrow and the literalist Bryan. Perhaps if everybody had been a modernist, everybody could have been religious and yet not tampered with the teaching of science in the public schools. To ask others to adopt your views, however moderate, is not the usual meaning of the word "compromise."

Taking the fundamentalists as they were, compromise was impossible. They scorned modernists as much as agnostics, and Bryan denounced the use of "weazel-words like 'poetical,' 'symbolical' and 'allegorical' to suck the meaning out of the inspired record of man's creation." If the fundamentalists hated Darrow, they would hardly have preferred Reinhold Niebuhr. They repeatedly stated their way of reconciling science and religion: anything that conflicts with the literal Bible is not science. This is not a compromise either.

III

While the reconciliation of science and religion was sometimes presented in terms of expedience, as compromise is a pragmatic necessity in any organized society, it was also presented in terms of truth, as the one valid view of the relations between these two areas of thought. Justice Chambliss of the state supreme court, in his concurring opinion, rode on both horses. He construed the Butler

Act as banning only those theories of evolution which denied to
God any role in man's creation. The legislature undoubtedly had
the power to ban such theories from the public schools, since the
Tennessee constitution declared that "no person who denies the
being of God, or a future state of rewards and punishments, shall
hold any office in the civil department of this state." This construction of the law, said the justice, allowed various interpretations of the details of the Scriptural account of Creation; it allowed one to believe that God had created man instantaneously or
over untold ages. Thus, he concluded, "the way is left open for
such teaching of the pertinent sciences as is approved by the progressive God recognizing leaders of thought and life."

This solution was congenial to some prominent scientists of
the time. In *The Earth Speaks to Bryan* (1925), Henry Fairfield
Osborn applauded the swing by scientists "away from purely materialistic and mechanistic interpretations toward spiritual and teleological interpretations . . ." He indicted John Dewey and William
McDougall because in their psychological investigations they had
lost sight of the soul. Writing kindly of the men who were re-
viving vitalism in biology, he said that his own major contribution
to the field was the contention "that living Nature is purposive . . ."

These statements were made by a scientist, but they are not on
that account scientific statements. When, in the same book, Osborn
writes that "every drinking man I knew in college in 1876 and every
drinking student of mine up to the year 1890 has paid the death
penalty," this does not prove that alcoholic beverages are lethal, it
only proves that Osborn was a temperance man who would use the
shoddiest evidence to promote his cause. When a scientist declares,
as many still do, that scientific findings bolster a religious view of
life, he may be a reflective man making the best interpretation he
can of the validated facts at hand. He may also be a timid man
who dislikes conflict and who wants very much to placate the pee-
vish forces of the vestry. He may be simply a man who was
reared in a pious home and who brought with him into adulthood,

as we all tend to do, the mode of thought learned in his youth. In the history of the world there has been nobody who dealt scientifically with all questions.

George Gaylord Simpson's recent *The Meaning of Evolution* (1949) is an extended refutation of the vitalist and teleological views of evolution. Simpson rejects Osborn's contention that the development of mastodons and elephants shows orthogenesis; it is, he says, impossible to square this view with the full body of facts. Evolution has been broadly oriented, and the orienting factor has been adaptation. But there are various workable adaptations to a given environment, and the one actually found is often not the best one conceivable. Every step in evolution results from an interplay of forces inside the organism with the external world. Several standards exist for appraising the progress in evolution; by some, man is "the pinnacle so far of evolutionary progress"; by others, he is not. On balance, says Simpson, he is. But this is not to say that the purpose of evolution was to produce man. The development of man resulted from the interaction of materialist forces. Purpose appears in nature only when man appears in nature.

Laymen are not ideally equipped to judge a conclusion of this kind that attempts to summarize and interpret hundreds of thousands of facts. The point here is a different one. Simpson is eminent enough to be chairman of the department of geology and paleontology at the American Museum of Natural History. He believes that his conclusions are scientific ones, founded on validated facts, and that no other conclusion is compatible with the validated facts. But under Justice Chambliss's construction of the Butler Act, Simpson could not teach his conclusions in the public schools of Tennessee. This mode of reconciling science and religion is likely to strangle science.

For anybody who really wants to effect this reconciliation, information about the two elements is essential: you must find out what science claims to know, what evidence it can offer, how the Bible should be interpreted and why. Authorities like Edmund M.

Morgan of the Harvard Law School have pointed out that originally expert witnesses were called by the court for its own enlightenment, not as witnesses for one of the parties. Morgan has recommended that this power should be restored to the court, especially in criminal cases where expert testimony is important to a fair trial. But in the Scopes case, only Justice Chambliss of the supreme court showed any interest in the expert testimony, and his grasp of it was far from perfect.

George Simpson's theorizing also challenges another mode of reconciliation which was advanced in the Scopes trial by several defense lawyers and witnesses. They argued in effect that science was one thing, religion another, and the two could not conflict because they never met. This was sometimes stated in terms of expedience, as when Arthur Hays said later: "It was felt by us that if the cause of free education was ever to be won, it would need the support of millions of intelligent churchgoing people who didn't question theological miracles." At other times it was put in terms of truth: Science deals with the body and material things, religion with the spirit; or Science deals with methods and processes, religion with first causes. However stated, the theory is basically that science and religion do not touch each other at any point. But Simpson's scientific conclusions clearly dispute the religious view that God has played some role in evolution.

It is true that science cannot answer some of the questions posed by religion. Science knows nothing of the human soul, cannot identify it, perhaps even suspects that it does not exist. Science does recognize the human mind as a distinct entity, and so far it has been unable to identify any electrochemical or other features of the brain that differentiate it from other parts of the nervous system. To that extent a vitalist view of the brain cannot now be decisively refuted in favor of a materialist one, but our knowledge of the physiology of the nervous system is currently progressing so rapidly that such a refutation may be forthcoming soon. The case is much the same regarding the origin of life and of the earth. Science now has no demonstrable interpretation of these occurrences. But research reported recently shows how the essential materials of living matter may have been created by heat and electricity working on simple chemical materials, and Winston Bostick has given experimental evidence of the possible origin of the universe of stars and galaxies. Science deals, always, with the transformation of something into something else, and thus cannot explain the ultimate origin of all matter and energy. But it adds that the question itself is spurious, that the total quantity of matter and energy now existing in the universe has always existed and always will.

The vital point is one of attitude. Science has explained everything it could explain, and it will continue to do so. Every effort to bar science from some areas on the ground that they were not susceptible to empirical investigation has had the effect of inhibiting science in other areas also. Man has progressed by exercising a humble confidence in the might of his own mind, not by throwing up his hands and shrugging his shoulders. A second quality of the scientific attitude was emphasized by Thorstein Veblen in 1897: "The modern scientist is unwilling to depart from the test of causal relation or quantitative sequence. When he asks the question, Why? he insists on the answer in terms of cause and effect. He wants to reduce his solution of all problems to terms of the conservation of energy or the persistence of quantity." The scientist, said Veblen, recognizes only the colorless impersonal sequence of material cause and effect, and refuses to go behind that sequence in search of any purpose in the process. Apart from human purposes, no Purpose exists.

Working from this attitude, science has steadily expanded our knowledge of nature and of man. The increments have come ever more rapidly: since every new idea, every new tool, is a combination of existing ideas or existing tools, it is inevitable that the larger the existing stock, the greater the number of possible new combinations. And the scientific knowledge has been accepted by more and more people, because it led to practical results, to a greater control of things and men which could be used to effect human purposes, and because the scientific habit of mind is itself cumulative.

Historically, religion has fought these encroachments. Nearly every major scientific idea was opposed by some creed. The rear-guard action tended to follow a pattern. First, the theologians de-clared that the new theory was not science at all, but only a new and especially superstitious heresy; then they tried to compromise between the new theory and received dogma; finally they said the idea had nothing to do with religion at all. The long-run result has been a withering away of religion, an expansion of secular thought at the expense of religion, an expansion of the area within which material causes were thought to rule and a concomitant shrinking of the area within which God's rule was regarded as operative.

Even if we credit Mencken's assertion that skeptics have ex-isted in all societies, there is no doubt that skepticism now infects more men and is applied to more objects. Only marginal Christian sects now agree with St. Augustine and Luther that the diseases of Christians show an infection by demons. Only the fundamen-talists now regard the story of Creation as a historical account, but in the 17th century it was accepted by Anglican and Puritan alike. At that time it was agreed that, while God was not present in the world, yet his supervision of it was direct and omnipresent. A New England parson was expounding the common creed when he preached in 1685: "His hand has made and framed the whole Fabrick of Heaven & Earth. . . . Those notable changes in the World in the promoting or suppressing, exalting or bringing down of Kingdoms, Nations, Provinces or Persons, they are all wrought by Him." To the same effect was Christopher Smart: "For the tides are the life of God in the ocean, and he sends his angel to trouble the great DEEP."

The same broad sweep shows, raggedly, in the history of im-aginative literature, if we trace the shifting locus of the core of darkness that major writers have tried to illumine. In the *Iliad* this lies substantially in the relations of men to gods, with gods exercising direct and often frivolous influence on the destinies of men. The meaning is far different when Gloucester exclaims in "King Lear" (IV,i): "As flies to wanton boys, are we to the gods; They kill us for their sport"; Shakespeare's focus is not on the relations of gods to man, but of man to man, and perhaps even more, of each man to himself. In our day we have gotten novels like André Malraux's *Man's Hope,* which focuses on group relations, and operates, without one or a few individual protagonists, at a social level of organization and inquiry.

Many religious modernists will feel that all this has no bearing, that Simpson's theories do not conflict with religion because the contention that God has played a role in evolution is not part of religion properly understood. But this raises the question of whether any Purpose exists other than human purpose. If not, how is religion defined? If so, we return to Bryan's questions: How can we reject some miracles expounded in the Bible and accept others? How can we accept some theories on grounds other than verifiable evidence and reject others that rest on the same absence of evidence?

Of course science has its defects. It cannot prove that anything is impossible. It deals only with probabilities. To believers in the Virgin Birth, it can merely say that no case of a virgin birth has ever been authenticated,* while the cause of hundreds of millions of conceptions can be proved. Science knows nothing of Absolute Truth. While it carries us closer and closer to the truth about countless relations, it will never reach the complete truth about any of them. For those who need the amniotic warmth of certainty, dogma is the proper womb.

IV

While William Jennings Bryan was desperately concerned with immortality, with majority rule, with asserting the claims of religion against those of science, he was equally concerned to up-

* Of course the biological possibility of nonmiraculous virgin birth is well established.

hold morality. "The spirit of brotherhood," he declared, "is impossible without faith in God, the Father, and peace, at home and abroad, is impossible without the spirit of brotherhood." Reverence for God and the resulting voice of conscience are so overwhelmingly the main cause leading men to right action that "one is appalled at the thought of what social conditions would be if reverence for God were erased from every heart."

In dealing with this question, Bryan was beset by conflicting loyalties. He thought himself a good Jeffersonian who believed in the separation of church and state. But he wanted to defend ethics, and the Butler Act was essential to that objective. So he had to contend that the statute was not an establishment of religion by law—a contention in which he was supported by a majority of the Tennessee supreme court.

If these logical difficulties are waived, Bryan's argument can be stripped down to a syllogism. Law, civilization itself, depend upon ethics. Ethics is derived from religion. Therefore government cannot be indifferent to religion. The major premise is valid. But what of the minor one?

It has been almost universally accepted. With rare exceptions such as the Crow Indians, savage tribes credit their moral beliefs to the gods, and ethical disputes are settled by reference to the clergy. In orthodox Christianity, from the idea of original sin burgeoned a belief that all men are perpetually on the verge of untold violence, and that chaos can be checked only by the unified power of church and state. St. Augustine and St. Isidore of Seville taught that all rulers are divinely appointed; St. Gregory said that men must submit even to evil rulers. Only rarely was ethics regarded as a higher law to be applied to government, as when Peter Crassus declared: "Render unto Caesar the things that are Caesar's, but not unto Tiberius the things that are Tiberius'; Caesar is good, but Tiberius is bad."

In the original American colonies the association of religion and government was fundamental. The Virginia Company in 1621 instructed the Council of State for that colony to aid the

Governor, "first and principally, in the Advancement of the Honour and Service of God," and secondarily in promoting the interests of the Crown. The Mayflower Compact names "the Glory of God, and Advancement of the Christian Faith" before mentioning "the Honour of our King and Country." The first written constitution in the colonies, the Fundamental Orders of Connecticut, January 14, 1639, set up a government "to mayntayne and preserve the liberty and purity of the gospell of our Lord Jesus which we now professe, as also the disciplyne of the Churches." The Massachusetts Body of Liberties, 1641, forbade that any man should be punished except under "some expresse law of the Country warranting the same, . . . or, in case of the defect of a law in any partecular case, by the word of god."

But especially after the late 18th century, government was increasingly severed from religion. In 1789, when only an estimated 5 per cent of the American population were church members, Congress was banned from passing any law "respecting an establishment of religion, or prohibiting the free exercise thereof." Most states made similar provision. Jews and Catholics were admitted to civil rights by states that formerly had denied them. But the process of secularization stirred anxiety in those who thought social order depended on religion. Visiting Europeans, including Englishmen, were often perturbed. So acute and civilized an observer as Anthony Trollope, who traveled widely in the United States in 1861-62, attributed much of the "rowdiness" of American society, many of our social and political evils, to the lack of a state church.

Although Bryan did not go so far as Trollope, he did think that government should protect the Bible as crucial to ethics and right action. But in important respects, Bryan's ethical theories were less in accord with the Bible than were Darrow's. Whereas Bryan's Gospel of the Second Chance could be construed as guaranteed forgiveness of repeated misdeeds, Darrow, like Scripture, was accomplished at paradox. He believed simultaneously in salvation by grace and by works. In his jury arguments, he repeatedly called on the jury to exercise mercy and love toward the defendant, to recognize that the alleged miscreant could not be held responsible for his actions. But Darrow accorded no such absolution to the jurors themselves. He assured them that if they were so evil as to punish the defendant, they and they only would be accountable for their act of hatred. This moral stance is one of the most profound of Biblical insights into the requirements of a humane ethics. After a man has erred, we should recognize that all humans are fallible, that each man always acts as he must act in view of the complex of pressures operating on the specific organism, and we should exercise grace, we should acknowledge the sinner as our brother and we should love him. But before a man has acted, while we can still alter by our actions the total complex of pressures upon him, while a chance exists that our demands upon him will influence his action, we should demand that he do his duty.

Erich Fromm has similarly distinguished fatherly from motherly conscience. The first, which is taught chiefly from the paternal side, demands that we face the harsher realities, that we accept our responsibilities and struggle to meet them. But we also judge ourselves in a softer, more gentle way, realizing that frailties are inevitable and that our worst trespasses cannot deprive us of the love that is due to all living things. This contradiction in conscience is innate to man's condition, and the ethical man will admit it gladly. "He may judge his fellow man with his fatherly conscience," writes Fromm in *The Sane Society,* "but he must at the same time hear in himself the voice of the mother, who feels love for all fellow creatures, for all that is alive, and who forgives all transgressions."

This the Bible teaches, that morality is a paradox distilled of duty and love. It projects for us a gripping vision of what man should be like. But the ideal it projects is impossible to reach. No man has ever been a perfect man; no man ever will be. We cannot reach the goal, we can only reach toward it. Because the goal is impossible, it does not permit us to become smug or complacent or feel superior to others. The ethical man lives under a remitless moral tension. He can only continue forever, in duty and in love, to struggle.

In the Bible this ethic is corrupted by other, more marginal, often conflicting views of ethics. The whole body of Scriptural ethics is not a system at all but a mosaic in which some tessera are lovely, others deformed, some moral, others loathsome. Two of its attitudes seem fatal to ethics. One is the contention that morality can be reduced to a few simple absolutes and embodied in Ten Commandments, or fifty, or five hundred. On the contrary, the moral man must act with infinite flexibility, with the closest regard to concrete details of who and what he is dealing with, with a comprehension of the total situation, the Gestalt, aiming always to promote life and health, to resist death and madness.

From the Biblical absolutes came a rigid authoritarianism in ethics. This is the voice that says: "I will tell you what to do, and you must do it; for if you do not, God will punish you." Such maxims give rise to a widespread sense of guilt that has come close to poisoning entire populations. The same authoritarianism tends to undermine any true sense of individual responsibility. Bryan is a good example. When he started his crusade against evolution, he acted with utter lack of responsibility. He did not know what the situation required, and he made no effort to find out. He acted in accord with the simple rules he had learned from his father, and he did so with absolute certainty that he was doing the ethical thing. His code of morality had led him into a tragically immoral course of action.

This result was possible because the authoritarian ethics that Bryan had imbibed in his youth had prevented him from ever growing up. He was terrified by the risks implicit in that farded temptress, an open universe. He fled back to Big Brother for reassurance and counsel. A clue to his character is found in the tendency of the human fetus to develop responsiveness to stimuli in an anterior to posterior direction, from the face to the lower limbs, with the greatest sensitivity in the region of the mouth. All his life, William Jennings Bryan liked to eat and to talk. He was tragically immature.

His juvenile grandiosity was manifest in his agreement to be examined by Darrow. In making the gesture, Bryan was the worst sort of rodomontade. It was a fatal error of tactics: if a person holds irrational ideas and insists that others should accept them because of their authoritative source, he should never agree to be questioned about them. The lesson was emphasized, thirty years after Bryan's downfall, by the Senate hearings regarding Joseph R. McCarthy, where the line of questioning was weak and compromised, but the mere fact that McCarthy could be forced to answer questions at all caused millions of people to see him in a new way. We cannot imagine the Pope condescending to debate with the opposition.

Although Bryan's scriptural morality was inadequate and hurtful, the Bible can yield a monumental offering to a truly human morality, as Reinhold Niebuhr has shown so brilliantly in his *An Interpretation of Christian Ethics*. The highest good in life, Niebuhr says, is the freedom of each man to "develop the essential potentialities" of his own nature. We are ethical to the extent that we help others to do this. But if religion does not tell us what those essential potentialities are, what can? To a great extent, an ever increasing extent, science can. Many scientists have abjured this cause. They have insisted that science deals only with techniques and instrumentalities, that it can tell us nothing about values.

The contention is absurd. The biological sciences can tell us much about the physiological needs and possibilities of all men. The social sciences have taught us that some values are common to all cultures: preserving the society by reproduction, raising the standard of living. Historical studies have illumined the persistence and universality of such values as democracy and the brotherhood of man, and have shown that an age can have its central problems, as war is the central problem today. To say that all this has no bearing on ethics is to reduce ethics to the single question: Is life worth living? Science teaches us also that anybody who asks this question is a desperately sick man.

To admit that we do not know everything, to admit that we are terribly ignorant of many things, is not to deny that we know much more than was known a century ago, and that science has been the method of the revelation. Psychology is still imperfectly developed, but already it has produced evidence about many problems posed by former systems of morality. It has revealed that men are happy when they are creating, unhappy when they are idle or destructive. It has shown that human nature is not infinitely plastic, as many cultural relativists seem to imply. From it we have learned that all men need to feel love and cooperativeness, that a craving for power or for prestige is a pathological symptom. Progress has been made toward a meaningful definition of the "mature person."

Science has its limitations, and some are intrinsic to it. The most serious of these is quite serious indeed: There is no science of the individual case, but to live is to cope with individual cases. Science cannot give us that total understanding of another specific being, that insight into the very core of a living man, that is needed if we are to love him and treat him in such a way that we help him. Much of the responsibility of the ethical life comes from the realization that an action that may cause one man to flourish will stifle another, that each situation is unique and makes its own demands upon us. For this sense of the unique individual and of the unique demands of his life at each moment, we must turn to art.

Our knowledge of man in general does us little good if we cannot weave ties of love and cooperation with other individuals. To do this we must know them. And fiction can serve us as a mighty resource. We know some characters in novels more deeply, more in terms of what is vital in them and what is tangential, more completely, than we ever know any living person. We become absorbed in their struggles; we recognize their entangled frailties and strengths, we accept the complexities in them, we become aware of the complexities in ourselves, we grasp the paradox that all men are alike and yet each man is different. What we learn from these created personalities equips us to see real people for what they are, not for what we wish them to be.

Yet, and yet, it does that too, in a sense, for it helps us to learn what we want ourselves to be. Art is not merely a projection of the realities about man. It is also a projection of ideals for man. All great art stretches and expands our sense of human possibilities. It teaches us how to see more clearly, move more surely, think more precisely, how genuinely to feel. It eliminates static. It teaches us to focus, and what to focus on. But no artist can teach these things until he has conquered them himself. The chief resource that an artist brings to his work is his life, for art arises from life, and the imagination can work only with the materials it has gathered from life. Art is a technique of discovery, not of invention, and the artist is the prime explorer. He stakes the trail for those who would follow, but he cannot travel the trail for them. They, too, must conquer it.

While art springs from life, it returns to shape life. Herbert Weisinger has recently shown how the ancient rebirth rituals were progressively modified until finally Shakespeare and his contemporaries found in them the essential plot of dramatic tragedy: from darkness through suffering to light. When Lear comes to see his kinship with all men, he is reborn, and so are we all. The artist becomes the architect of the human soul. This is fitting; even Plato, for all his distrust of art, acknowledged that poets had once been regarded as "the fathers and authors of wisdom." They can be so again. They can teach us that human life is nothing without purpose, and that a proper eye will fix on nothing less than the re-creation of the earth and of man. Man can transform himself when he wills to do so.

Such is one message of the Bible. Bryan saw this. He taunted his opponents with the failure of modern man to produce a greater book than the Bible. This failure, he said, was proof of the divine inspiration of Scripture. It is proof rather of the immense creative powers of men who are moved by a worthy purpose. We need not cheapen man by denying him glories that he has won honestly.

But this is exactly what Clarence Darrow often did. He liked to proclaim that man has no freedom of will, that he is a machine, that he can never be anything but the puppet of heredity and environment. This mechanism in philosophy was strengthened by Darrow's contact with clients like Loeb and Leopold, until it sometimes became a cynicism in life. If Darrow felt a brooding compassion for others, he did not respect them enough to love them; we may doubt that he was genuinely intimate with anybody during the final years of his life. He was fearful, and kept his distance. His fate, while different from Bryan's, was in some ways no better. Darrow could have gotten a more realistic view of human possibilities by pondering some of his other clients—Eugene Debs, Jim McNamara, John Thomas Scopes. Or he could have read more deeply in Aeschylus, or Shakespeare, or the Bible.

Perhaps the example of Bryan comes to a final irony: the Bible is a magnificent book, but like any book it must be read with a scientific and human mind, not with the mind of a superstitious, frightened, and ungenerous past.

Sources and Acknowledgments

In writing this book my purpose has been twofold. First, I wanted to get the facts straight. An effort has been made to track down every piece of pertinent evidence, whether it exists in legal records, personal correspondence and other manuscripts, stories in newspapers and magazines, books, or the memories of surviving participants in the events. It would be foolish to pretend that I have perfectly achieved this aim. There are gaps in the available evidence that I have not managed to fill, and doubtless I have erred at times in appraising the evidence that does exist. But I do think that the story as told here corrects many mistakes in previous accounts of the episode, and that it comes much closer than do those accounts to telling what actually occurred.

Second, I have tried to view the Scopes trial in the broadest possible context. This has meant seeing how occurrences at Dayton were shaped by national, sectional, and statewide forces. It has also meant seeing how this episode, so often described almost purely in terms of its ludicrous aspects, was simultaneously an episode that involved some of the most profound and lasting of all human hopes. The anti-evolution movement, far from having been a simple manifestation of ignorance and bigotry, was a terribly confused and complex phenomenon. I have wanted to understand the full range of meanings that the events here described had to the men and women who acted them out, in the hope that a close study of this brief episode would let us see into some of the persisting mysteries of the human mind.

These aims have dictated the form of the book. I have aimed at recording in a straightforward and direct way the moving chaos that was this specific chunk of historic reality. But I wanted to do so in a way that would suggest significances far beyond the narrow story being told.

In such an effort, an elaborate system of footnotes would be misplaced. A score of sources could be cited for some statements in this work. Others do not rest on any direct evidence at all but on my general understanding of the situation, of the types of people involved, and of how these people would think under these circumstances. All statements about what was said and done rest directly on sources that were deemed sound; it will be obvious from the text that most of them are based on the trial record or on newspaper stories.

These notes are intended to show what sources proved most valuable in ascertaining and analyzing the various parts of the story. Since I hope that some readers will be encouraged to go on thinking and reading about the major problems raised in these pages, I have cited sources in the form, such as cheap paperbound books, that can be most readily obtained by the general reader.

242

The indispensable sources were of course the official records of the Scopes case. The stenographic transcript of the trial was published in two versions in 1925. *The World's Most Famous Court Trial: Tennessee Evolution Case* (Cincinnati: National Book Company) prints an unabridged text; Bryan's undelivered speech is given as a supplement. In Leslie H. Allen, ed., *Bryan and Darrow at Dayton* (New York: Arthur Lee), parts of the transcript are given verbatim and parts are summarized. Both versions are often garbled or punctuated in a way that obscures the meaning of what was said; I have not hesitated to alter punctuation where this would clarify the intended meaning.

The other invaluable source was the Scrapbooks containing the office files of the American Civil Liberties Union. Volumes 273, 274, 275, 277, 278, and 317, of about 300 pages each, relate to the Scopes trial and the anti-evolution movement. They contain both incoming and outgoing correspondence. The massive collection of press clippings is mainly from New York City and Tennessee newspapers, but there is also a sampling from other parts of the country. When I first used these Scrapbooks in 1951, they were located in the New York Public Library. They have since been removed to the Princeton University Library, but their former depository still has a complete set of microfilms.

The Kirtley F. Mather Scrap Book of Newspaper Clippings for 1924-1930, loaned to me by Dr. Mather of Harvard, also covers newspapers in various areas. Dr. Arthur S. Link of Northwestern University generously loaned me his notes on the evolution controversy, many of them based on Southern newspapers and religious publications.

The three full-length studies of fundamentalism and anti-evolution are Maynard Shipley, *The War on Modern Science: A Short History of the Fundamentalist Attacks on Evolution and Modernism* (New York: Alfred A. Knopf, Inc., 1927), by the head of the small but militant Science League of America, useful for its state-by-state survey and its personal acquaintance with many of the events recounted; Stewart G. Cole, *History of Fundamentalism* (New York: R. R. Smith, Inc., 1931), a sound book; and Norman F. Furniss, *The Fundamentalist Controversy, 1918-1931* (New Haven: Yale University Press, 1954), which describes the controversy over evolution and modernism in each of the various denominations. Although I have often disputed the facts or interpretations of these earlier works, my debt to them is nonetheless heavy.

Participants in the Scopes trial who told about it in autobiographical volumes are William Jennings Bryan, *Memoirs,* which was completed by his widow, Mary Baird Bryan (Philadelphia: John C. Winston Company, 1925); Clarence Darrow, *The Story of My Life* (New York: Charles Scribner's Sons, 1932); and Arthur Garfield Hays, *Let Freedom Ring* (New York: Liveright, 1937). None can be recommended as infallibly reliable, but all are revealing for what they show of the qualities of mind of the respective authors. Lucille Milner, *Education of an American Liberal* (New York: Horizon Press, 1954), tells how the American Civil Liberties Union became involved in the Scopes case.

My analysis of the meaning of the Butler Act has been influenced by Kenneth Burke's writing in many books about symbolic action, and by Robert Merton's distinction between manifest and latent function; see his *Social Theory and Social Structure*, 2nd ed. (Glencoe: The Free Press, 1957). My account of the passage of the law and the early events in Dayton is drawn from Bryan's *Memoirs*, Shipley's book, and a variety of journalistic accounts. Especially useful were pieces by George Fort Milton; Dixon Merritt's "The Theatrical Performance at Dayton," *Outlook*, Vol. 140 (July 15, 1925); and Marcet Haldeman-Julius, "Impressions of the Scopes Trial," *Haldeman-Julius Monthly*, Vol. 2 (Sept., 1925), which contains a surprisingly balanced and full picture of John Washington Butler.

Scholarly and often perceptive accounts of the various facets of postwar repression are Robert K. Murray, *Red Scare: A Study in National Hysteria, 1919-1920* (Minneapolis: University of Minnesota Press, 1955); John Higham, *Strangers in the Land: Patterns of American Nativism, 1860-1925* (New Brunswick: Rutgers University Press, 1955), not only the best source on the immigration restriction movement but also containing an acute discussion of the Ku Klux Klan; and Bessie L. Pierce, *Public Opinion and the Teaching of History in the United States* (New York: Alfred A. Knopf, Inc., 1926), which reminds us that textbooks were often censored for reasons other than religious. For shrewd commentary on prohibition and the Klan, see Richard Hofstadter, *The Age of Reform: From Bryan to F.D.R.* (New York: Alfred A. Knopf, Inc., 1955). My own understanding draws on Hofstadter's analysis of the "status revolution," and also on the analysis of urban-rural conflicts given by Samuel Lubell, *The Future of American Politics*, rev. (New York: Anchor Books, 1956).

Any investigation of the South should begin with W. J. Cash, *The Mind of the South* (New York: Alfred A. Knopf, Inc., 1941). Of comparable quality are the works of C. Vann Woodward, *The Origins of the New South, 1877-1913* (Baton Rouge: Louisiana State University Press, 1951) and *The Strange Career of Jim Crow*, rev. (New York: Galaxy Books, 1957). The politics of the region are keenly appraised in V. O. Key, Jr., *Southern Politics in State and Nation* (New York: Alfred A. Knopf, Inc., 1949). The best general history is Francis Butler Simkins, *A History of the South* (New York: Alfred A. Knopf, Inc., 1953). Directly pertinent were Howard Odum, *Southern Regions of the United States* (Chapel Hill: University of North Carolina Press, 1936); W. T. Couch, ed., *Culture in the South* (Chapel Hill: University of North Carolina Press, 1934); Edwin Mims, *The Advancing South* (Garden City: Doubleday, Page, 1926); and Virginius Dabney, *Liberalism in the South* (Chapel Hill: University of North Carolina Press, 1932) and *Below the Potomac* (New York: D. Appleton-Century, 1942). My total sense of the South in this century has been greatly influenced by fiction, especially the novels of Ellen Glasgow and T. S. Stribling.

All of the biographies of Bryan are disappointing. So are the Bryan Papers in the Manuscript Division of the Library of Congress, which yielded only a few interesting items such as the correspondence with Louis F. Post. My interpretation of Bryan is based almost exclusively on published primary sources. His works that were most useful for my purposes, besides his *Memoirs*, were *The Prince of Peace* (New York: Fleming H. Revell Co., [1909]), *In His Image* (New York: Fleming H. Revell Co., 1922), and *Seven Questions in Dispute* (New York: Fleming H. Revell Co., 1924). On his role at the Democratic national convention of 1912, see Arthur S. Link, *Wilson: The Road to the White House* (Princeton: Princeton University Press, 1947); on his actions as Secretary of State, see Walter Millis, *Road to War: America, 1914-1917* (Boston: Houghton Mifflin Co., 1935). Part of my analysis is lifted from Walter Lippmann's "Bryan and the Dogma of Majority Rule," *Men of Destiny* (New York: Macmillan, 1927). Altgeld's letter to Henry Demarest Lloyd, August 2, 1899, is in the Lloyd MSS, Wisconsin Historical Society.

In Darrow's case also, we are confronted with poor biographies and a disappointing set of papers in the Manuscript Division of the Library of Congress. Although this collection holds little except readily available printed material by and about Darrow, it is the source of the quoted letter, probably written about 1895 to an anonymous person, in which Darrow expounds his professional ethics. A copy of the letter to Fremont Older, July 14, 1923, is in the Theodore Dreiser Papers at the University of Pennsylvania, that to Jane Addams, October 21, 1932, in the Addams Papers at Swarthmore College. My picture of Darrow is drawn from a variety of sources examined during eight years of research aimed toward a biography of him.

The historiography of Tennessee is amazingly slight, that of Dayton much slighter. Philip M. Hamer, ed., *Tennessee: A History, 1673-1932* (New York: American Historical Society, 1933), 4 vols., yielded little pertinent data; more useful was Donald Davidson, *The Tennessee*, Vol. II (New York: Rinehart, 1948). Essential information was found in U. S. Bureau of the Census, *Religious Bodies, 1926*, and the follow-up study for 1936. But most of my description of the state and the town was pieced together from contemporary journalistic accounts and the books already cited.

This is even true, I should admit, of my account of Scopes' application for an injunction from the U. S. District Court, Middle District of Tennessee. In spite of numerous press references to this petition, Mr. Robert D. Hall, chief deputy clerk of the court, informed me in 1956 that no official records of the occurrence could be found.

But, except for transcripts of some of the oral arguments before the Tennessee supreme court, I was able to assemble a complete set of official records of the appeal. The "Brief and Argument" for Scopes, the "Reply Brief and Argument for the State of Tennessee," and the "Amicus Curiae Brief" filed for the Unitarian Laymen's League, were all loaned to me by Professor Louis H. Pollak of the Yale Law School. The "Supplemental

Argument" for Scopes, the "Brief and Argument of the Tennessee Academy of Science as Amicus Curiae," and a typewritten transcript, corrected in pencil, of Darrow's oral argument before the state supreme court, are located in the Darrow Papers of the Library of Congress. Citations of the court decisions are given in the text.

Useful information about the Scopes case, especially about its financial aspects, is given in the published annual reports of the American Civil Liberties Union for 1925-1927.

Perhaps the most enchanting feature of studying the Scopes case is its diversity, the range of subjects that it touches in some fashion. On many of these subjects I was at best an informed layman; on few indeed was I a specialist. My efforts to expand what William James called "the apperceptive mass" led me to plunder ideas shamelessly, and I am glad to acknowledge the books that I found most profitable and most pleasant.

Anybody writing today about civil liberties from a legal perspective must be conscious that he follows after Holmes, Cardozo, Zechariah Chafee, Roscoe Pound. An incisive treatment of another celebrated case of three decades ago is G. Louis Joughin and Edmund M. Morgan, *The Legacy of Sacco and Vanzetti* (New York: Harcourt, Brace, 1948). But two more individual factors have played the major role in shaping my understanding of our legal system: conversations during the last fifteen years with dozens of lawyers, law students, and law professors; and my own detailed pondering of many cases in which Clarence Darrow was the attorney for the defendant.

Some of the best writing being done in this country now—writing that is clear and coherent but not vulgarized—is in books explaining scientific topics for the outsider. A model of its kind is George Gaylord Simpson, *The Meaning of Evolution,* rev. (New York: New American Library, 1951). I have also benefited from Julian Huxley, *Evolution in Action* (New York: New American Library, 1957), and from two works by Ruth Moore, *Man, Time, and Fossils: The Story of Evolution* (New York: Alfred A. Knopf, Inc., 1953), and *The Earth We Live On: The Story of Geological Discovery* (New York: Alfred A. Knopf, Inc., 1956). An earlier work which argues that science proves the truth of religion is Henry Fairfield Osborn, *The Earth Speaks to Bryan* (New York: Charles Scribner's Sons, 1925).

Of the many recent books on Judaism and Christianity, the ones I found most stimulating are Robert H. Pfeiffer, *Introduction to the Old Testament,* rev. (New York: Harper & Brothers, 1948); Millar Burrows, *What Mean These Stones? The Significance of Archeology for Biblical Studies* (New York: Living Age Books, 1957); and A. Powell Davies, *The Ten Commandments* (New York: New American Library, 1956), which emphasizes the "evolution" of the moral code. Even persons who are not convinced, as I am not, that ethics must rest on theological sanctions are likely to appreciate, as I do, the profundity of Reinhold Neibuhr, *An Interpretation of Christian Ethics* (New York: Living Age Books, 1956). H. L. Mencken, *Treatise on the Gods,* 2nd ed. (New York: Alfred A. Knopf, Inc., 1946), is informed and pithy. The chapter on religion in Harold J. Laski, *The American Democracy* (New York: Viking Press, 1948), is highly relevant.

Sound studies of the psychology of religion are rare indeed. The classic work, although more than a half-century old, is William James, *The Varieties of Religious Experience* (New York: Modern Library). The book that so excited Bryan's wrath is James H. Leuba, *Belief in God and Immortality* (Boston: Sherman, French & Co., 1916). An excellent description of a revival in Cincinnati a century before the Scopes trial is in Frances Trollope, *Domestic Manners of the Americans* (New York: Alfred A. Knopf, Inc., 1949), Ch. VIII. The account of the Holy Roller meeting near Dayton, quoted in the text, is by Allene M. Summer, in the *Nation*, Vol. 212 (July 29, 1925); see also H. L. Mencken, "The Hills of Zion," *The Vintage Mencken* (New York: Vintage Books, 1956). Two well-known novels about fundamentalist ministers, Sinclair Lewis's *Elmer Gantry* (New York: Harcourt, Brace, 1927) and Thornton Wilder's *Heaven's My Destination* (New York: Harper & Brothers, 1935), seem to me overdrawn; far more suggestive is a short story by Wilbur Daniel Steele, "The Man Who Saw Through Heaven," in Bennett Cerf and Angus Burrell, eds., *Bedside Book of Famous American Stories* (New York: Random House, 1936). The agonizing Chapter III of James Joyce's *A Portrait of the Artist as a Young Man* recounts a sermon about hell, and its effects on an adolescent.

My effort to interpret Bryan and other fundamentalists has drawn on a variety of psychological concepts and data: the Gestalt concept of premature closure, Else Frenkel-Brunswik's studies of "intolerance of ambiguity," the notion of "free-floating" anxiety and guilt. I have been impressed by the evidence that parents who are "restrictive" in rearing their children, as the fundamentalists sought to be toward all children, are themselves likely to be submissive people with little self-assurance. Anybody who broods awhile on the father-son similarities in the cases of Bryan, Darrow, and Scopes is likely to conclude that religion is learned behavior and that it involves an emotional tone as well as an intellectual orientation.

William Sargant, *Battle for the Mind: A Physiology of Conversion and Brain-Washing* (New York: Doubleday, 1957), persuasively argues that certain types of conversion follow a functional breakdown of the cortex arising from prolonged and severe emotional stress. For the statement by Thomas Mann about father-images, see "Freud and the Future" (1936) in his *Essays of Three Decades*, trans. H. T. Lowe-Porter (New York: Alfred A. Knopf, Inc., 1948), p. 426.

Much of my argument on the relations of science to ethics is a paraphrase of Abraham Edel, *Ethical Judgment: The Use of Science in Ethics* (Glencoe: The Free Press, 1955), a pioneering summary that yet makes me wish more philosophers and social scientists would learn to write a clean prose. A large part of Erich Fromm, *The Sane Society* (New York: Rinehart, 1955), treats of the same subject from a psychological perspective. Richard Hofstadter, *Social Darwinism in American Thought*, rev. (Boston: Beacon

Paperbacks, 1955), shows how the theory of evolution was incorporated into a type of social science that denied any meaningful morality at all.

I do not see why anybody should fail to read Lord Raglan's *The Hero: A Study in Tradition, Myth, and Drama* (New York: Vintage Books, 1956), a masterly and delightful book. In Herbert Weisinger's *Tragedy and the Paradox of the Fortunate Fall* (East Lansing: Michigan State College Press, 1953), seminal analysis is frequently marred by a turgid style. I also found useful insights in Samuel H. Hooke, ed., *Myth and Ritual* (London: Oxford University Press, 1933).

Several participants in these events shared their memories with me, in interviews or by correspondence; they filled several troublesome holes in the written record and also imparted to the historical facts a warmth and immediacy which I have tried to retain in my account. My gratitude is great to Justice Felix Frankfurter; Roger N. Baldwin of the American Civil Liberties Union; Judge William H. Holly; Watson Davis of Science Service; William K. Hutchinson of the International News Service; Dr. Kirtley F. Mather of Harvard University; and Dr. Charles Frederick Wishart, president emeritus of Wooster College. Miss Nellie Kenyon, who reported the Scopes trial for the Chattanooga *News,* graciously allowed me to quote from her article in the *Nashville Tennessean Magazine,* June 10, 1956. Mr. John Thomas Scopes, in the interests of factual accuracy, read portions of the manuscript.

I regret that this list is not longer. By the time my research into the written records was complete, most of the important actors in this story had died. Of those surviving, several either refused or neglected to comply with my letters of inquiry. Obviously their course was unimpeachable, and the fact is mentioned only by way of saying that I have not knowingly ignored any potential source of information.

Some general obligations have also been incurred. This volume grew out of research begun in 1950-1951 under a grant from the Committee on Midwestern Studies of Michigan State University and the Rockefeller Foundation. The Reverend Roger Ortmayer, editor of *Motive,* showed various courtesies, as did Professor T. Harry Williams of Louisiana State University. For the chapter about Darrow, I have drawn on my article analyzing his career in the *Antioch Review,* Spring, 1953, and on the sketch I prepared for the forthcoming Supplement Two (Vol. XXII) of the *Dictionary of American Biography;* my thanks for permission to use this material are due to the editors of the two publications. The late Mrs. Clarence Darrow kindly allowed me to quote from the correspondence and other unpublished writings of the late Mr. Darrow. The letter from Arthur Garfield Hays to Walter Nelles, September 9, 1925, is quoted by permission of the Executors of the Estate of Arthur Garfield Hays.

Professor Louis H. Pollak of the Yale Law School read the entire manuscript, and Dr. George Gaylord Simpson read the sections pertaining to science; both men were most generous in their efforts to save readers from my ignorance. If they have not entirely succeeded, the fault is mine. My wife Evelyn contributed all the typing, and criticism besides. My chief debt, in this as in much else, is shown by the dedication.

R. G.

Index

Aaron, 14
Addams, Jane, 61
Agassiz, Louis, 28
agnosticism, 11, 112, 118, 172
Alexander the Great, 187
Allegheny College, 50
Allyn and Bacon, 211
Altgeld, John Peter, 24-5, 35, 50, 55, 57, 62
American Association for the Advancement of Science, 81, 126, 143, 161, 202
American Association of State Geologists, 154
American Bar Association, 197, 210
American Civil Liberties Union, 18-20, 66-7, 74-8, 81, 193-202, 210
American Federation of Teachers, 82
American Legion, 11
American Medical Association, 74
American Men of Science, 30
American Mercury, 45
American Museum of Natural History, 31, 76, 101, 229
American Psychological Association, 154
American Society of Naturalists, 126
anti-evolution bills and campaigns, 62-7:
    Fla., 33-4, 64, 213
    Tenn., 44-5, 79
    Miss., 11-2, 212
    West Va., 33, 213
    Ga., 33
    S. C., 63
    Ky., 6, 33, 63-4, 213
    Tex., 64, 211, 213
    Iowa, 79
    Okla., 64, 213
    N. C., 64, 65, 213
    Calif., 64-5, 213
    Minn., 65, 79, 213
    N. D., 79, 213
    Ore., 79
    Del., 79, 213
    La., 212
    Ark., 212
    Cleveland, 213
    Mo., 213
    Va., 312
    N. H., 213
    Me., 213
    and big business, 12-3, 16, 67
    unpublicized, 65-6
    constitutional amendment, 85
    after Bryan's death, 211-3
    See also Butler Act
Anti-evolution League of America, 65, 85
anti-radicalism, 10-3, 15, 17, 66-7, 78, 204
Aquinas, Thomas, 15
art:
    change in focus of, 232-3
    and ethics, 239-41
Associated Press, 180
atheism, 11, 74, 78, 172-3, 204
Atkin v. *Kansas,* 203-4
Atlanta, 215
atonement, 29, 42-3, 63

Bagehot, Walter, 185, 223
Bailey, Forrest, 75, 194-7, 198, 199, 200, 201, 206, 207
Baldwin, Roger N., 18, 20, 67, 75, 201-2, 206-7
Baltimore *Post,* 215
Baltimore *Sun,* 129, 178, 193, 215
Baptist church, 4, 7, 14, 29, 63, 65, 71, 81, 99, 101, 148, 208, 212, 214, 216
Bateson, William, 161
Baylor University, 64, 213
Beamish, Richard, 117
Belmont, August, 26
Bible, 85, 99, 192:
    infallibility of, 4, 5, 15-6, 28, 29, 33, 37-41, 63, 82, 86, 91, 101, 111, 135-6, 168
    translations of, 101, 122-3, 162-3, 166

interpretations of, 130, 135-6, 147, 163-74, 181-3, 203
morality of, 181-3, 188-9, 207, 235-7, 238, 240
as art, 240-1
See also Creation; names of books of; morality
Bible Crusaders of America, 212
Bible Institute of Los Angeles, 214
Birge, Edward A., 31
Bland, Richard P., 24
Boas, Franz, 171
Bogard, Ben, 212
Bolshevism. *See* anti-radicalism
Bostick, Winston, 231
Boston, 11, 199
Bristol, Tenn., 217
British Association for the Advancement of Science, 214
Brooklyn, 81, 211
Brown, John, 62
Bryan, Silas Lillard, 22-3, 49
Bryan University, 140-1, 196, 216
Bryan, William Jennings, 5-6, 11, 21, 46, 61, 62, 79-80, 84-5, 94, 101-2, 112, 116, 119, 124, 125, 137, 138, 143-4, 145, 176, 179, 192, 212, 224, 225:
    on government, 12-3, 34-6, 90, 135-6, 181
    religion of, 12-3, 23, 34, 37-44, 88, 90-1, 115, 167-74
    on evolution, 29-34, 90-1, 181
    on education, 21, 33, 36, 67, 88, 90, 134, 181
    as a lawyer, 21, 183
    and father, 22-3, 185-6, 237-8
    career, 22-7
    Altgeld's evaluation of, 24-5
    wealth of, 34, 196
    on prohibition, 27, 34-5
    absolutism of, 35-6
    on morality, 37-43, 235
    attacked, 73-4, 78-9, 137-8, 143, 151
    speeches by, 88-91, 133-6
    as defense witness, 147-8, 166-75
    undelivered speech, 180-9, 192, 204
    questions to Darrow, 190-1
    dies, 192-3, 195
    and ritual, 220-1
    immaturity of, 237-8
    See Bible; rebirth; religion and science

Bryan, William Jennings, Jr., 94, 131
Bryan, Mrs. William Jennings (Mary Baird), 23, 34, 36, 94, 115
Burbank, Luther, 80
Bury, J. B., 204
Butler Act, 221, 224-7, 234:
    text of, 3
    legislative history of, 2-8
    and Baptist-Methodist rivalry, 4-5
    lack of opposition to, 5, 86-7, 115-6
    governor's message on, 7-8, 150
    as symbolic action, 7-8, 18, 217, 225-6
    ignored, 18
    plans to challenge, 18
    Scopes arrested, 20
    Scopes indicted, 69-70
    views on, 73-4, 78-9, 80, 81, 82, 101-2, 194
    enforcement of, 74
    pro and con, 78, 79-80
    federal injunction against, 83, 195
    constitutionality of, 103-8, 118-9, 130-42, 150, 195, 200, 202-10
    meaning of, 120-1, 130, 132, 139-40, 141-2, 167, 176, 181, 196, 202-3
    a practical nullity, 209-10, 217
    never repealed, 217
Butler, John Washington, 2-8, 17, 82-3, 86, 94, 122, 145-6
Butler, Nicholas Murray, 78
Butler, Pierce, 210
Byrd, Howard G., 102

Cabell, James Branch, 45
California, 65
Campbellites, 6, 99
Carden, Frank L., 147
Carlson, Anton J., 56
Carroll County, Tenn., 74
Case, Shirley Jackson, 56
Catholic church, 11, 85-6, 199, 214
Cattell, James McKeen, 77
Chamber of Commerce, of the United States, 12-3; of Chattanooga, 147
Chambliss, Alexander W., 208-9, 227-8, 229
Channing, William Ellery, 92
Chase, Harry W., 65
Chattanooga, 19, 68, 69, 70, 71, 86, 147, 150, 162, 216
Chattanooga *News*, 100, 146, 174-5

Chattanooga *Times*, 18, 115-6, 193-4
Chautauqua, 29, 151
Chicago, 11
Chicago *Tribune*, 32, 46, 85, 148
Chicago, University of, 56, 135, 154, 199
Christian Fundamentalist, 214
Christian Fundamentals, 15
civil liberties. *See* Bryan; Darrow; evolution; majority rule; religion and science
Clark, Edgar Young, 211
Cleveland, 213
Cleveland, Grover, 24
Colby, Bainbridge, 45-6, 77, 85
Cole, Fay-Cooper, 56, 154, 214-5
Columbia University, 78
Commonweal, 85
Congregational church, 78, 114, 126, 199
Cooksville, Tenn., 83
Corinthians, 193
Creation, Biblical story of, 2, 3, 120, 133, 136, 163-4:
　multiple-creation theory, 28
　meaning of, 7, 31, 32, 106, 130, 139, 167-74, 203, 227-8
　disputed by science, 121, 181-2
　myths, 186-7
　See evolution; fundamentalism; religion and science
Curtis, Winterton C., 154, 162, 164

Dabney, Virginius, 217
Darrow, Amirus, 49
Darrow, Clarence S., 9, 17, 83, 85, 87-8, 94-105, 109-15, 118-20, 123-7, 130-3, 135-7, 140, 141, 193, 217:
　public letter to Bryan, 32, 148
　enters case, 45-6
　nonconformity of, 47-9, 92
　and father, 49
　career, 49-55
　on government, 55-6, 59, 61-2, 107-8
　on science, 56-7, 87-8
　philosophy of, 56-9, 61, 136-7, 205-6, 241
　on courts, 59-60
　on education, 60, 222
　on religion, 60-1, 190-1
　attacks on, 74-8, 193-202
　strategy of, 87-8, 147-8
　speech by, 105-8
　clash with judge, 142-5, 149-50
　confessional by, 151-3
　examines Bryan, 166-75
　answers to Bryan, 190-1
　in state supreme court, 205-7
　praise of, 214-5
　narrates film, 215-6
　ethics of, 235-6
Darrow, Mrs. Clarence (Ruby H.), 108, 109
Dart, Raymond A., 157
Darwin, Charles, 149, 182, 215. *See* evolution
Darwinism. *See* evolution
Daughters of the American Revolution, 11
Davenport, Charles B., 77
David, 187
Davies, A. Powell, 168
Davis, John W., 18, 75, 76, 197
Davis, Watson, 94, 191
Day, Bill, 99
Dayton, Tenn., 19-20, 44-5, 69-74, 80-91, 100, 109-10, 112, 115-6, 128-9, 146, 152, 161, 180, 191, 193, 215-6
Dayton Progressive Club, 84, 109-10
Debs, Eugene V., 9, 51, 55, 62, 193, 207, 241
DeKalb County, Tenn., 74
Democratic party, 72, 102, 161, 174
Deuteronomy, 91
Devil, 187-8
Dewey, John, 228
Dostoyevsky, Fyodor, 190

Ecclesiastes, 47, 174
Eddy, D. Brewer, 199, 202
education. *See* Bryan; Darrow; evolution; majority rule; religion and science
Einstein, Albert, 80
Elhuff, Lewis, 124
Elijah, 187
El Paso *Times*, 66
Episcopal church, 162, 205
Erie, Pa., 215
ethics. *See* morality
Europe, 10, 11
evolution, theory of:
　and religion, 2, 3, 28, 63, 163-4
　and morality, 27-31, 39, 85, 134-5, 164, 181-3, 195
　truth of, 45, 73, 87-8, 95-6, 134, 138

evidence for, 91, 125-8, 154-62, 181, 203
meaning of, 132, 134, 142-3, 161, 227-33
See Bryan; Butler Act; Scopes trial; Simpson
Exodus, 89
Ezekiel, 2

Fayetteville, Tenn., 80
Ferguson, Miriam, 211
Five Points, 29, 33
flood myths, 169-71, 186
Florida, 34, 141, 184
Fosdick, Raymond B., 201-2
Foster, George Burman, 56
Frankfurter, Felix, 75, 76, 77, 196, 198
Fromm, Erich, 236
fundamentalism, 10, 12, 13-8, 29, 63, 85-6, 97, 98, 106, 114, 128-9, 171-2, 174, 192, 211-4, 221-2. See anti-evolution; Bryan; Butler Act; Scopes trial
Fundamentals, 29
Furniss, Norman F., 211

Genesis, 30, 31, 70, 111, 121, 125, 139, 148, 163-4, 186-7. See Creation
George, Henry, 28-9, 50, 55
Georgia, 15
Georgia Federation of Labor, 78
Gizzards Cove, Tenn., 69
Godsey, J. L., 79
Gore, John, 83
Green, Grafton, 208

Haeckl, 49
Haggard, A. P., 70, 71, 100, 110, 129
Haggard, Wallace C., 19
Hagley, Charles, 125
Haldeman-Julius, Emanuel, 92
Hamilton, Thomas, 68
Hanna, Marcus A., 24
Harding, Warren G., 10
Harvard University, 12, 15, 28, 148, 154, 198, 230
Hayes, Carlton J. H., 214
Hays, Arthur Garfield, 76, 78, 85, 104, 112, 116-7, 119, 120, 122-3, 125, 131, 132, 134, 139-40, 142, 143, 147, 148, 150, 151, 153-4, 164, 165,

166, 174, 176, 178-9, 196, 198, 199, 209, 210
Herrick, Charles Judson, 56
Hicks, Sue K., 19, 20, 21, 78, 104, 132
Hill, Lew, 6
Holt, Henry, and Company, 211
Holy Ghost, 5
Holy Rollers, 86, 128-9
Holy Trinity Church v. U. S., 203, 206
Hughes, Charles Evans, 72, 75, 197, 198, 210
Hull, Cordell, 17, 72, 73
Hunter, George, 19-20, 122-3, 124-5, 133
Hutchinson, William K., 113-8
Huxley, Julian, 82

Illinois, 22-3
Illinois College, 23
immigration, 8, 11
immortality, 16, 41-3, 94, 181-3, 188-9, 191, 202, 204. See rebirth
Indiana, 8, 12
International News Service, 113-6
Isaiah, 97, 188-9
Israel, 1. See Judaism

Jackson, Andrew, 4, 222
Jackson, Tom, 98
Jasper, Tenn., 192
Jefferson, Thomas, 55, 121, 222, 234
Jeremiah, 118
Job, 52
John, 17, 42, 153, 189
Jonah, 167-8
Jones, Charles R., 193
Jordan, David Starr, 214
Joseph, 187
Joshua, 168
Joughin, G. Louis, 167
Judaism, 114, 146, 153, 168, 186-7, 188, 213, 214
Judd, Charles Hubbard, 154

Kafka, Franz, 14
Keebler, Robert S., 80-1, 197, 199, 216-7
Keith, Arthur, 214
Kellogg, Vernon, 30
Kentucky, University of, 19
Kentucky Wesleyan College, 64
Kimberly, Hal, 15
Kinsman, Ohio, 49

Kirkland, James H., 79
Knights of Columbus, 11
Knoxville, Tenn., 70, 79, 114, 162, 215
Knoxville *Journal*, 194, 215
Krutch, Joseph Wood, 86-7, 138
Ku Klux Klan, 9, 11, 12, 44, 211

LaFayette, Tenn., 2
Lake, Kirsopp, 12
Last Judgment, 94
League of Nations, 10, 72
Leeper v. *Tennessee*, 105, 119
Leuba, James H., 30
Leviticus, 14
Lipman, Jacob G., 154, 205
Lippmann, Walter, 11, 35, 65-6, 221-2
Little Rock *Gazette*, 191
Littleton, Martin W., 75
Lloyd, Henry Demarest, 24-5, 35
Loeb, Jacques, 57
Loeb-Leopold trial, 53-5, 59, 60, 75, 109-
    10, 131, 135, 136-7, 182, 204, 241
Long, Huey, 15

McCarthy, Joseph R., 238
McDougall, William, 228
McKenzie, Ben G., 93, 100, 104, 105,
    109, 112, 120, 130, 132, 137, 165,
    166, 170, 217, 224
McKenzie, J. Gordon, 93, 165
McKinley, William, 24
McKinney, Colin P., 209
McNamara trial, 51-2, 62, 241
McReynolds, James C., 210
Machaut, Guillaume de, 189
Macon County, Tenn., 2-3
Macon *Telegraph*, 211-2
majority rule, 34-6, 61-2, 135-6, 221-7.
    See Bryan; Darrow
Malone, Dudley Field, 45-6, 74, 75, 76,
    77, 81, 85, 93, 100, 105, 112, 115,
    119, 120, 121, 136-8, 139, 140, 143,
    145, 148, 151, 165, 166, 171, 172,
    180, 191, 199, 202
Malraux, André, 233
Mann, Thomas, 22, 184-5, 221
Manufacturers' Record, 13
Mark, Jerome, 146
Marquette University, 85
Marr, W. B., 5, 79-80
Marshall, C. T., 196

Martin, T. T., 12, 85, 212
Massachusetts, 141
Massingill, J. P., 98
Masters, Edgar Lee, 52
Mateer, Horace, 33
Mather, Kirtley, 66, 148, 152, 154, 159,
    162, 163-4, 172, 174
Mathews Shailer, 162, 163
Matthew, 188-9
Meadville Theological Seminary, 49
Mencken, H. L., 45, 85, 94, 128-9, 138,
    146, 193, 232
Metcalf, Maynard M., 125-8, 130, 132,
    154, 162
Methodist church, 4-5, 14, 22, 64, 69, 71-
    2, 80, 81, 82, 85-6, 98-9, 102, 162,
    192, 213, 216
Meyer v. *Nebraska*, 105, 119
Micah, 29-30
Michigan, University of, 50
Midwest, 31, 44, 65
Millikan, Robert A., 64
Milner, Lucile, 18
Milton, George Fort, 174-5, 192
miracles, 29, 39, 182-4, 191, 233. *See*
    Bryan; immortality; rebirth; Virgin
    Birth
Missouri, University of, 154
modernism, religious, 4, 39, 86, 199, 202,
    214, 221, 226-7, 233. *See* Bryan;
    fundamentalism; Virgin Birth
Moody Bible Institute, 12
Moon, Truman J., 211
morality, 128-9:
    Catholic versus Protestant, 8-9, 11
    and Bible, 4, 7, 135, 181-3, 190, 234-5
    Biblical, 188-9, 235-6, 238, 240
    and science, 238-9
    and art, 239-41
    See Bryan; Darrow
Morgan, Edmund M., 167, 229-30
Morgan, Howard, 123-4, 128, 136
Morgan, Mrs. Luke, 128
Moses, 89, 187
Murkett, Herman E., 162
Murray, George Gilbert, 78
"Mystery of Life," 215-6

Nagel, Charles, 202
Nashville, 4
Nation, 128

National Association of Manufacturers, 12-3
National Education Association, 82
National Research Commission, 126
Neal, John Randolph, 44-6, 75, 77, 80, 83, 84, 100-1, 104, 115, 117, 119, 131, 194-7, 199, 209, 210
Nebraska, 23, 27
Nehemiah, 1
Nelles, Walter, 75, 76, 194, 197-9, 201
Nelson, Wilbur A., 154
New Jersey, 154
New Orleans *Times-Picayune,* 212
New Republic, 194, 210
New York City, 11, 45-6, 76-7, 79, 101
New York, 11, 133
New York *Mirror,* 215
New York *Times,* 31, 87, 147, 215
New York *World,* 78
Newark *News,* 215
Newman, Horatio Hackett, 154
Niebuhr, Reinhold, 40, 227, 238
Nietzsche, Friedrich, 29, 54, 135
Norris, J. Frank, 17, 64
Northwestern University, 214
North Carolina Academy of Science, 65
North Carolina, University of, 65
Nott, Josiah, 28

Oberlin College, 126
Ohio, 196
Oklahoma, 191
Older, Fremont, 57
Omaha *World-Herald,* 23
Oregon, 11
original sin, doctrine of, and guilt, 10, 14, 41, 128
Osborn, Henry Fairfield, 31, 64, 76, 81, 87, 101, 228

Paducah, Ky., 81, 102, 213
Page, Walter Hines, 15
Parshley, H. M., 215
Pascal, Blaise, 226
Peay, Austin, 6-8, 45, 74, 79, 130, 150, 184, 195, 200, 202, 217
Peter, 5
Philadelphia, 215
Philadelphia *Inquirer,* 117
Pickett County, Tenn., 17
Pierce v. *Society of Sisters,* 119

Pikeville, Tenn., 147
Popular Science Monthly, 28
Portland, Ore., 11
Post, Louis F., 31
Poteat, William L., 65
Potter, Charles Francis, 85, 86, 116
Pound, Roscoe, 198
Powell, Thomas Reed, 198
Powell, W. F., 4, 7
Prendergast trial, 50-1
Presbyterian church, 29, 32-3, 65, 207
Price, George M., 12, 171
prohibition of alcoholic liquors, 11, 12, 27, 78, 133, 177, 214, 216, 217, 228
Proverbs, 22, 184
Psalms, 2, 42, 101
Pupin, Michael I., 81, 146-7

Raglan (F. R. Somerset), 183-4, 185, 187-8
Raleigh *News and Observer,* 65
Rappelyea, George W., 19-20, 68-9, 81-2, 86, 123, 141, 195, 196, 216
Raulston, John T., 69-70, 73, 85, 87, 93, 94-7, 99, 102-6, 108, 111-27, 131-3, 135, 139, 141-54, 164-6, 167, 168, 169, 170, 171, 175-9, 180, 192, 196, 200, 208, 210, 217
rebirth, 53, 63, 69, 94, 140, 153, 191, 193:
    general desire for, 1
    Bryan's emphasis on, 41-4, 90-1, 94, 134, 136, 181-3
    revival meeting, 128-9, 184-9
    myths, 183-9
    Christian rituals, 188-9
    secular rituals, 218-21
    See ritual
Red Hunt. *See* anti-radicalism
redemption. *See* rebirth
religion and science, 3-4, 7, 31, 64, 85, 101-2, 111-3, 121, 130-8, 141-2, 148, 163-4, 181-3, 195, 208-9, 227-33. *See* Bryan; Darrow; evolution
Republican party, 72, 102
Resurrection. *See* rebirth
revival meeting. *See* rebirth
Rhea County, Tenn., 69, 70-4, 81-91, 128-9, 217. *See* Dayton
Richmond, 45
Riley, Jim, 98

Riley, William Bell, 12, 29
ritual:
in Scopes trial, 21, 44, 94, 97, 105, 136, 151-3, 180-9, 219
in life, 153, 218-21
elements of, 218
functions of, 220-1
See rebirth
Robinson, Fred E., 19, 123, 124-5, 136, 141, 191, 195, 216
Robinson, James Harvey, 44
Rogers, Will, 191, 213
Roosevelt, Theodore, 9, 72
Rose, John, 73, 162
Rosensohn, Samuel, 76, 77
Rosenwasser, Herman, 101, 162
Russell, Bertrand, 214
Ryan, Thomas Fortune, 26
Ryan, John A., 85, 199

salvation. *See* immortality; rebirth
Samuel, 105
Sanford, 210
science and religion. *See* religion and science
Science Service, 94
Scopes, John Thomas, 1, 13, 19-20, 44-6, 55, 68, 69, 76-7, 79, 84, 93-4, 102-3, 123-4, 178-80, 184-5, 191, 195, 199, 200, 207-8, 214, 227, 241
Scopes, Thomas, 45, 99, 102-3, 207
Scopes trial:
motives for, 19-21, 68-9, 80, 147, 224
defense strategy, 78, 87-8, 193-202, 207, 209-10
prosecution strategy, 79-80, 168, 175
financing defense, 81, 201-2, 214
scientific witnesses, 80, 81, 87-8, 95-6, 100, 115, 130-42
trial opens, 93
Scopes re-indicted, 94-5
jury, 96-100
prayers in, 94, 103, 111-3, 114, 149, 200
motion to quash indictment, 103-8, 118-9
press leak, 113-8
testimony against Scopes, 119-25
meaning of Butler Act, 120-1, 130, 132, 139-40, 141-2, 167, 176, 181, 196, 202-3
scientific testimony, 125-8, 143-6, 150-1, 154-64
jury excused, 127
Darrow clashes with judge, 142-5, 149-50, 151-3
and interest in evolution, 153-4, 214-6
outdoors, 153, 167-74
examination of Bryan, 166-75
Scopes convicted, 175-8, 179
sentence, 176-8
appeal to supreme court, 176, 197, 198-9, 200-1, 202-9
Scopes not guilty, 180
case throttled, 209
aftermath of trial, 211-7
Seay, E. T., 205
Shakespeare, William, 233, 240, 241
Shaw, George Bernard, 78
Shelton, Harry, 124, 128
Shelton, John A., 6
Shelton, Mrs. William R., 128
Simpson, George Gaylord, 161, 229-30
Slovenian National Benefit Society, 202
Smith College, 215
Smith, T. V., 56
social Darwinism, 28-9
Social Gospel, 9, 11
Soil Science, 154
Sout, Morris, 125
South, 13-8, 31, 44, 63, 65, 88, 90-1, 184-5, 191, 213, 220-1, 224-5
Southern Methodist University, 64
Spencer, Herbert, 28
Spenser, Edmund, 189
Spring City, Tenn., 217
Sprouls, Jesse W., 73
Spurlock, Frank, 150, 197, 199, 200
Stanford University, 214
Starr, Frederick, 56
Stevens, Doris, 141
Stewart, A. T. (Tom), 94, 96, 99, 100-1, 103, 105, 110, 112, 116-7, 118, 120, 121, 122, 124, 125, 130, 139-40, 142, 143, 150-1, 152, 168, 170, 172, 175-8, 180, 192, 196, 208, 217
Straton, John Roach, 12, 101, 196, 211
Strong, Charles H., 197, 201, 205
Sumner County, Tenn., 2-3
Sumner, William Graham, 28
Sunday, Billy, 60-1, 211

Supreme Court, U. S., 20, 77, 81, 201, 209, 226
Supreme Kingdom, 211-2
Sutherland, George, 210

Taft, William Howard, 210
Tampa, Fla., 116
Ten Commandments, 11, 237. *See* morality
Tennessee, 8, 17-8, 138, 142-3, 147, 149, 154, 184, 205, 216-7, 225-8
Tennessee Academy of Science, 154, 205, 208, 210
Tennessee Bar Association, 80-1
Tennessee Department of Education, 5
Tennessee, University of, 5, 44-5, 79, 212
Thompson, J. R., 98-9, 179
Titus, 42
Trollope, Anthony, 235
Trousdale County, Tenn., 2-3
Turnerbund, American, 78
Tutankhamen, 31-2
Tylor, E. B., 171

Unitarian association, 85, 86, 102, 114, 116
Unitarian Laymen's League, 78, 197, 205
Universal Pictures, 215
urbanization, 8-9, 13-4, 180-1

Van Devanter, Willis, 210
Van Loon, Hendrik, 82
Vanderbilt University, 6, 79, 205
Veblen, Thorstein, 231
Virgin Birth, 4, 5, 29, 43, 63, 233. *See* miracles; Bible

Voliva, Wilbur Glenn, 73-4
Volstead Act, 11, 27
Voltaire, François, 62

Wake Forest College, 65
Walden's Ridge, 89-91
Walsh, Frank P., 75
Walsh, Thomas J., 75
Washburn, George F., 141, 212
Washington, D. C., 77
Washington, University of, 214
Watson v. *Jones,* 202-3
Weisinger, Herbert, 240
Wells, H. G., 20
Wesley, John, 4, 72
Whitaker, Walter C., 162
White, Walter, 19, 69, 79, 88, 122-3, 140-1
Wilson, Woodrow, 5, 26-7, 72, 161
Winchester, Tenn., 85, 192
Winrod, Gerald, 214
Winthrop College, 214
Wisconsin, 11
Wisconsin, University of, 31
Wishart, Charles F., 33
woman suffrage, 18, 34, 75, 141
Woodward, C. Vann, 17
Wooster College, 33
World War I, 9-11, 18, 26-7, 29, 53, 70, 138, 223
World's Christian Fundamentals Association, 21, 29, 213

York, Alvin, 72
Youmans, E. L., 28-9